LOOKING BACKWARD

LOOKING BACKWARD

True Stories from Chicago's Jewish Past

WALTER ROTH

ACADEMY CHICAGO PUBLISHERS
in association with
THE CHICAGO JEWISH HISTORICAL SOCIETY

Printed in 2002 by
Academy Chicago Publishers
363 West Erie Street
Chicago, Illinois 60610

Published in association with The Chicago Jewish Historical Society

Printed in the U.S.A.

Library of Congress Cataloging-in-Publication Data

Roth, Walter, 1929-
Looking backward : true stories from Chicago's Jewish past / Walter
Roth.
p. cm.
ISBN 0-89733-513-9
1. Jews--Illinois--Chicago--History. 2.
Jews--Illinois--Chicago--Biography. 3. Chicago (Ill.)--Ethnic
relations. I. Title.
F548.9.J5 .R65 2002
977.3'11004924--dc21
2002008032

TO MY WIFE CHAYA,
OUR CHILDREN AND GRANDCHILDREN

CONTENTS

—

IV

CHICAGO JEWS AND ZIONISM: RENOWNED VISITORS

V

CHICAGO JEWS AND THE ARTS: THE PAGE AND THE STAGE

VI

CHICAGO JEWS ON BOTH SIDES OF THE LAW: COLORFUL CHARACTERS

FOREWORD

WHEN WALTER ROTH ASSUMED the presidency of the Chicago Jewish Historical Society, it was expected that he would provide each issue of the Society's quarterly with a short personal message from the president, a common feature in such publications. This he has done regularly with topics of interest and worth.

But Walter Roth is not a typical organization president, a man with mere leadership abilities. He is a gifted writer with unusual research ability and an abiding interest in Chicago Jewry. This combination of talents has resulted, in addition to his messages, in a steady stream of vigorous articles on different aspects of the Chicago Jewish experience. His interests have led him, and us, into many fascinating and unexplored byways. He has opened doors and lifted curtains on obscure, half-forgotten and sometimes hidden incidents. He has introduced us to a broad variety of characters, a few of whom we may be glad we never met but who too are part of our history. His research activities have already resulted in one well-received book, *An Accidental Anarchist*.

This felicitous selection of stories, written during the past fifteen years, provides interesting and valuable insights into local Jewish history. Those accustomed to thinking of history mainly in terms of organizations, institutions and momentous events will be reminded that, in the end, history is people. The reader will meet some of the most colorful and interesting of them in these pages.

Irwin Suloway
Professor Emeritus
Chicago-State University

INTRODUCTION

—

FOR SOME PEOPLE, HISTORY is a series of stories devised by the mind to give one a sense of belonging to the community in which he or she lives. This is certainly true for me; I relish stories which create a sense of joy and that euphoria impels me to write about them.

The true stories in this anthology were first written for *Chicago Jewish History*, published more or less quarterly by the Chicago Jewish Historical Society (CJHS) and this book is being published as part of a celebration of the 25th anniversary of the CJHS. As a practicing attorney since 1954, I have always been fascinated by history. I majored in English history at the University of Illinois (I identified with some of the English kings) and then researched and wrote about my family's history in Germany, from which we fled in 1938.

In 1987, after I chaired a CJHS panel discussion featuring a number of German Jewish refugees who had built new lives in Hyde Park, a community on Chicago's South Side, I became interested in American history, and particularly in the history of Chicago Jews. My activities with CJHS grew and I was fortunate enough to be elected its president. Most of my time with CJHS was spent on research and writing for its newsletter.

My research sources were the Regenstein Library at the University of Chicago, the Archives at the University of Illinois at Chicago, the Newberry Library, the Chicago Historical Society and, most of all, the Spertus Library, where, with the assistance of its librarian Dan Sharon (a brilliant source of information), I pored over old Chicago newspapers and many other books and magazines. The anchor work in my studies was H. L. Meites' classic *History of the Jews of Chicago*, originally published in 1924 and reissued in 1994 by the CJHS.

Walter Roth
November, 2002

ACKNOWLEDGMENTS

———

THE INSPIRATION FOR THIS anthology came from my children Ari, Judy and Miriam and their respective spouses Kate, Steven and Mark. At a "milestone" birthday party, they presented me with a booklet of clippings of stories I had written and which subsequently formed the basis for this book. My daughter Judy merits a special mention because it was her work that was the springboard for the book. My wife Chaya, of course, has my gratitude and love for her patience, understanding and encouragement in bringing this project to fruition.

My special thanks go to Irwin Suloway, Joe Kraus and Bev Chubat who, as editors of *Chicago Jewish History* during the times when these stories were published, were of immeasurable assistance in helping to edit my material.

My gratitude is extended to my publishers, Anita and Jordan Miller of Academy Chicago Publishers, whose editing and patience (sprinkled with humor) have been inspiring, and to Sarah Olson for her first-rate design and production of the book. Finally, the Chicago Jewish Historical Society and a number of its members, particularly Norman Schwartz and Charles Bernstein, have been extremely helpful with their advice and assistance in the research necessary to unfold these stories. The entire CJHS has my gratitude.

I
CHICAGO JEWS AND THE SECULAR CITY: BUILDERS, MOVERS, SHAKERS

MEITES' *HISTORY OF THE JEWS OF CHICAGO*

—

H.L. MEITES' CLASSIC *History of the Jews of Chicago* was first presented to the public at a meeting of the Chicago Historical Society on May 19, 1924, the year of its original publication. This invaluable work contains nearly 900 pages of illustrated entries about individuals, organizations and buildings in Chicago from the early 1800s to 1924. A small supplement was added to the book's second edition published in 1927.

Meites, an immigrant from Odessa, Russia, loved his adopted city and wanted to document the Jewish contribution to Chicago's success. He begins his history with the pre-Civil War Jewish settlements along Clark and Wells Streets in what is today downtown Chicago. In 1840, Jews also bought land in what is now northwest suburban Schaumburg in an unsuccessful attempt to settle there. During the Civil War, the Jewish community, numbering less than one thousand, were able to raise a company of soldiers in two days, immediately after the call for volunteers from President Lincoln.

Meites talks about Abraham Kohn and his family, merchants who had originally set up business in Massachusetts. They soon discovered that they had settled in a colony of Christians who, convinced that the end of the world was at hand, had little interest in purchasing anything from anybody. So the Kohns moved to Chicago. Abraham Kohn's daughter later married the architect Dankmar Adler, son of Liebman Adler, an avowed abolitionist and the German-speaking rabbi of Chicago's first Congregation, Kehilat Anshe Ma'ariv, K.A.M. In

1861, Abraham Kohn, then president of K.A.M., presented Abraham Lincoln, on the eve of the newly elected president's departure for Washington, with an American flag inscribed with a Hebrew quotation from the Book of Joshua "Be strong and of good courage."

From the Civil War to the Great Fire in 1871, Jewish immigration to Chicago increased markedly. These immigrants were primarily Jews from small towns or villages in Germany, many of them merchants who set up shops and founded the first Jewish hospital, along with synagogues and early charitable institutions.

Then came the Great Fire of 1871, in which a number of congregations lost their buildings and many merchants saw their stores go up in flames. K.A.M temple at Wabash Avenue and Peck Court survived the fire, while everything immediately north of it burned to the ground. Meites says that the Reverend Ignatz Kunreuther, the first rabbi of K.A.M, always insisted that it was his prayers that had saved his congregation. He offered no explanation of why those prayers hadn't saved the B'nai Sholom synagogue across the way, but it was suggested by a wag of the day that "It was probably because Kunreuther's prayers were in accordance with Minhag Askenaz [the German prayerbook] while B'nai Sholom's prayer book was Minhag Polen [the Polish one]." However, the K.A.M. temple was destroyed in a smaller but still disastrous fire three years later.

It was after this second fire that Jews began to cross the Chicago River and settle along Canal Street. The Mariampoler Congregation, whose synagogue was in ruins, crossed the river and became the first Russian-Polish congregation to be established in what was to become a large new Jewish community on Chicago's West Side as immigrants poured in from Eastern Europe in the latter part of the nineteenth century.

With the arrival of these Eastern Europeans came all the social problems that beset poor immigrants. Meites does not dwell on the perennial German-Russian Jewish tensions, but writes at great length about the charities set up to help aid West Side Jewry. Over and over again, the name of Julius Rosenwald appears as the benefactor of West Side institutions.

Meites deals briefly with the labor movements that emerged from the turmoil of the West Side; he was not equipped, he said, to deal with them in depth, and in fact he had little interest in the working classes. His chapter on the Jewish unions—the Cloakmakers Union, the Cigar Makers Union, and the Carpenters Union—is informative, but skimpy. He does attempt to dispel the apparently widespread notion that Jews were heavily involved in the Haymarket riot. In early May, 1886, August Spiess, one of the Haymarket anarchists, addressed the largely-Jewish Cloakmakers Union, headed by Abraham Bisno. On May 4 nearly 400 Jewish strikers began a march to the Haymarket area, where female Loop factory workers planned to join them. However, the strikers were intercepted by the police, who broke up their march by clubbing them. It was only later that day when the strikers were meeting to discuss the police action, that a worker rushed in to tell them he had just read in a German paper that "an anarchist had exploded a bomb" at the Haymarket.

Meites calls himself the first "card-carrying" Zionist in Chicago, and some of the most valuable research in his book concerns the founding and activities of the Zionist organizations where, by 1900, the Knights of Zion had taken over the leadership of the city's Zionist movement. He includes an unforgettable picture of the Volunteers of Zion, young men dressed in military uniforms, marching in "soldierly precision with a Zionist flag seen for the first time on Chicago streets ... head[ing] parades, preserv[ing] decorum at public gatherings, and guard[ing] the dignity of the Jewish name." These Zionist military units and bands marked the death of Theodore Herzl on July 3, 1904, with a mass parade on the West Side. Poale Zion, the workmen's branch of the Zionist organizations, was organized in Chicago about this time; and a few years later, in 1916, local Zionist leaders founded the original American Jewish Congress in the city.

As an intriguing aside, Meites includes the entire text of "The Blackstone Memorials" by the Reverend William E. Blackstone, a Christian evangelist who advocated the return of the Jews to Palestine, and whose work Meites obviously considered a valuable contribution to the Zionist movement in Chicago. Blackstone's first Memorial was widely circulated and presented to President Benjamin Harrison in 1891; the second Memorial was presented to President Woodrow Wilson in 1916. Blackstone was motivated by the fundamentalist belief that the return of the Jews to Palestine would result in the "Second Coming" of the Messiah. Whatever his motivation, Blackstone was a favorite of the American Zionists and often spoke at their gatherings.

Meites records patriotic Jewish activities in the First World War, including the numbers of Jewish volunteers, the names of Chicago Jewish ranking officers and those men who died; the proportion of Jewish combatants to non-combatants; decorations and citations awarded to Chicago Jews; lists of those who were involved in Liberty Loans and Four Minute Men, who took part in loyalty demonstrations, served on draft boards, and helped to entertain servicemen. He lists also the contributions of Jewish women to the war effort.

After that war, American Jews undertook a great drive for relief for the six million Jews of ravaged Eastern Europe. Julius Rosenwald pledged $1,000,000 on the condition that a total amount of $10,000,000 be raised in the entire nation. Woodrow Wilson wrote to Rosenwald acknowledging his gift and adding, in words strongly applicable today: "The Russian Revolution has opened the door of freedom to an oppressed people. It is to America that these starving millions look for aid; and out of our prosperity, fruit of free institutions, should spring a vast and enabling generosity. Your gift lays an obligation even while it furnishes inspiration."

There are many chapters in Meites' book on the work of Jews in public office; in industry, commerce and finance; in the labor movement; and in athletics. Other chapters deal with religious, cultural, educational, welfare, fraternal and social organizations, and with homes and hospitals.

When this book was published in 1924, America was peaceful and prosperous in the main. Jewish life was developing in Chicago. On May 18, 1924, Congregation Rodfei Zedek laid the cornerstone of a new temple, designed by Abraham Epstein, at 54th Street and Greenwood Avenue. In that same year on September 5, K.A.M., the oldest congregation in Chicago, dedicated a new temple at Drexel Boulevard and 50th Street, and on September 12, Isaiah Israel dedicated its new temple at 51st and Greenwood. The Jews of the South Side were then at the peak of growth and prosperity. Many other new religious buildings would be built in other parts of the city during the ensuing years.

Meites could feel justifiably optimistic about the future of the Chicago Jewish community. But in his remarks at the 1924 celebration of the book's publication, Judge Harry M. Fisher of the Circuit Court pointed out that a new immigration bill had just come into effect, closing American borders for the first time in its history, except for those who could be included in a yearly quota for each country. The Polish quota was about 3,000 persons a year. Does this immigration bill, asked Judge Fisher, portend a new era? "Is there not some little cloud upon the horizon that may spread and overhang and darken the next chapter? Who knows?" And indeed, this "little cloud" spread until it prevented the escape of millions of Jews from the Holocaust.

WHO WAS LAZARUS SILVERMAN?

—

IN THE OCTOBER 1909 issue of *The Market World,* a New York Wall Street publication, an article entitled "A Portrait of Lazarus Silverman" begins:

> Born and educated in Bavaria, a pioneer banker in Chicago, a contributor to the equipment of regiments for the Union army in the Civil War, a more than generous philanthropist in the days following the Chicago fire of 1871, author of the bill for the resumption of specie payments by the United States Treasury in 1873, a charter director in the company which first exploited the Mesaba Range and Vermillion County as the richest source of iron ore in the then coming age of steel construction, and a prominent figure in that group of men who have guided Chicago to the position of the second city in the Western world—such is the brief record of the life of Lazarus Silverman, who died at the age of seventy-nine in Chicago, last June—a record which will be more of a monument than stone."

Meites says that Silverman was a "banker from the '60s and an authority on finance for a half century, whose service to the United States government in connection with the Sherman measure (the resumption of specie payment following the Civil War) has been characterized as the greatest national service ever rendered by a Jew."

Who was this man, acclaimed locally and nationally during his lifetime but now virtually forgotten?

Lazarus Silverman was born in Oberschwarzag, Bavaria, on February 29, 1830, and immigrated to the United States in 1849, at a time when many young German Jews were leaving Bavaria for the New World for political, social and economic reasons. As many of his countrymen had done, he first went to a small town in the South, in Alabama, and earned his living as a peddler. In April, 1853, he moved to Chicago and by 1854 had set up a note-brokering and banking business and begun to make real estate investments in and around the city. His Silverman's Bank was established by 1857, surviving despite a severe national economic downturn, and on April 12, 1859, he married Hannah Sachs of Louisville, Kentucky. During the Civil War, Silverman lent the government large sums of money for the purchase of saddles, bridles and other necessities for the Federal Army.

In 1870, a Chicago business publication described Silverman as a "thorough and completely successful businessman," whose bank was well-known in Europe as well as the United States. The bank survived the great Chicago fire of 1871, although the material cost to Silverman was great. Nevertheless, Meites says, he was "instrumental in assisting and helping many poor and deserving people, filling his own house on Calumet Avenue near Twenty-Second Street, with the destitute and homeless, and erecting for others temporary structures for their protection and comfort, also purchasing at that time large amounts of flour and other food products, gratuitously distributing the same among the needy and homeless."

Silverman was frequently involved in large financial operations, and financiers and politicians sought his advice. In 1873 the "specie payment" law, considered Silverman's signal contribution, was enacted. Silverman himself dictated an account of this affair, "His Own Account During His Last Illness," which was published after his death in *The Market World*. In the aftermath of the Civil War, the currency of large American cities, and of the federal government itself, fluctuated wildly, often causing great economic distress. Silverman's business was of course also affected. He developed a plan to stabilize U.S. currency by making it attractive for foreigners to pay their American debts in gold, thus enabling the U.S. to build a gold reserve to back its own currency. He presented this plan in Washington to Illinois Senator John Alexander Logan, Senator John Sherman, Chairman of the Finance Committee, and other prominent statesmen. The plan was Silverman's, but Sherman apparently adopted it as his own, since it is known to posterity as the Sherman Plan.

By the end of the 1880s, Silverman, at the height of his success, was living in a mansion at 2213 S. Calumet Avenue. He was involved in many ventures with Marshall Field, Potter Palmer and other Chicago financiers; was one of the founders of the Duluth & Iron Range Railroad and the Minnesota Iron Company (later merged into U.S. Steel); and owned acreage in Upper and Lower Michigan, farmlands in Iowa, Washington and Wyoming and many buildings in Chicago.

He was active in a number of charities, the Cleveland Orphan Home apparently being one of his favorites, and he was also a member of the Jewish Agricultural Society, the goal of which was to settle Jews in farming communities. His purchases of farmlands were undoubtedly made in connection with this organization. In many cases, he advanced the funds for farm equipment to help these early farm communities.

Strangely enough, little is known about Silverman's synagogue or other local Jewish affiliations. But Meites says that Silverman was a member of K.A.M. in the 1850s; and that in 1860 he was on a committee that rejected a new reform prayerbook for the Congregation, causing a split among the membership, with the reformists leaving to establish Sinai Congregation, the city's first reform synagogue.

In 1893 the World's Columbian Exposition focused international attention on Chicago. But suddenly that summer several Chicago banks failed, and just as suddenly, the United States was caught in another financial depression—this one, the Panic of 1893, was more serious than most of the others.

Henry Ericsson, a builder, was Silverman's friend and client. In his 1942 book *Sixty Years a Builder*, Ericsson describes the scene in June, 1893 in front of Silverman's Bank in the Commonwealth Building at LaSalle and Washington Streets, where a long line of anxious bank customers had formed:

As they crowded his bank to withdraw their money, Lazarus
Silverman stood beside his trusted nephew, Minzesheimer, and on
the counter back of the old-fashioned cage heaped up piles of glis-
tening gold and silver and stacks of paper money. Unperturbed and
with superb showmanship, he would go outside and mingle with
the throng to hear what the people were saying. All along the line,
at the sight of him, one- time peddlers, who had become merchants,
small perhaps but successful, remembering how he had helped to
equip them with their first shop would slip out of line and leave
without asking for their money.

Silverman's Bank survived this crisis. He resumed his activities,
and Ericsson built a four- story building for Silverman on Edina Place,
now named Plymouth Court, the site of the Standard Club. However,
on August 1, 1893, the "pork and lard corner" at the Board of Trade,
supported by a number of Chicago's largest meat operators, collapsed
and many fortunes vanished overnight. Panic gripped the city. Herman
Scheffner, a Jewish businessman whose bank had failed, drowned himself in Lake Michigan. No matter what happened on the Board of
Trade, people considered that Lazarus Silverman had infinite resources
and his bank would always be safe. But this time, his luck had run
out. He left immediately for New York to raise cash to meet the expected demands of his depositors. But the collateral he had to offer
was not adequate, and he could not avoid bankruptcy.

When he returned to Chicago, the court hearing on his bankruptcy
was set for Saturday. This was ironic, because Silverman's Bank was
always closed on Saturday, and his checks and notes were imprinted
with the phrase, "No business on Saturday." Ericsson notes: "What
his inward feelings were no man could discern, as on his Sabbath
Lazarus Silverman appeared in court before a Gentile pretrial judge.
But there were people who thought it at least poetic justice, for had he
not always kept his bank open till noon on the Christian's Sunday
and spent his Sunday afternoons inspecting his properties?"

At the bankruptcy hearings, it evolved that many of Silverman's
depositors were "small Hebrew merchants and peddlers," and his total

unsecured indebtedness amounted to $650,000. His lawyer was Julius S. Grinnel, who had been state's attorney at the Haymarket trial and was now general counsel of the Chicago City Railway Company. Silverman had for many years been an active investor in Chicago tractions enterprises.

Levi Mayer, a prominent Jewish lawyer, represented the secured creditors. Silverman testified that his bank had paid out $600,000 to $700,000 in cash during the summer of 1893 and that he had assets to pay all of the unsecured creditors. All he requested was an extension to permit him to resume his banking business.

But despite efforts by his friends, Silverman's Bank never reopened. He removed his real estate business to the Plymouth Court building. From there, true to his word, he devoted his remaining years to liquidating his many holdings so that he could make good on his promise to pay off all of his depositors. He did make good on that promise, even though he was under no legal obligation to do it.

Lazarus Silverman died, aged 79, on June 9, 1909 at the home of his daughter at 2213 Calumet Avenue, where the funeral was held. Interment was at Mount Maariv Cemetery. An announcement in the *Chicago Tribune* requested that members of the Independent Order of B'nai B'rith, especially those of the Ramah Lodge, attend the funeral.

From the papers filed with the Probate Court of Cook County, it appears that Silverman's fortune was gone by the time of his death. Only a few parcels of vacant real estate were listed on the inventory for his estate. Nearly all his worldly possessions were gone, but as *The Market World* had written at the time of his death, his life was his monument. Though his name is generally unknown today, Chicagoans should remember Lazarus Silverman for his many accomplishments on behalf of the city and the nation.

THE UNIVERSITY OF CHICAGO CENTENNIAL

———

THE UNIVERSITY OF CHICAGO is probably unique among top American universities in the extent to which Jews (and particularly Chicago Jews) have played major roles in its founding and development. Not only were Chicago Jews instrumental in founding the university, they have benefited from it, since it is one of the few major American universities that has never had a policy restricting the admission of Jewish students. With Jews active from the beginning as students, faculty and trustees, the interaction between the university and the Jewish community has gone through many phases.

There had been an earlier University of Chicago, near 34th Street and Cottage Grove on land donated by Stephen A. Douglas. When that school ceased operations, several Chicago groups began to plan a new university. But the campaign flagged until, in 1890, members of the Standard Club came together to raise funds. Under the chairmanship of Berthold Loewenthal, a banker and president of Sinai Congregation, and with the assistance of Sinai's Rabbi Emil Hirsch and of Eli Felsenthal, a prominent attorney, roughly 400 people met and pledged to raise $25,000.

Citing the importance of the campaign in his 1916 *History of the University of Chicago*, Dr. Thomas Wakefield Goodspeed wrote, "The committee assumed the entire labor of securing the subscriptions. . . . This generous co-operation was one of the essential factors in the final success achieved." In a letter to the Standard Club in 1891, Goodspeed had gone even further:

> I am reminded that a year ago, when we were in utmost danger of failing in our efforts to secure the establishment of the University of Chicago, the Club came to our relief . . . It has been felt by the denomination that inaugurated the movement and by the Board of Trustees of the University that the action of the Standard Club was one of notable public spirit and liberality.
>
> It will be held in lasting and grateful remembrance, and we hope to erect on our campus a memorial that will tell the story to coming generations.

The denomination Goodspeed referred to was Baptist: the University of Chicago was founded as a Baptist institution. Despite this religious affiliation, it quickly established itself as a school that refused to follow the common university practice of sharply limiting Jewish enrollment. As we have pointed out, in contrast to many prestigious East Coast universities, Chicago consistently made a place for Jews as students, faculty, administrators and trustees. Through the 1920s and 1930s—an era when anti-Semitism in the U.S. may well have been at its peak—Jewish enrollment at the university was between twenty and thirty percent of the student body.

The university's founding president, Dr. William Harper, was a brilliant Old Testament scholar who had taught Hebrew at the Morgan Park Baptist Theological Seminary and then at Yale University. His presence at the infant university ensured its survival. His appointment caused John D. Rockefeller, who had already given $600,000, to donate an additional $2,000,000. The Baptists themselves raised another $400,000, and ten acres of real estate on the Midway were donated by Marshall Field. Thus the university was able to build its campus and hire faculty. The $25,000 the Standard Club members had been able to raise may not have been a significant part of the total, but it did represent broad public support at a critical initial stage.

Jewish contributions to the university did not stop with that first donation, however. Several campus buildings are named for Jewish donors: Henry Crown Field House and Mandel Hall and the Samuel Kersten, Jr., Physics Building. The business school is still known informally as Rosenwald Hall, despite Julius Rosenwald's reluctance to allow any building to be named for him. In the school's medical complex are the Max Epstein Clinic, the Goldblatt Cancer Research Center, the Bernard Mitchell Hospital and the Arthur Rubloff Intensive Care Tower. The medical school itself is named for the Pritzker family. And the Regenstein family underwrote the cost of housing the university library.

There have been a number of other examples of Jewish donations to the university as well. The Nathan Cummings family gave funds to establish an endowed faculty chair in Jewish studies. The university's Hillel House was established through monies given by B'nai B'rith and the Karasik family, whose son, a marine, was killed in World War II. Ludwig Rosenberger donated an immense collection of German Judaica that remains one of the best collections of its kind in the world. In his 1934 history, Philip Bregstone included a two-page list of such donations ranging from the $75,000 given by Mr. and Mrs. John Hertz "to be expended by the University of Chicago in the study of disorders of the pituitary gland and related conditions," to the $250,000 received from Louis Kuppenheimer by the department of opthalmology.

Apart from financial support, there was also Jewish leadership at the school. Eli Felsenthal and Julius Rosenwald were members of the original Board of Trustees and both served in that capacity for many years. In 1972, on the university's 80th anniversary, Edward Hirsch Levi, grandson of Rabbi Emil Hirsch and son of Rabbi Gerson B. Levi, was appointed its president.

Hundreds of Jews have served as faculty members. Among the original faculty was Rabbi Hirsch, who taught at the university until his death. In 1902, Julian Mack, then a city judge and later a federal judge and leader of the American Zionist Movement, was a professor at the law school for many years. Many current faculty members are

Jewish, including several who have won Nobel prizes while with the university.

On a lighter note, Jewish culture may well remain most evident through the ongoing annual "Latke-Hamentash" debates. The tradition began when Rabbi Maurice Pekarsky brought together Anthropology Professor Sol Tax and History Professor Louis Gottschalk to argue the competing merits of the Purim pastry, the hamentash, and the Chanukah potato pancake, the latke.

The university, now in its second century, promises to remain what it always has been for Chicago Jews: a place that has challenged, recognized and welcomed them.

WORLD'S COLUMBIAN EXPOSITION:
JEWS ON THE MIDWAY

THE WORLD'S COLUMBIAN EXPOSITION of 1893 was an audacious undertaking. In the words of Mayor Carter Harrison, "Chicago has chosen a star and looking upward to it, knows nothing it cannot accomplish." The great fair brought the accomplishments of Chicago to the attention of the world—just two decades after the Great Fire had nearly destroyed the city.

An 1890 Act of Congress specified that the exposition was to provide an exhibit of arts, industries, manufactures, and the products of the soil, mine, and sea, in the city of Chicago. The nations of the world were invited to take part. Jackson Park, a large tract of swampy land on the South Side, was designated as the location of the fair, and within little more than two years, a dream city—the "White City"— had been erected there. Noted architects, including Dankmar Adler, and sculptors under the direction of Daniel Burnham, had designed huge exhibition halls in a variety of elaborate European architectural styles. These white buildings, illuminated by electric lights, shone brilliantly at night.

Chicago's mercantile elite, the department store magnates of State Street, heavily promoted the White City. Marshall Field's; Carson Pirie Scott; the Fair Store; Mandel Brothers, Rothschild & Co., Spiegel, Cooper & Company—all displayed a variety of merchandise from around the world that could be bought from courteous sales clerks. But many civic leaders felt that beyond this display of material achievements, however magnificent, "something higher and nobler is demanded by the enlightened and progressive spirit of the present age." The result was the World's Congress Auxiliary of the World's Columbian Exposition, which sponsored meetings of people whose ideas represented virtually the entire spectrum of human thought and endeavor. These congresses were convened from May 15 to October 15 in the newly built Art Institute of Chicago.

The Congress on Women, chaired by Bertha Honoré Palmer, opened the series. Its success was surpassed only by the last congress, the World's Parliament of Religions, where Emil G. Hirsch, Chicago's leading Reform rabbi, spoke for Judaism. Hannah Greenebaum Solomon, a member of Rabbi Hirsch's Sinai Congregation who moved in the same social circles as Mrs. Palmer and her associates, was invited to serve on the governing committee of the Parliament of Religions, where she organized a Jewish Women's Congress. One result of this was the formation of what would eventually become the National Council of Jewish Women.

Another, very different, but increasingly interesting part of the exposition was the Midway Plaisance, a mile-long stretch of land connecting Washington Park with the White City in Jackson Park. A poem published in the *Chicago Daily News* praised the "wisps of loveliness" at the Midway Plaisance, with its Algerian dancers and "lithe Moorish maidens with bangles of gold/and eyes that will set you afire at a glance . . ." In addition to these enticing beauties, the Midway held a wealth of colorful commercial amusements. Its main attractions were the gigantic Ferris Wheel and a collection of villages presenting the "native populations, products, food, and games of the world's population."

Dr. Barbara Kirshenblatt-Gimblett's "A Place in the World: Jews and the Holy Land of World Fairs," provides an in-depth look at the background of the villages along the Midway. Earlier fairs, most recently the Paris International Exposition of 1889, had included foreign and, especially, exotic French colonial entertainers, but the 1893 Midway exposition was meant to have a more serious ethnological and anthropological purpose.

Frederic C. Putnam, Harvard Professor of Ethnology, was appointed to organize exhibits of historical and cultural interest on the Midway, and he retained Cyrus Adler, a Jewish scholar at Harvard and the Smithsonian Institution, as a consultant. Putnam planned to construct ethnic villages showing the evolution of mankind—beginning in Africa and culminating in Europe, with the Near and Far East arranged between them. There were no plans for a Jewish village, since Adler and others believed Jews to be members of an acculturated religion with no particular homeland. To Putnam, Jews were a race, while Adler strove to present Judaism as a religion, one of the groups that lived in Biblical lands. He believed that "everything which makes for the higher life in modern man derived directly from a few groups of people that lived about the Mediterranean, and that knowledge of this civilization is essential to an understanding of the higher history of human thought." Adler clashed with those scholars who believed that Western civilization developed largely from Aryan sources.

When under Putnam, the planning and construction of the Midway exhibits proved to be poorly organized and behind schedule, the professor was replaced as manager of Midway concessions by Sol Bloom, who was to become a publisher of popular music and later an influential congressman. Although Bloom, who was born in Pekin, Illinois, was only twenty-two years old in 1893, he had had years of experience in theatrical management in San Francisco. At the 1889 exposition in Paris, he had negotiated a contract to exhibit the Algerian Village—the most exotic and spectacular of the French colonial attractions—in America, and he brought this troupe to Chicago. In his autobiography Bloom describes the unruly behavior of some of the Algerians as they waited for the fair to open. He had, he said, to hire members of Buffalo Bill's Wild West Show, encamped near the Illinois Central railroad tracks, to round up the wandering artists.

Bloom mentions no other Jews on the Midway beside himself, although Isidor Lewi in his 1901 article "Yom Kippur on the Midway" says that Jews constituted about four-fifths of the population of the Midway Turkish Village. The exposition hired Jewish translators and guides to explain the Oriental Villages to visitors. Robert Levi, the manager of the Turkish Village, who had brought many Jews from that country to work at the fair, also hired some Jewish Chicagoans, passing them off as Turks. There was a report in the *Chicago Tribune* of a controversy that arose when these Midwesterners refused to wear Oriental costumes, "including gorgeous bloomers."

Some of these Jews may have owed their jobs to Cyrus Adler, who had been appointed Commissioner of the Chicago Exposition to Turkey, Palestine, and Morocco. Since Palestine was under the rule of the Ottoman Empire in 1893, and many Jews lived in and around Jerusalem, it is fair to assume that performers and workers from Palestine were present. Their physical appearance and costumes made it easy for them to pass as "Mohammedans."

The *danse du ventre*—the "belly dance"—was the sensation of the Midway. It was performed in the Egyptian Theater on the Cairo Street, and a popular song at the fair, "She Never Saw the Streets of Cairo," incorporated the "hootchy-kootchy" melody. Some of the most famous belly dancers on the Midway were Jewish—among them Nazha Kassik, a Syrian, and Rahlo Jammele, "a native of Jerusalem." They performed in the theater in the Moorish Palace. Rossiter Johnson's 1897 history of the exposition notes that the chief Algerian dancing girl was beautiful, mysterious, and popular, "but she was less fascinating to young men visitors than Fatima, of the Persian theater, who was more lithesome, and executed the *danse du ventre* with a wild abandon that called for repression by the authorities."

Of course, there is much more about the Midway than can be covered here. Frederic Putnam created a large photographic exhibit on his favorite subject, "The Development of Man," in which Jews were presented as a racial type. A decade later, at the St. Louis Fair of 1904, the Jews of Jerusalem were recognized in their own right, not as "Mohammedans." But it was not until the 1933 Chicago World's Fair that there was a Jewish Day when a great pageant, "The Romance of A People," staged in Soldier Field, presented the history of the Jewish people and their dream of a national homeland in Palestine.

JULIUS ROSENWALD AND
THE MUSEUM OF SCIENCE AND INDUSTRY

———

JULIUS ROSENWALD IS SAID to have given nearly sixty-three million dollars for philanthropic purposes in his lifetime because he believed in "giving while I am alive." This was an enormous sum of money at the time of his death in 1932, although subsequent inflation tends to reduce its impact. Of all the causes, institutions, and buildings that Rosenwald fostered, the most widely known today is undoubtedly the Museum of Science and Industry, on South Lake Shore Drive at Fifty-Seventh Street.

According to legend, says Rosenwald's biographer M.R. Werner in his 1939 book *Julius Rosenwald: The Life of a Practical Humanitarian*, Rosenwald first conceived the idea of the museum when his eight-year-old son William wandered away from his parents who were visiting Munich, Germany, and was found in an industrial museum there. However, the Rosenwald archives at the University of Chicago contain a number of articles and papers from subsequent years dealing with the great industrial European museums as well as one then being contemplated for New York City. Jacob Schiff, a New York philanthropist and close friend of Rosenwald, is mentioned in these papers. Thus Rosenwald must have gotten the idea of an industrial museum from a number of different sources.

The opportunity to realize this museum project came when in the 1920s many of the grand buildings left standing after the 1893 World's

Columbian Exposition, burst into flames, or had deteriorated because they had not been intended to be permanent structures. Of the few buildings that remained, the grandest, and the most well-constructed, was the Palace of Fine Arts. It had temporarily housed the Field Columbian Museum—now the Field Museum of Natural History—until 1920, when that museum's permanent home was completed. Then it remained empty, deteriorating rapidly.

It was about that time that Rosenwald began to discuss his idea for the establishment of an industrial museum with many of his Chicago business contacts. He asked his close friend and attorney, Leo Wormser, to help implement the project. The two visited industrial museums in Munich and Vienna in 1926, and on their return Wormser filed the papers incorporating the Rosenwald Industrial Museum. On September 16, 1926, the Secretary of State of Illinois granted articles of incorporation to the new museum, which was to be housed in the old Fine Arts building. Among the founding trustees were Rosenwald, Wormser and a number of Chicago's most prominent businessmen, including Sewell L. Avery as president, Rufus Dawes, T. E. Donnelly, John V. Farwell, Joseph T. Ryerson, Albert A. Sprague, Harold H. Swift, and Charles H. Thorne. Julius Rosenwald agreed to contribute three million dollars initially for the repair and maintenance of the building. A five-million dollar reconstruction bond was issued by the city.

Much more money was needed for the tremendous project, which involved turning an immense wood and stucco building into a highly decorative steel and dressed-stone structure. Some of the money came from Rosenwald, and a great deal came from the public-works-minded Roosevelt Administration. When the museum was finally opened to the public in 1933, to coincide with the Chicago World's Fair: A Century of Progress, only a small portion of the original building had been rebuilt and, alas, Rosenwald was dead. A full generation passed before his vision became a complete reality. The enormous building now stands completed, but—unlike the Field Museum, the John G. Shedd Aquarium, and the Adler Planetarium (donated by and named for Rosenwald's brother-in-law)—it does not bear the name of its major benefactor.

There had apparently been a misunderstanding among the trustees when the museum was originally named. Without consulting him,
they had determined to call it the Rosenwald Museum. He protested
almost immediately to Wormser, who replied that since the charter
had already been issued, nothing could be done about it. Rosenwald
maintained his consistent position that his name not appear on any
objects of his charity, and on July 12, 1929, an amended certificate
was filed by the museum changing its name to the Museum of Science
and Industry, but stipulating that "whenever the name 'Museum of
Science and Industry' is used on behalf of this corporation (except in
legal papers and documents), it shall be immediately followed by the
words 'founded by Julius Rosenwald.'"

In this way, the museum trustees bowed to Rosenwald's refusal to
allow the museum to bear his name, despite his crucial contributions
to its creation. But they obviously felt that his efforts had to be acknowledged somehow, and for many years museum literature contained the words "founded by Julius Rosenwald," and Chicagoans
called it "the Rosenwald Museum."

Almost sixty years later, on January 21, 1986, when Julius
Rosenwald had been dead for more than a half century, his wish was
granted in its entirety. On that date the museum filed an amendment
to its articles of incorporation deleting the requirement that the words
"founded by Julius Rosenwald" appear on all museum papers. Thence-
forth the institution was known simply as the "Museum of Science
and Industry." This was a kind of tribute to the modesty of Chicago's
most notable Jewish philanthropist.

CENTURY OF PROGRESS: JEWISH DAY PAGEANT

———

THE GREATEST JEWISH SPECTACLE ever staged in Chicago took place on Monday evening, July 3, 1933 at Soldier Field, before more than 125,000 people. Sponsored by the Jewish Agency for Palestine, "The Romance of A People" was the culminating event of Jewish Day at A Century of Progress, the world's fair held along Chicago's lakefront. The fair was a colossal effort, planned for over five years, designed to emphasize the progress made by the United States, and by the city of Chicago, in the areas of technology, science and industry over the preceding hundred years.

Why a Jewish Day and why sponsorship by the Jewish Agency for Palestine? The Fair Committee had designated over two dozen special days, one for each of the nationalities that made up the immigrant population of Chicago, and was building a Hall of Religion for displays by Chicago's religious groups. Chicago's Zionists considered Palestine their homeland, and since the Jewish Agency represented the Jewish community in its dealings with the British Mandate authorities in Palestine, the Jewish Agency was the obvious choice to represent Jewish national aspirations. At least this was the choice of Meyer Weisgal, Executive Director of Zionist Activities for the Midwest. In his autobiography, *So Far*, Weisgal writes that in the early 1930s he formulated plans for a Chanukah pageant at Chicago's Opera House. The pageant was so successful that by 1932 he could proclaim, "The Zionist Organization is today on the lips of every Jew and non-Jew in the city of Chicago."

Weisgal had arrived in Chicago with his family from Kikl, Po-land, in 1908, at the age of fourteen. His father, Shloime Chaim Weisgal, had come to work as a *chazan*—a prayer leader—at the Tell Place Synagogue on the West Side. In 1911, Chazan Weisgal decided that "Kikl on Lake Michigan was not Kikl in Poland" and moved his family to the Bronx, where Meyer became interested in Zionism. By 1921, at the time of the struggle between Chaim Weizmann and Louis D. Brandeis for control of the Zionist Organization of America, Weisgal was a propagandist for the Weizmann group and editor of *The Maccabean*, the first ZOA monthly magazine in English.

According to Weisgal, when Chicago Jews were asked to partici-pate in the fair, discussions went on for months about whether the Jews were a race, a religion, or a nation; whether they should be rep-resented by a building; and if so, what kind of building? After the success of his 1932 Chanukah pageant, Weisgal felt inspired: "Not a building, not an exhibit, but a pageant portraying five thousand years of Jewish history. It would have everything—religion, history, the long-ing for Zion, the return to Zion, and it would be called 'The Romance of A People.'" Weisgal asked for and received the support of Rabbi Solomon Goldman and Judge Harry Fisher, two Chicago Zionist lead-ers. Then he went to see Rufus C. Dawes, president of the fair, a deeply religious man who loved his Bible. Weisgal was able to con-vince Dawes that Jews had "four thousand years of history, from Abraham down to the present that no one has!" Dawes agreed to schedule a special Jewish Day at the fair, the grand finale of which would be a huge spectacle produced by Meyer Weisgal.

In addition to the Jewish Day program, a Jewish exhibit, to be housed in the Hall of Religion for the duration of the fair, was organized by non-Zionist Reform Rabbis Louis Mann and Gerson Levi. It consisted of a display of Jewish artifacts and portraits of famous Jews through the ages, illustrating their contributions to the fields of social science, education, religion, literature, medicine, philanthropy, agriculture, states-manship, music, art, drama and child welfare. The design and planning was done by the architectural firm of Alfred S. Alschuler and Com-pany. A. Raymond Katz was the painter of the murals.

Weisgal gave the pageant all his time. By his account, he was the man in charge. He followed the general pattern of his Chanukah festival, but on a grander scale. Instead of dealing with a single holiday, the "Romance" would cover the period from the Creation to the twentieth century. The authors of the text included Weisgal, Rabbi Solomon Goldman and Weisgal's close friend Maurice Samuel, a talented writer and influential Zionist. The music director, who also wrote the score, was Isaac Van Grove, a composer who had been a conductor of the Chicago Civic Opera and who had worked with Weisgal on the Chanukah celebrations. Cantor Avrum Matthews, an opera and concert artist, was the leading singer.

Weisgal says that he had learned from his father and brother, who were cantors, how to stage a show with singers and dancers—particularly on the Jewish holidays. He recruited 3500 singers, actors and dancers from Jewish performing arts groups in Chicago, Milwaukee, Waukegan and Indiana Harbor. Among the music directors were Hyman Reznick, director of the Halevy Choral Society and musical director of the Board of Jewish Education in Chicago, and Evelyn Hattis Fox, a prominent community leader. The broadcasting director was Ralph Schoolman. Among the stage directors were Ben Zion Gordon and Ralph J. Halperin. Nathan Vizonsky directed the dancers.

Weisgal decided that he needed a famous speaker to fill Soldier Field, with its seating capacity of nearly 100,000. Who was the most famous Zionist Jew in 1933, and a brilliant orator at that? Chaim Weizmann, of course. Weisgal telephoned Weizmann, who was living in London. Weisgal describes their conversation:

WEISGAL: Hello, Dr. Weizmann, this is Meyer in Chicago.
WEIZMANN: *Vos, bistu meshugge gevorn?* Have you gone out of your mind? Is Chicago on fire again?
WEISGAL: No, but it will be when you come here. I want you to come to Chicago for Jewish Day.
WEIZMANN: What's that?
WEISGAL: (I explained as fast as I could.)

WEIZMANN: What's in it for the movement?

WEISGAL: (with impressive emphasis and prayer in my heart) If you will come to Chicago for one day, and make only one speech, even if for only five minutes, I will give you $100,000 for any Zionist fund you designate.

WEIZMANN: Put it in writing.

Weisgal promised in writing to raise $100,000 for Weizmann's Central Refugee Fund, which helped German Jews to settle in Palestine, and Weizmann agreed to come to Chicago. Weisgal warned Weizmann that he was limited to only one speech. If he made two speeches, the fee would go down to $50,000; if three, to $25,000.

Weisgal now had his star. By 1933, Chaim Weizmann, who had had a humble birth in 1874 in the village of Motol, near Pinsk in the Russian Pale of Settlement, had become an internationally famous organic chemist, the hero of the Balfour Declaration and the great populist leader of the Jewish people. Suddenly national Jewish organizations decided to participate in Jewish Day. The Zionist Organization of America shifted its convention to the Palmer House; the B'nai B'rith moved its annual meeting to Chicago, and national youth groups, including Avukah, the Zionist youth organization, scheduled a rally there for July 3.

In the days preceding Jewish Day, Jews flocked to Chicago, and on the day itself hundreds of extra police had to be called to handle the crowds. Thousands were already in Soldier Field in the afternoon, when Harry Berkman, a noted athlete, led 3,000 youths in marches and performances. Among the many prominent Jewish community leaders who came to Chicago was Nathan Strauss, Jr., the New York philanthropist.

The "Romance" began at 8:15 p.m. The next day, under a front-page headline, "125,000 Witness Jewish Spectacle," Chicago *Tribune* reporter James O'Donnel Bennett wrote: "One hundred and twenty-five thousand men, women and children of Chicagoland's Jewry unrolled on Soldier Field last night a gigantic scroll emblematic of the resounding Pentateuch and thereon they read the story, now tragic, now triumphant, of their race's march down forty centuries to the new Palestine of today."

The giant Torah was placed on a huge four-level stage at the center of the arena, where a chorus of thousands of singers and dancers were massed. In an innovation at that time, forty-six performers were positioned in a small room under the stage, unseen by the audience. Except for the massed chorus, these hidden performers supplied all the sound for the pageant. Twenty of the performers were singers, mostly cantors, and the rest were orchestra members, except for Ralph Schoolman, who read the narrative and was the Voice for the "Romance." They were led by a conductor who in turn watched Isaac Van Grove, standing in the center of the stage to conduct the entire proceedings. The stage was decorated with Stars of David and the new Zionist blue-and-white flag. A huge six-pointed star towered over the entire stage. Seven hundred and fifty dancing girls strewed flowers around the Torah. The *Tribune* report continued: "The solemn, weighty voices of cantors intoned in Hebrew the opening lines of Genesis—And God said Let there be light—and there was light. Trumpets and multitudes of voices heralded the coming of the earth's first dawn."

The pageant, which lasted about ninety minutes, was a tremendous success. The *Tribune*, having devoted fourteen columns to a description of it, was apparently so impressed that the newspaper underwrote a reenactment of the pageant for the following Thursday evening, July 6. This was accomplished, writes Weisgal, through Herculean efforts by the entire cast, but this time before a crowd estimated to be about 55,000.

As for Chaim Weizmann, he arrived in Chicago on July 1, and was greeted by an honorary reception committee of more than 100 people, headed by Bernard Horwich, a leading Chicago Zionist businessman and philanthropist. Weizmann delivered a ten-minute speech on July 3 before the pageant began. The exact text of his brief remarks is not quoted anywhere; he did not apparently deal with any substantive matter. He wrote to his wife Vera on 6 July 1933, "It is hot here and difficult to work . . . Generally speaking, it's been a

success, but there is not much money here . . . The Jewish Day went
off well. Everyone is praising the performance, though it was not to
my taste." He spent most of his stay in Chicago at the ZOA convention, where he did give a series of substantive speeches about the situation in Palestine, pleading for funds to strengthen the refugee German Jewish community there and discussing his plans for dealing with
the Arab-Jewish problem.

The British were reneging on their commitment to a Jewish homeland, and Arab unrest was increasing in Palestine. In 1931, Weizmann
had been defeated in a bid for reelection as president of the World
Zionist Organization, but he remained active in the movement, de-
voting much of his time to rescuing European refugees, and especially
helping German scientists escape to Palestine. After meeting with Emir
Feisal at Aqaba in 1918, he had hoped to reach an understanding
with Arab leaders over the conflicting national aspirations of Jews
and Arabs, saying that he believed that the 600,000 Arabs then living
in that territory had "exactly the same right to their homes [there] as
we have to our National Home." In his speeches to the Zionist convention in Chicago in 1933, he expressed his hopes for Arab-Jewish
reconciliation. But the Arabs did not respond to him and their attacks
on Jews in Palestine in succeeding years doomed Weizmann's hopes.

Weisgal comments that he raised the $100,000 promised to
Weizmann and sent it to him without deducting anything for the additional speeches. Immediately after Jewish Day, Weisgal attempted
to take the "Romance" on the road, but the God who had been so
cooperative in Chicago let the rains come down in New York. The
pageant had to be delayed and then performed indoors, though again
with great success.

Though not to Weizmann's taste, "The Romance of A People"
left fond memories for Chicagoans who were there as participants or
members of the audience. The Zionist conference at the Palmer House
was debating the growing crisis of German Jewry, but at the Pageant,
Chicago Jews, despite the Great Depression, could still exhibit pride
in their history, not foreseeing the tragedy about to engulf their people
in Europe. This was to be the last pre-World War II public spectacle

of its kind. A few years later, such a celebration would be unthinkable.

Weisgal's successful pageant did not make a profit. He could never stay within a budget and the organizations that backed his efforts did not like his exorbitant spending. Some critics claimed that Weisgal had taken Weizmann's $100,000 from the New York receipts of the "Romance," causing a loss there. In any case, after that pageant, Weisgal plunged into an even more spectacular project: a production of *The Eternal Road* by Franz Werfel, directed by Max Reinhardt with Norman Bel Geddes, and music by Kurt Weill. After expenditures that exceeded all expectations, the production opened in New York to critical praise and large audiences, but the investors lost all their money. *The Eternal Road* was produced again in Germany nearly seventy years later.

After that Weisgal went on to manage the Palestine Pavilion at the 1939 World's Fair in New York City, where he repeated his Chicago success. He presented Jewish Palestine as a nation among the nations of the world, raising the blue-and-white flag with its Star of David along with those of other sovereign nations, even though the State of Israel would not be recognized until 1948. World War II ended Weisgal's theatrical career. Weizmann lived to be elected the first president of Israel in 1948. Upon his death four years later, he was buried at Rehovot, the site of the Weizmann Institute of Science, which he had founded, and of which Meyer Weisgal eventually became president.

Weisgal applied his showmanship, bravado and fund-raising skills—first displayed so flamboyantly in Chicago in 1933—to his later work on behalf of the State of Israel and the Jewish people, for which he received deserved recognition. He died in 1977.

II
CHICAGO JEWS AND ANTI-SEMITISM: TRAGEDY ABROAD, CHALLENGES AT HOME

ADOLF KRAUS: EFFORTS TO HELP RUSSIAN JEWS

——

AT THE BEGINNING OF the twentieth century, Jews in Europe who hoped to immigrate to the United States received help from the earlier generation of immigrants who, feeling secure as Americans and possessing new political power, lobbied for increased Jewish immigration and favorable foreign policy decisions. It is difficult even now to determine how successful their efforts were. But Chicago's Jewish community played a central role, and one man, Adolf Kraus, was an important contributor to that role.

Kraus was a prominent Chicago attorney who, like many others, was horrified by widespread press reports of the Kishnev pogroms of 1903, which sparked a mass protest meeting addressed by Clarence Darrow and Jane Addams. Even before that, Czar Nicholas II had come under heavy criticism from many non-Jewish quarters One of the last absolute monarchs in the world, he was a symbol of the worst aristocratic abuses. When one of his ministers, Viacheslav Van Plehve—said to have been responsible for many pogroms—was killed by a bomb thrown by university student Igor Sazanov, many Americans applauded. The *Chicago Daily News* editorialized, "[t]he Cubs should hire [Sazanov] as a pitcher."

In 1904, when the Japanese attacked the Russian naval base at Port Arthur, setting off the Russo-Japanese war, Americans initially supported the Japanese. Jacob Schiff, a prominent New York financier, used the vast resources of his investment banking firm to float huge bond issues for the Japanese. But American opinion began to shift as terrorist assassinations of Russian officials increased and the Japanese inflicted a series of stunning defeats on the Russian armed forces. When the Russian Baltic fleet was wiped out in the Battle of Tsushina in May, 1905, and the sailors of the battleship *Potemkin* mutinied, President Theodore Roosevelt expressed the opinion that the potential collapse of Russia was a greater peril than the czar's continued tyrannical rule. After Japanese incursions into Manchuria and Korea, the American press began to label the Japanese the "yellow scourge." In this atmosphere, the czar sent representatives to the United States to negotiate a peace treaty with the Japanese under American auspices. Among these representatives was Russian finance minister Sergei Witte, soon to become prime minister and the man to whom Adolf Kraus would address most of his appeals.

Witte, unlike most of the czarist officials, seemed gracious and agreeable. With the American government now friendly to the czar Witte decided, in his own words, "that in view of the considerable influence of the Jews on the press and other aspects of American life, especially in New York, [it would be better] not to exhibit any hostility toward them." In August, 1905, Witte agreed to meet with some Jewish bankers, businessmen and community leaders to demonstrate that the Czar had no animus against these people. Kraus says in his 1925 autobiography *Reminiscences and Comments*, that it was at his request that Witte came to meet with this delegation on August 14, 1905 at Portsmouth, New Hampshire. Besides Kraus and Jacob Schiff, among those present were Oscar Straus, a New York businessman whom Theodore Roosevelt would soon appoint as the first Jewish member of a U.S. presidential cabinet, and Witte's official interpreter Gregory Wilenkin, a Russian Jew.

Kraus's goal at the meeting, as well as in his subsequent contacts with Witte, seems to have been to use his personal charm to demonstrate that Jews could be civilized citizens of the modern world. He wanted to show by his own example that Jews deserved full civil rights. His description of a key point in the meeting showed that hope:

Many questions were asked and answered during the interview. To Mr. Schiff's question, "Will you please tell me why you, as a Russian, have full rights in your country while he (pointing to Mr. Wilenkin), also a Russian, has none?", Witte, without hesitation, answered that the restrictive Russian laws applicable to Jews, if printed would fill a large volume; that they were unjust, that they ought to be repealed, but that that should be done gradually, for if they were repealed at once it might create a revolution; that only the Czar could repeal the laws, but that not much could be expected from the Czar so long as the young Jews were leaders among the Revolutionists; that we ought to use our influence to convince the young Jews that it was to our interest to be loyal to the Czar; that if that could be done, the Czar would probably grant relief.

To this remark, Jacob Schiff made a sharp retort which was, however, toned down by the more balanced judgment of the other members of the delegation.

This version of the events was more controversial than might at first appear. Philip Bregstone, in his 1933 *Chicago and Its Jews*, notes that, according to some Chicago newspapers, Witte demanded that the delegation members use their influence to keep Russian Jews from revolutionary activities, issuing an "ultimatum as a condition for the removal of restrictive laws" and the members of the committee promised to use their power to influence their Russian brethren.

Bregstone says that when Kraus returned to Chicago, a public meeting was arranged at Anshe Knesseth Israel Synagogue, on the corner of Clinton and Judd streets, at which Kraus was to report the results of his mission. However, a group of Jewish "radicals" incensed at the "incorrect" reports of the conference, came to the synagogue with the avowed purpose of causing a disturbance, and did almost succeed in breaking up the meeting. The police were called and about a dozen protesters were arrested. Bregstone himself became part of the Kraus-Witte affair because, as an assistant city attorney assigned to the Maxwell Street police court, he was called upon to prosecute the cases. Clarence Darrow's law firm was engaged for the defense with Darrow's partner Peter Sissman in charge. Sissman demanded a separate jury trial for each defendant.

When the first trial resulted in a guilty verdict, Bregstone felt he had made his point and he asked Kraus, the aggrieved party, for permission to drop charges against the other defendants. Bregstone reports that Kraus said, "I cannot blame these people for feeling as they do. They received the wrong impression through the reports of the press concerning our interview with Count de Witte and although they probably acted too rashly, I believe they have already been punished . . ."

Witte returned to Russia, where the czar appointed him premier of Russia and proclaimed a new constitution, supposedly granting new freedoms to the Russian people. There followed immediately a wave of pogroms against Jews in Odessa and other Russian cities. Kraus, as president of B'nai B'rith, telegraphed Witte demanding that he protect the Jewish population. Witte replied by wire: "You may be assured that the government will use all possible measures to prevent violence against peaceable inhabitants without regard to what nationality they belong." The *Chicago Daily News* St. Petersburg correspondent reported on April 25, 1906: "The publication of a letter written by Adolf Kraus of Chicago and Premier Witte's reply thereto has caused a sensation in Russia. The entire press recognizes the Chicagoan's communication as statesmanlike and humane."

The question of whether these Kraus-Witte communications would have any effect soon became moot when Witte died suddenly and the czar's constitution turned out to be a fraud. The revolution that was shaking Russia was crushed and the attacks on Jews continued. Adolf Kraus, however, went on trying to convince the czarists that there were "civilized" Jews, in the belief that this would cause them to drop their anti-Semitism.

In 1907 when the Russian Grand Duke Boris visited Chicago, Kraus arranged a luncheon where the Grand Duke and Baron Schlipenbach, the Russian consul, would meet forty recent Jewish immigrants from Russia, neatly shaved and appropriately dressed for the occasion, so the Duke "might see for himself what good citizens they become when offered the advantages of a friendly environment."

Kraus notes that the "Grand Duke outdid himself in affability and amiability. He had a few words to say to each one as my guests were introduced to him and responded most cordially to a toast to his health."

But Kraus's hope of convincing Duke Boris by his luncheon that Jews were "likeable" was doomed to disappointment. When he wrote the Duke later to protest the continuing pogroms, he never received an answer.

In the end, it is obvious that Kraus's efforts to ameliorate the situation of Russian Jews were a failure. But his attempts were interesting in themselves. He epitomized the Jewish immigrant who was able to prosper within his first few years in America. Born in Bohemia in 1850, he immigrated to the United States at the age of fifteen, came to Chicago a few years later and was admitted to the bar in 1877. He had a successful practice; many of his clients were non-Jewish Middle Europeans. He was corporation counsel under Mayor Carter Harrison and from 1895 to 1896 published and edited the *Chicago Times*. In 1899 he was elected president of Isaiah Congregation on the South Side. With his election as president of B'nai B'rith in 1905, he became deeply involved in Jewish communal affairs, becoming also an active member of the Jewish Committee.

His activities reflect the optimism of those prominent Jews who believed that their quick success in America could be replicated by Jews in other countries under improved political conditions. Kraus felt that if he could only convince the czar's ministers that Jews were really not different from other Russians, anti-Semitism would wither away.

Kraus remarked at one point that he was disappointed that his Reform Jewish background had taken him so far away from Jewish tradition that he was never a bar mitzvah. He may also have regretted his useless efforts to appease the czar's anti-Semitism with protestations of Jewish propriety. For all of their success in their new land, the Jews of America achieved uncertain results when they tried to use that success as leverage on the world political scene.

RETURN OF RUSSIAN REFUGEES PREVENTED

—

IN LATE 1908, CHICAGO was teeming with thousands of recent Jewish immigrants who had fled Russia and her provinces as a result of revolution and pogroms. The United States itself was in the throes of one of its cyclical depressions, and mass unemployment prevailed in Chicago. The new immigrants lived primarily in the so called "ghetto" area on Chicago's near South Side, west of the Chicago River. They were a frightened lot, without indigenous leadership. Spokesmen for the community were the earlier Jewish settlers from Germany, Middle Europe or, to a lesser degree, Lithuania—men like Rabbi Emil G. Hirsch, Judge Julian Mack, Julius Rosenwald and Bernard Horwich. The new immigrants had reasons to be afraid, still traumatized by a savage police and media onslaught on Russian "anarchists" which had occurred in March, 1908, when a young Russian Jewish immigrant from Kishineff, Lazarus Averbuch, was shot dead at the home of Chicago's chief of police because the chief thought he was an anarchist-assassin.

Within six months, another disturbing situation arose in Chicago, this time involving one of the most sensitive of all issues: the right of the Czarist police to demand extradition of persons wanted for crimes committed while they were in Russia. The case in question was formally entitled the "Matter of the Demand of the Imperial Russian Government for the Extradition of Christian Rudovitz." In her classic 1910 work *Twenty Years in Hull House*, Jane Addams wrote, "It is impossible for any unacquainted with the Russian colony to realize

43

the consternation produced by this attempted extradition. One old man, tearing his hairs and beard as he spoke, declared that all his sons and grandsons might thus be sent back to Russia; in fact all the younger men in the colony might be extradited, for every high-spirited young Russian was, in a sense, a revolutionist."

For Jane Addams, the "Russian colony" was the Jewish ghetto as it existed in 1908—a neighborhood adjoining Hull House in the Halsted Maxwell Street area. The Russian-Jewish immigrants, streaming into the United States by the tens of thousands, were also deeply concerned with other immigration problems. Congress was continually considering new legislation to stem the flood of "anarchists" from Russia—legislation that would, it was feared, prevent families from uniting in the U.S.

In addition, a bitter debate was raging between the Jewish community and the State Department and its secretary, Elihu Root, over the "Passport Question." In a circular letter dated May 28, 1907, State declared that henceforth, pursuant to existing treaties with Russia, passports would not be issued "to former Russian subjects or to Jews who intend going into Russia, unless it has assurance that the Russian government will consent to this admission." While the State Department withdrew parts of this directive early in 1908, the "Passport Question" continued to be an area of open concern to American Jews, particularly those who were recent immigrants from Russia.

The State Department circular arose out of provisions contained in trade treaties between Russia and the United States in the 1880s, one of which, concluded in 1887, provided for the extradition of persons charged with certain crimes. In 1908 the Czarist government apparently decided to test this treaty by seeking the extradition of two refugees: Jan Pouren, in New York, and Christian Rudovitz, in Chicago.

Rudovitz, born in 1873 in the Baltic states, had fled to Chicago in the late fall of 1907 and worked as a carpenter in West Pullman. As his name indicates, he was not Jewish. He was arrested on a charge by Baron Ernst Schilling, the Imperial Russian Consul at Chicago, that he had committed the crimes of 'murder, arson, burglary, robbery and larceny on or about January 3, 1906 at the estate of Benen, District of Tukkum, in the Government of Courtland, in the Empire of Russia."

The extradition trial began in Chicago on December 1, 1908 before Mark A. Foote, United States Commissioner for the Northern District of Illinois, who was not a lawyer. At that time commissioners were not required to have legal training, and their expenses had to be paid by the country seeking extradition.

Rudovitz's arrest caught the attention not only of Jane Addams but also of many other settlement workers and liberal intellectuals active in Chicago's civil struggles. Graham Taylor of the Chicago Commons, Raymond Robins, another settlement worker and leading Progressive; and Louis Post, editor of the periodical *The Public*, came forward to protest the extradition. Some of Chicago's leading newspapers, however, did not appreciate the views of the settlement leaders. The *Inter Ocean* branded Rudovitz's supporters "precisely those who are always expressing sympathy, for the murderers and would-be murderers." It was the interest of Jane Addams and her friends, however, that undoubtedly made Rudovitz a landmark case, for Addams was instrumental in bringing in Clarence Darrow, who in 1908 was already a well known figure on the Chicago legal scene.

Darrow had only recently returned to Chicago from Boise, Idaho, after contracting a near-fatal illness at the trials of "Wild Bill" Heywood, a labor leader indicted for the murder of the governor of Idaho, who had been killed by a bomb when he opened the gate to his home. Darrow had won not-guilty verdicts at these trials and was now back in Chicago practicing law with the firm of Darrow, Masters & Wilson. An associate at this firm was a Jewish attorney and socialist, Peter Sissman, who joined Darrow in working on the Rudovitz case. Sissman himself was an immigrant from Russia.

The Russian government charged that Rudovitz and his accomplices had broken into the house of a Leskinsky family in Benen on January 3, 1906, killed mother, father and daughter, burned their house and stolen their valuables. Darrow argued that these acts, if they had occurred as claimed, were all political crimes, not extraditable under the treaty with Russia.

Darrow drew a harrowing picture of Russia and the Baltic states during the Revolution of 1905 and after, presenting reports of tortures inflicted by the Czarist police in Benen of such a ghastly nature that "gasps went up from those gathered to witness Rudovitz's fight for liberty." Prisoners were beaten until the flesh fell from their bones, pencils were stuck into their eyes and police jumped on a young boy's chest until his chest bones and ribs were broken.

A principal witness for the defense was Martin Jurow, another Russian immigrant and a friend of Rudovitz, who testified that these tortures were inflicted on his own young brothers when they refused to disclose Martin's hiding place. When asked on cross-examination to disclose the names of fellow revolutionists, Jurow refused to answer, and his refusal was sustained after lengthy argument before a federal judge. Jurow explained that he and Rudovitz were members of the Social Democratic party; their aim "was to overthrow the present government and establish one for the people. We robbed the barons and disarmed the soldiers. We broke into houses and stole guns and ammunition. We adopted resolutions that those who gave evidence against our leaders should be killed." Jurow said that those who had been killed were spies who had betrayed their comrades.

On December 6, 1908 in an overcrowded courtroom, Clarence Darrow made his final plea to Commissioner Foote. The *Chicago Tribune* reported:

> The final argument for the defense began with a fiery denunciation of Russian oppression and autocracy. Charges that the czar is plotting to stretch the arm of despotism over the United States were coupled with the statement that there are more than 100,000 political exiles from Russia in America and that if the barriers which stand between Rudovitz and trial by Russian court martial are broken down, it will establish a precedent under which the czar may seek and reclaim countless other fugitives here.

The attorney for the Russian government, William C. Rigby, argued that the crimes involved were not political in motive: "He is not a bona fide revolutionist; he is a common murderer and robber, a common criminal, and should be sent to Russia to stand trial for his crimes." Immediately after the closing arguments, Commissioner Foote ruled that Rudovitz should be extradited to Russia. Darrow then announced that the defense would file an administrative appeal to Elihu Root, Secretary of State, the only legal recourse left, in order to quash the extradition.

Darrow, Sissman and a law professor prepared and filed a sixty-nine-page brief with Secretary Root, setting forth the facts and their view of the law with respect to extradition for "political crimes." In a lengthy review of all existing authorities, the lawyers for Rudovitz argued that his "crimes" were clearly political in light of the revolutionary activities occurring in the Russian territories in 1908. The brief concluded:

> The political aspect of an offense is not affected by reason of the brutality of the act committed, or by presence of malice which the actor may have towards the victim. It is also immaterial whether the act is generally described as a common crime; also, whether the victim is actually a nonparticipant in an attempt to suppress the uprising.
>
> In the present case, there was at the time of the Benen expedition a political uprising throughout the Baltic provinces and extending over a large portion of the Russian Empire. Benen, Zhagarn and Mitau were in the center of the revolutionary area. Every act placed at the door of the accused was directly connected with, incidental to and formed a part of the political disturbance. If Christian Rudovitz was himself a member of the Benen expedition, and committed any of the acts charged against him, the demanding Government is not entitled to his surrender in view of the beneficent provision of Article III of the Extradition Treaty of 1887, which declares that, "If it be made to appear that extradition is sought with a view to try or punish the person demanded for an offense of a political character, surrender shall not take place (Treaties in Force, 1904, 673)."

For that reason counsel for the accused respectfully request that
he be not surrendered to the demanding Government, and that he
be discharged from custody.

While the brief was being prepared, a new organization was formed
in Chicago: the Political Refugee Defense League of America. Philip
Angaten, a former member of the Chicago Board of Education, was
installed as president; Isabel McLain as vice-president; Raymond Robins as secretary and Jane Addams as treasurer. The group planned to
have mass meetings and to appeal directly to President Theodore
Roosevelt. These mass meetings began on December 14. One gathering at Hull House attracted hundreds of people who were addressed
by, among others, according to the Chicago *Tribune*, "Samuel Mervis
and Maurice Seskind. The last two spoke in Hebrew." At another
meeting, held at the Chicago Opera House, Israel Zangwill's play *The
Melting Pot* was presented.

The Chicago Federation of Labor adopted resolutions demanding
that Rudovitz be granted asylum. Other meetings and groups adopted
resolutions calling on the U.S. to abrogate the existing treaties with
Russia. Congressman A. J. Sabath, Judge Julian Mack and Rabbi Emil
G. Hirsch became active in these protest meetings.

Professor John Henry Wigmore of the Northwestern University
Law School, a leading legal intellectual whose "Wigmore on Evidence"
is still in use today, sent a lengthy opinion to Secretary Root comparing the Russian revolutionists to the "operations around Boston in
1775, before the American colonists' military organization was per-
fected in Philadelphia." As to the crimes themselves, Wigmore as-
serted that they were merely incidental to the revolution, which was
"political in nature." On the last day of his term in office in January,
1909, Root granted asylum to Rudovitz and Pouren, stating that
Rudovitz's crime was a political offense and therefore "under the terms
of the treaty in effect between the U.S. and Russia . . . he was not
extraditable." Rudovitz, who had been held in the Cook County Jail
since his arrest, was released on January 28, 1909.

Root's ruling came as a surprise to many. He was not known for his liberal attitudes on immigration, and the Roosevelt administration in general had been extreme in its call for restrictive legislation against radical elements, particularly immigrants from Russia. Perhaps the motivation was a desire for new political support on the part of a man about to become a U.S. Senator from New York. Or the ruling might have reflected some disillusionment with the Czar's oppressive actions in Russia. The *Chicago Daily News* reported that "in the Jewish quarter, the news caused general rejoicing." It did not matter that Rudovitz was a Lutheran.

With this decision, the Russians ceased their attempts to extradite Russian immigrants from the United States. Several years later the "Passport Question" also became moot when the United States abrogated its treaty with the Russians which had given the Russian government the right to deny an American passport to Jews wishing to travel to Russia.

Many historic gyrations have occurred in American relations with Russia since the Rudovitz case, particularly in connection with immigration issues. Within ten years of the case, undesirable immigrants were being deported by America to Soviet Russia. In the twenties, America closed its borders to mass immigration from Eastern Europe and, of course, under Stalin Russia closed its own borders to Jewish emigration.

A more personal footnote to history: three years after the Rudovitz case, Darrow became involved in the notorious McNamara litigation in Los Angeles, where the McNamara brothers were indicted for dynamiting the headquarters of the *Los Angeles Times* and killing twenty people in a bitter labor dispute. As a result of this litigation, Darrow was accused of bribery and subjected to difficult and expensive trials in order to clear his name. When he returned to Chicago in 1913, penniless and discouraged, he told friends that he was through with the law. It was Peter Sissman, the Russian Jewish immigrant and co-counsel in the Rudovitz case, who approached Darrow offering to join in a law partnership with him. The partnership of Darrow and

Sissman lasted for over ten years. One of the last cases handled by the firm was the defense of Nathan Leopold and Richard Loeb for the murder of Bobby Franks in 1924.

BLOOD LIBEL: PREJUDICE ON THE SOUTH SIDE

―――

UNLIKELY AS IT SOUNDS more than eighty years later, there was a ritual murder accusation on Chicago's South Side in 1919, and some Chicago Jews had to seek safety from their neighbors who had been inflamed by a story without foundation. Although apparently no one was seriously hurt, criminal charges and some strong police action were necessary before sanity reigned again.

On July 4, 1919, a mostly Polish-American mob began roaming the neighborhoods along Buffalo Avenue between 81st and 84th Streets. The mob had been incited by one Casimir Lota who was circulating a story that H. Kahn, a merchant, had murdered a Christian child as part of a secret Jewish blood-letting ritual.

This "blood libel," as the Jews called it, had most recently occurred eight years earlier, in 1911, when a Russian Jew named Mendel Beilis was accused by the Czarist authorities of perpetrating a ritual murder. The absurdity of the charges and the treatment of Beilis sent shock waves around the world, Chicago being one of many places where people demonstrated against the Russian government. For the next two years, until he came to trial in 1913, Beilis was imprisoned, and Chicago newspapers kept their readers informed of the case. Hearst's daily *Chicago American* went so far as to put out an extra edition on October 20, 1913, mostly in Yiddish.

Chicago community activists and area politicians were outspoken in their outrage against the Russians. Judge Julian Mack, Hannah

Greenebaum Solomon, and Jane Addams were just a few who met to plan a mass meeting to protest the Russian trial. U.S. Representative Adolph Sabath and Senator J. Hamilton Lewis, both of Illinois, introduced resolutions in Congress condemning the Russians.

An October 16, 1913, mass meeting—so large that the crowd filled the Garrick Theater and organizers had to arrange for the overflow to go to Cohn Opera House across the street—marked the height of Chicago's concern about the case. Speakers from across the country and from all religious denominations came together to condemn Russia's actions.

Jane Addams opened the proceedings to great applause. Father O'Callaghan, a leading Chicago Catholic priest, said that he worked incessantly to discourage anti-Semitism in his flock. Booker T. Washington condemned the trial, but expressed the hope that it would help usher in an era when prejudices of every sort would break down before the realization that the "brotherhood of man" was the most important common link of all humanity. It was Jenkin Lloyd Jones of Lincoln Center, however, who best delivered the outrage of the gathering. It was Russia, he said, not the Jews, who was on trial. Rabbi Emil Hirsch declared, "The Russian government wants somebody to justify the Russian Pale. The atrocities in Cuba for which we went to war are child's play compared to the treatment by the Czar and his police of the six million people whose only crime is their refusal to adopt the orthodox religion of Russia."

If, indeed, it was Czarist Russia that was on trial in the Beilis case, then Czarist Russia was found guilty. On October 28, a jury of Russian peasants acquitted Beilis of the crime of ritual murder. Within five years, Czarist Russia would no longer exist. In its place, Lenin would have established the Union of Soviet Socialist Republics. The Beilis case itself was not at all a factor in the Russian Revolution, but it was emblematic of the barbarism that had made the Russian government almost universally despised. Certainly Chicago Jews did not expect a ritual murder charge to surface only six years later in their own community.

Chicagoans did not seem to know how to react to the events of July, 1919. Mainstream newspapers that had lavished attention on the Beilis case completely ignored the Kahn accusation. The earliest extant press account of the incident comes from the July 8 *Chicago Jewish Courier*, the city's leading Yiddish newspaper, which reported only that Kahn had filed charges against Casimir Lota for inciting mob violence against his family and property. A hearing of the charges was set before Judge Gemill for July 24.

The *Courier* reported that because over one hundred extra police were on patrol, the streets were quieter by July 8. Along with that good news came some bad: "The boycott against the Jewish stores in South Chicago is growing. Poles are still whispering about a murdered Polish youth, and thus the boycott propaganda advocated in the local Polish newspapers has spread." The *Courier* picked up the story again on July 25, reporting that at the hearing the day before of the case against Lota and seventeen other Poles, the courtroom was packed with Polish men and women, and consequently a number of Jews who were scheduled to appear as witnesses for the plaintiffs were afraid to testify.

Kahn's two sons did testify that Lota had spread rumors of ritual murder about their father and that he had brought other Poles into Buffalo Avenue to terrorize the Jewish community. Lota, they said, had gone into Kahn's store accompanied by police and a group of Poles, and was allowed to search the entire place, including the basement. This despite the fact that no body had been found and that the police outside announced that no harm had come to a single soul. Lota had gone about the neighborhood shouting that the Kahns had killed a Polish boy and that the police had been paid to cover up the murder.

Called to testify at the hearing, Lota, "in broken English," denied all the charges against him. Judge Gemill, apparently stunned by the nature of the case before him, was prompted to comment, "Alas, what citizens we have." The *Courier* reported that, upon examination by two assistant state's attorneys, Lota was shown to be a liar and that he and his cohorts "are rioters and deserve punishment." The judge immediately found Lota guilty of inciting mob violence and fined him $100. The other seventeen defendants were called up one after the other, found guilty by Gimmel, and fined $10 each. All the defendants paid on the spot.

The *Courier* concluded with a bit of humor: "When everyone had already left the courtroom, shouts were heard outside. Casimir Lota was arguing with his lawyer, Bill O'Connor, to return the twenty dollars he had given him in return for the assurance that O'Connor would free Lota from the charge against him. In the end, O'Connor spat and left in his automobile amidst the ringing laughter of some Americans there."

Though the incident was ignored by Chicago's mainstream press, a local newspaper, the *Daily Calumet*, ran a long editorial on the riots on July 7, 1919, saying they had stirred up "race prejudices." It decried the rumors that a Polish boy had been murdered despite the fact that no body had been found. "There was absolutely nothing to the story, but nevertheless, there are people who like to believe such things, and it has been found extremely difficult to stamp out these false reports." The editorial did not point out the particular anti-Semitic nature of these riots but dealt with them as stemming from "race prejudice" and "rumor spreading" which should be avoided in the future.

An interesting article by Ann Friedman, "Life Among the Poles in Old South Chicago," appeared in the June, 1989, issue of *Chicago Jewish History*. Her family owned a store near Buffalo Avenue, and she describes the frequent attacks on Jews living in that area. In the disturbances of 1919, she recalls that Davey Miller and his gang, a "tough bunch" from Chicago's West Side, came to the assistance of these South Side Jews: "I don't know who asked him to assist us, but this time Miller used brains rather than brawn. He visited the priest at St. Michael's Church at 83rd Street and South Shore Drive, the parish of the Polish people in our area. Miller also had a reputation for being a diplomat. He requested the priest to ask from the pulpit if any of their children were missing. There was no response. The rumors ended, calm was restored to the area, and Jews in this South Chicago neighborhood called The Bush were able to continue their sometimes uneasy lives among Polish Americans."

With Lota's conviction, the blood libel faded away. One reason it is forgotten today may be that, a few weeks later at the end of July, 1919, notorious race riots shook Chicago when predominantly Irish-American mobs killed hundreds of African-Americans, and the city's attention focussed on another violent prejudice.

AMBIJAN: AUTONOMOUS JEWISH REGION OF USSR

While Zionists and their supporters worked to create a Jewish state in Palestine in the 1920s, some Jewish leaders, Chicagoans among them, sought alternatives to a state in the Middle East. Some called for the development of political autonomy within existing governments, proposing, among other things, settling Jews as farmers in thinly populated areas of the United States. There was talk of a Jewish state in Uganda or somewhere in South America. But it was in Stalin's Soviet Union that these discussions led to the formation of a nominal Jewish state in Birobidjan, a vast, inhospitable area in Eastern Siberia, the only country in the world where Yiddish would be the official language. A Chicago attorney named Jacob Grossberg played a tragic role in this story.

There was a large Jewish population in the fertile Crimea, where they suffered serious religious persecution. In 1926, a group of American Jews met in Philadelphia to form *ICOR*, an organization devoted to raising funds for the establishment of Jewish collectives in the Crimea; the name means "farmer" in Hebrew. Julius Rosenwald was the biggest backer of *ICOR*, ultimately contributing $2,500,000 of the $15,000,000 the group would raise. Rosenwald and other *ICOR* supporters broke with world Zionist leaders who considered the project a distraction from the more pressing work of settling Jews in Palestine. Dr. Stephen Wise, on behalf of the Zionist leadership, opposed placing any funds in the hands of Soviet officials. He insisted that the Soviet government would never keep its word to the Jewish settlers and that sooner or later the Jews would be removed from the land. While Rosenwald opposed the philosophy of the Soviet government, he felt it was nevertheless essential to take a chance on the good faith of the Soviet leaders.

In any event, the *ICOR* funds were passed on to the Soviet Union, where officials sent back glowing reports of Jews settling in the Crimea and using the American donations to purchase farm equipment. There were no practical ways for *ICOR* to determine the truth of these reports and within a couple of years the Soviets turned their attention to the even more ambitious project of settling Jews in Birobidjan. *ICOR* simply faded away.

Jacob Grossberg was a prominent Chicago attorney, a leader in numerous civic and Jewish communal activities and in 1916 a founder of the American Jewish Congress. Always an independent spirit, he had his differences with the leaders of the Congress and with the Zionist Organization of America. In February, 1936, Grossberg convened a meeting at his home of some leading Chicago Jews to discuss forming a Chicago chapter of Ambijan, a New York group founded to support Jewish settlement in Birobidjan. Among the people reported to have been present at that first meeting were Mr. and Mrs. Henry Koenig, Nicholas J. Pritzker, Julius Schaffner, S. B. Komaiko and Charles Komaiko, Jr.

Since this group was largely ignorant of the inhospitable conditions of Birobidjan, the possibility must have sounded appealing. For two years, the Soviet Government had recognized Birobidjan as an Autonomous Region for Jewish settlement, with Yiddish as its official language. Soviet officials held out promises that Birobidjan would one day become a full-fledged republic and the Jewish cultural center of the Soviet Union. The Zionists' political state in Palestine was still just a dream—no one could guess that its establishment was only twelve years away—and here was a Jewish state that already existed, one that awaited only financial support from world Jewry.

As could be expected, the Chicago Ambijan Committee immediately encountered Zionist opposition just as *ICOR* had a decade earlier. In reply to an invitation to a fund-raising dinner, Judge J. M.

Braude, a Chicago Zionist, replied that he would not attend and that help for the Jews in Palestine was of greater importance. H.L. Meites wrote in *The Chicago Jewish Chronicle* in February, 1936, that Jacob Grossberg had "completely retired from communal activity of Jewish interest" in unwisely choosing to work for Ambijan.

Grossberg replied, "We are confronted with a situation even worse than the one which originally called into being the Jewish Congress. With the inhuman persecutions from which Jews are suffering in Central Europe, all existing places of asylum, including Palestine, are wholly inadequate. Birobidjan not only constitutes a very substantial addition to these places, but holds out hope of being ultimately of the greatest capacity."

In a recent biography, Grossberg's grandson Edmund Grossberg writes about his grandfather's Ambijan work. His first effort was a dinner in June of 1936 to raise money and elect a delegation to visit Birobidjan. He planned originally to hold the dinner in the Standard Club, but the club manager kept dragging his feet, so the meeting was shifted to the Hotel Sherman. Grossberg fired off a letter of complaint about the manager's discourteous behavior to Edward Felsenthal, and received an apology from the club president, A. G. Ballenger.

Grossberg wrote also to Samuel A. Goldsmith, executive director of the Jewish Welfare Board—predecessor of the United Jewish Appeal—about including Ambijan in the distribution of charitable funds raised by the Chicago Jewish community. Goldsmith was not receptive to this plea. But in November Grossberg organized another dinner at which Lord Marley was the featured speaker. A fairly substantial amount of money was raised and forwarded to the New York headquarters. The immediate objective was to resettle a first contingent of 1,000 Polish Jews in Birobidjan.

This fundraising success was a testimony to Grossberg's impressive standing in the community. He had brought the issue before the Chicago public and managed in a matter of months to make it possible for those first 1,000 Jews to begin settling in Birodbidjan. It must have seemed then that Ambijan was about to create a massive resettlement that would save thousands of Jewish lives. But immediately after that, things slowed down. Deciding to wait for a response from New York Ambijan headquarters before the Chicago branch went on with fund raising, Grossberg began a stream of one-sided correspondence. He wrote letter after letter to New York and received evasive responses or none at all.

Weeks turned into months and months into more than two years before Grossberg finally acknowledged to himself and Chicago Ambijan that their efforts had been in vain. In November, 1938, he telegraphed New York demanding the return of all monies sent from Chicago, noting that the Ambijan committee had failed to move a single person from Eastern Europe to Birobidjan. Although it took relentless effort, Grossberg eventually did manage to recover the money from the New York office. Embarrassed at the failure of his and the committee's efforts, and after consultation with the major donors, the committee donated the funds to the American Organization for Rehabilitation through Training (ORT).

As Edmund Grossberg puts it: "The story of Birobidjan is another historical footnote on the efforts to prevent the Holocaust by getting the Jews of Europe out of harm's way. [Grossberg], like other thinking and caring people of the time, tried to do something and failed. In their worst nightmares nobody foresaw the full extent of what was about to occur."

The Chicago Ambijan Committee appears to have been revived after World War II when a new group of Chicago Jews raised money on behalf of the Jews of Birobidjan. As late as 1948, J. Jessmar wrote in the *Chicago Sentinel* 's "100 Years of Chicago Jewry," that over 30,000 Jewish war orphans had been settled in Birobidjan after World War II and that more than 115,000 Jews were living there. Jessmar said that Birobidjan offered to Jewish survivors, "a Jewish environment and the hope of a richer life for themselves and their children." Such a conclusion could be possible, of course, only if one ignored Stalin's anti-Semitic policies, many of which were hostile to the very idea of a Jewish identity, let alone a Jewish state.

In a few years the Chicago Ambijan Committee was gone, as were most of the Jews who actually had settled in Birobidjan. With them went not only the dream of a Jewish state in Europe but also the work and honest efforts of Jacob Grossberg and others whose good intentions blinded them to the insurmountable obstacles of their project.

KRISTALLNACHT HAUNTS CHICAGO

—

FROM NOVEMBER 9 TO 10, 1938, the infamous government-sanctioned Kristallnacht was carried on throughout Germany. Hundreds of German and Austrian synagogues were vandalized or destroyed; 30,000 Jews were arrested and sent to concentration camps where many were murdered; and thousands of Jewish-owned stores were looted and their windows shattered—hence the Nazi euphemism "Kristallnacht." Shortly afterward the German government levied a huge fine on the German-Jewish community, making them pay for their own destruction. In addition, numerous new restrictions were imposed, designed effectively to hasten the exclusion of Jews from German society.

The Nazis officially declared that all this vandalism and destruction was a spontaneous reaction of the German people to the assassination of Ernst Vom Rath, a German embassy official in Paris, by Herschel Grynszpan, a seventeen-year-old Polish-Jewish refugee. A week earlier, Grynszpan's parents, along with thousands of other Polish Jews, had been forcibly transported by the Nazis from Germany to Poland. Vom Rath's assassination was the tormented son's revenge.

The governments of Poland, Romania and Hungary were actively anti-Semitic and the tragic deadlock in Arab-Jewish relations in Palestine came to a head in 1938. As country after country seemed to be caught up in the fury of anti-Semitism, American Jews, confronted with the appalling prospect of millions of Jews being driven out of Europe, were powerless to provide a haven, since U.S. immigration laws allowed entrance only to a few. To make matters worse, anti-Semitism and isolationism were growing in America in 1938 and millions were still unemployed as the Great Depression continued. Immediately after Kristallnacht, Chicago Jewry responded as a community with public protests, prayers, fund-raising and support for a boycott of German goods—this last a controversial issue. At that time, the city had the second largest Jewish community in America; it was also fairly representative of political life in America. It was possible for some individuals to help a few European Jews reach the United States by signing affidavits, often backed by funds put in escrow, guaranteeing that these refugees would not become public charges. Unfortunately these affidavits saved only a very small number of the millions of endangered German, Austrian, Polish and Hungarian Jews.

Fifty years later, Jewish organizations, including the Jewish press, have come under heavy criticism for their passivity, their failure to demonstrate, protest and lobby vigorously against the U.S. lack of positive action to save Hitler's victims. A number of books have analyzed the events of the 1930s and their tragic consequences: *The Transfer Agreement* by Edwin Black; *The Deafening Silence* by Rafael Medoff; *Beyond Belief* by Deborah E. Lipstadt; Haskell Lookstein's *Were We Our Brothers' Keepers?: The Public Response of American Jews to the Holocaust 1938-1944* and David Kranzler's *Thy Brothers' Blood—The Orthodox Response During the Holocaust.*

The year 1938 started with ominous stories from Europe of impending attacks on Jews. On January 27, the *Sentinel* headlined a full-page story: "100,000 Jews Flee From Romania Districts." On the same day, another article, headed "German Jewry's Obituary," begins: "The world press has become more or less silent about the situation of the Jews in Germany." On February 24, 1938, the *Sentinel's* headline was "Anticipate Emigration of 25,000 German Jews—5,000 to Palestine and 10,000 to the U.S.A."

In March, 1938, Germany annexed Austria. Thousands of Jews were assaulted and arrested. Many were killed or commited suicide. The Nazi rampage in Vienna was unprecedented, exceeding anything that had occurred in Germany up to that time, and received full coverage in the Chicago press, both Jewish and mainstream. The March 19 issue of the *Sentinel* carried these banner headlines: "Nazi Hordes Swarm over Austria," "Suicidal Wave Sweeps Austria" and "Extend Boycott to Austria." On March 31 the paper reported that Jews were being forced to sweep the streets of Vienna at gunpoint, and that Goering had warned, "All Jews Must Go." An editorial in the *Reform Advocate* strongly backed a boycott of Austrian goods.

On April 7 the *Sentinel* carried a long story about the launch of an anti-Semitic program in Hungary, and reported that at a dinner celebrating the fiftieth anniversary of the *Chicago Jewish Courier* at the Sherman House, Secretary of the Interior Harold J. Ickes had sharply attacked the Nazi actions. All through the late winter and spring of 1938 the papers carried alarming stories about the condition of Polish Jewry, detailing the policy announced by the Polish government in May, 1938, that the "Jewish problem" was to be solved by the reduction in the number of Jews "to be achieved by furthering their emigration to Palestine and other countries." (Madagascar was a destination favored by the Poles.) "Special benches" had been set up for Jewish college students and authorities had ordered a boycott of Jewish businesses. At that time there were nearly three million Jews in Poland.

In June, 1937, Rabbi Stephen Wise and other Jewish leaders had met with Secretary of State Cordell Hull to ask for official American condemnation of the anti-Semitic actions of the Polish government. But things were getting worse. The June, 1938, Evian-les-Bains conference, called by the United States and other countries to find havens for refugees after the Austrian invasion, was a disaster. The Polish government insisted on the "resettlement" of at least 50,000 of its Jews every year. Country after country, including the USA, whose quota for all Polish immigrants remained a mere 6,000 per year, made clear that they were not willing to amend their immigration laws to help the refugees. It should be noted that the Nazis often pointed gleefully to the Evian conference as proof that the world did not want German Jews.

Romania too was often in the news in early 1938. The previous December, Octavian Goga had taken over as premier with the avowed purpose of destroying or expelling the Jews, and he implemented anti-Jewish laws with lightning speed. King Carol dismissed Goga in February, but for the Jews of Romania the pattern had been set for the future. For Romania and other "new" post-World War I countries like Hungary and Czechoslovakia, the U.S. had virtually no immigration quota at all.

The Jewish community in Palestine was also under siege in 1938. In 1937 the British Royal Commission for Palestine, the Peel Commission, issued a report recommending partition of the country. Its immediate effect was to divide all elements in Palestine—and elsewhere—into pro- and anti-partition camps. In Chicago numerous articles and editorials addressed the issue. At the Jewish Agency meeting in London in March, 1938, the majority of American non-Zionists opposed partition. Their representative Felix M. Warburg declared, "We believe that no lasting peace in Palestine can be obtained until the parties directly affected, namely the Jews and the Arabs, have been given a full opportunity to endeavor to arrive at a peaceful understanding."

The opposing positions attracted a great deal of attention in the Jewish press. An anguished editorial by Ludwig Lewisohn in the *Sentinel* on March 31 attacked the anti-Zionists for opposing the Zionist leader Chaim Weizmann, calling them "assimilationist forces" impeding the creation of a Jewish state which could serve as a haven for Jews. "Do you want," Lewisohn asked rhetorically, "to wait till a new world war is on us and you cannot rescue the Jewish youth of Germany, Austria, Poland, Romania? Or don't you want to rescue that youth at all?" The final resolution of the Jewish Agency meeting was a compromise designed to seek further negotiations with the British. In any event, in early 1938 there were reports of widespread fighting in Palestine between the British and Arabs and increased tension between Arabs and Jews. The papers reported that in June, 1938, Shlomo Ben Joseph, the first Jew to be executed by the British, was hanged in Acre Prison for shooting at an Arab bus.

The macabre world scene was concisely summed up in an editorial by William Zuckerman in the *Sentinel* on April 6, 1938, headlined, "Is European Jewry Finished?": "Thus there is not now a Jewish community in Europe that can come to the succor of the Austrian Jews. Perhaps salvation lies with American Jewry. European Jewry cannot stand up to the new tragedy."

Beginning in June, 1938, the *Chicago Tribune* carried almost daily front-page stories about attacks on Jews in Berlin and other German cities. The *Tribune*'s coverage of events in Germany during this period was remarkable in its clarity, revealing in graphic detail the fury being unleashed on the Jews of Germany. Considering that Robert R. McCormick, the paper's publisher, was an isolationist who detested the British and supported Hitler as a bastion against the "Communist menace," these articles on the plight of the Jews in Germany are astonishing. For example, next to the news that Johnny Vander Meer had pitched his second successive no-hit game in five days for the Cincinnati Reds on June 16, 1938, was a column by Sigrid Schultz about the terrorizing of the Jews of Berlin, where Nazi gangs were roaming the streets, attacking Jews and Jewish businesses. Jews were driven out of movie theaters and some were arrested. There were reports of deportations to Buchenwald, "a concentration camp."

On June 18 and 19, 1938, the front page headlined the "Berlin War on Jews." Schultz reported that fifty Jewish stores had been smashed in Berlin, two new concentration camps were being built, and the June campaign against the Jews was said to have been provoked by the Czechs. (The American Jewish Yearbook for 1938-1939 suggests that the disorders were intended to impress participants at the Evian conference that the Nazis were serious about driving the Jews out of Germany.) Sigrid Shultz was the *Tribune*'s trusted Berlin bureau chief, who, born in Chicago, had lived for years in Germany. She was openly critical of the Nazis, and her reports gave Chicagoans eyewitness accounts of the Nazi rampage. After Pearl Harbor, she returned to America and in her 1944 book *Germany Will Try Again*, urged the total dismantling of Germany.

As summer ended, Czechoslovakia and its Jews were in mortal danger. In September, 1938, the mass exodus of Jews from the Sudeten area, which was soon to be ceded to Germany, began. The Munich "settlement" at the end of September completed the expulsion of the Jewish community from the Sudetenland. Thousands of Jews fled to Prague and its environs. Over 20,000 Jews had been driven out of their homes by the Nazis, and panic gripped all the Jews of Czechoslovakia.

On November 8 and 9, 1938, the *Tribune* headlined results of Congressional elections at the same time that the Kristallnacht riots were beginning in Germany. Under the paper's banner headline of election results on November 10 there was a second headline, "Mobs Wreck Jewish Stores in Berlin," over a story by Sigrid Schultz. On November 11 under the front-page headline "Hitler Seizes 20,000 Jews," Schultz wrote an eyewitness account of the destruction of synagogues and stores in Berlin:

> Systematic destruction of Jewish property, looting, arson and wholesale arrests of Jews without charges swept Germany today. It is estimated that 20,000 Jews were arrested in Germany and what was Austria. The Nazi violence far outdid anything that happened along this line in Germany in the darkest days of the Red Revolution. Then hungry mobs stormed the food stores. Today the mob gloated over the smashed stores of Jews. They helped themselves to clothes, furs and toys and scattered the goods in the streets for their friends to pick up.
>
> In the days of the revolution the police tried to intervene. Today they walked unconcernedly through the . . . crowds as if everybody was out for an enjoyable afternoon stroll. . . . Two Jews were shot to death during the anti-Semitic riots. . . .Twenty synagogues were destroyed in Vienna. . . . Nine of the twelve Berlin synagogues were set afire at dawn. . . . Many Jews were arrested and carried off to unknown destinations. . . . In villages, homes of Jews were set afire. Terrified Jews fled into the countryside, hiding in the woods. . . . In Berlin an American walking down the Kurfuerstendamm, one of the city's principal thoroughfares, saw a mob haul a Jew out of a store, knock him down and trample on him until his shrieks stopped.

Newspapers and magazines sold in Chicago deplored the German action. The *Tribune* and the *Daily News* ran editorials attacking the Nazis and their assault on the Jews. But some reporting was strange. Henry Luce's *Life* magazine of November 28, 1938, carried several pages of pictures of the destruction in Germany. But on the next page there are six photographs of Hitler and Goering cooing over the christening of Goering's child. The caption reads, "Germany's Two Head Men Try Out Their Charms on a Five-Month-Old Baby."

Of all the papers and periodicals reviewed, only the *New Republic* urged a change in U.S. immigration laws. A November 30 editorial headed "Let the Jews Come In!" demanded more than simple indignation:

> Five hundred thousand German Jews are in the most desperate predicament of modern times. . . . The question is where can they go? Even Palestine is being barred to them, and every country is creating difficulties. At the present time, German-Austrian combined quota is about 27,000 a year. The total quota from all countries is about 153,000, but many lands do not use up their allotments; and in a number of recent years, more people have left America than have entered it. We can see no possible reasons why the unused quotas from other countries should not be transferred to the refugees. Even the bitterest anti-Semite will recognize that the total number who could possibly come in would be an insignificant addition to our present population.

In the aftermath of Kristallnacht, Roosevelt recalled the American Ambassador Hugh R. Wilson for consultation, and openly deplored the Nazi attacks. These actions were applauded by the Jewish press as courageous and welcome. But the Chicago press also reported that President Roosevelt had said at a news conference on November 15 that he did not contemplate a change in the quota system. They noted that on November 18 Roosevelt had extended the visitor's visas of 15,000 Germans then living in the United States, many of them Jews. On November 20, the *Tribune* reported that this extension of

visas had come under sharp attack by Congressman Martin Dies, chairman of the House committee investigating "un-American activities."
A *Tribune* editorial objected to any loosening of immigration restrictions, even in the face of the existing crisis in Europe.

A reading of the general Chicago press at the time indicates that
there was absolutely no sentiment among the vast majority of the
American public for a change in U.S. immigration quotas, especially
at a time when jobs were hard to get. Even the Jewish press, while
agonizing over the plight of the Jews in Europe, looked to other countries as havens for the refugees.

But the Chicago Jewish community did take some steps to try and
relieve its beleaguered brethren in Europe. A Joint Boycott Council of
Nazi Goods and Services was organized in Chicago in 1936 by the
American Jewish Congress and the Jewish Labor Committee head-
quartered at 8 South Dearborn Street. It was a successor to the original boycott committee started by the American Jewish Congress in
1933. By 1938 the organization was publishing a periodical, *Boycott*;
distributing lists of merchants cooperating and not cooperating with
the boycott, and selling stamps marked "Stamp Out Nazism," which
could be affixed to correspondence. In March, 1938, the Joint Council added Austrian goods to its boycott list and later in the year included goods from Sudetenland.

In its December issue *Boycott* optimistically announced that the
boycott was succeeding in fighting Nazi terror. It claimed the full co-
operation not only of many Jewish groups but also of the American
Federation of Labor, certain Roman Catholic groups and area universities. A boycott rally at the University of Chicago was said to have
drawn 2,000 students and was addressed by outstanding members of
the faculty including Professor—and future U.S. Senator—Paul H.
Douglas. *Boycott* editorialized after Munich, that, "As heretofore,
this battle will have to be fought with the most effective peace-time
weapon available to the masses—the boycott of German-made goods
and services." The December issue made no special reference to
Kristallnacht. Interestingly enough, the boycott movement was op-

posed by many American Jews, and, initially, perhaps under duress, by Germany's Jews themselves.

Some insight into the rationale of the anti-boycott faction could be found in Bernard Horwich's 1939 autobiography, *My Eighty Years*. Horwich, who had been born in Russian Lithuania in 1863, and immigrated to the United States in 1880 to become a successful manufacturer and banker, was president of the Chicago Section of the Zionist Organization of America from 1898 to 1901, was the first president of the Federated Jewish Charities of Chicago and an active leader in the American Jewish Committee.

Horwich expressed the opinion that some Jewish leaders "acted very unwisely" when the "Hitler regime suddenly and unexpectedly fell upon the Jews like a wild beast." In the past, he said, when there were outrages against the Jews in Russia, Jewish leaders had been able to relieve the situation by "talking things over calmly with the appropriate officials." Unfortunately, when Hitler came to power and attacked the Jews, Horwich wrote, "several of the so-called leaders, acting without proper authority, or due consideration, became excited and made use of demonstrations, mass meetings, abuse and slander and finally the boycott.

"We Jews must do something, they shouted through loudspeakers and headlines. We must not be 'sha-sha' men . . . cowards, like the assimilators. We must fight to the bitter end." This boycott movement, Horwich went on, had continued despite pleas by German Jews for its cessation because the boycott was causing Hitler to lash out at German Jews. With quiet diplomacy and pleadings, as in the past, the Nazis might not have acted so violently against the Jews. "Not only the German Jews, but Jews all over the world have been jeopardized," and it would be far better if Jewish leaders concentrated on anti-Semitism in the United States instead of "heroically attacking Hitler verbally from America." He argued that the American Jewish Committee and its leader, Dr. Cyrus Adler, were opposed to the boycott, as were B'nai B'rith and the American Jewish Joint Distribution Committee.

The only recourse, Horwich concluded, "should be one of de-
fending and not offending . . . We must regain a demeanor and conduct that will unceasingly appeal to the conscience of the world. We
must unceasingly drop all aggressiveness and restore, in its place, an
age-old policy of 'dignified endurance'. . . . Our aim is not to destroy
Hitlerism but to survive it. We cannot destroy Nazism. That is the
world's job, and let us hope it will be accomplished soon . . . That is
the sort of fight to which we must devote our energies—a fight for
ourselves and not against someone else."

The bitterness that divided the Chicago Jewish organizations on
the boycott issue is exemplified by a memo in Max Kopstein's files at
the American Jewish Congress. The files are now housed in the Chicago Jewish Archives at the Spertus Institute. Kopstein, then a young
attorney, was an officer of the American Jewish Congress and a leader
of the Chicago Joint Boycott Council. Kopstein, like other local Congress leaders, was closely identified with the national president of the
Congress, Rabbi Stephen Wise, considered the leading proponent of
the boycott and other anti-Nazi demonstrations and protests.

In his undated memo, probably written some time in 1938,
Kopstein attacked those American Jewish organizations which were
not democratically elected as was the Congress. He said that in Chicago the Congress had a total individual membership of 5,000 and
had 255 affiliated Jewish organizations, congregations, vereins and
landsmanschaften, thus having a total membership of some 40,000.
Each organization voted to send a representative to the Congress's
Executive Council, unlike other Jewish organizations which selected
their leaders from the "wealthy" without any democratic participation. Kopstein wrote that while the "democratic" and "liberal" Jewish organizations supported the boycott, other Jewish organizations
whose leaders favored "quiet action," withheld their support.
Kopstein's memo is sharply critical of these "so-called" Jewish leaders who advocated behind-the-scenes action. Differing attitudes in
Chicago toward the boycott apparently had roots in older community differences as well as honest disagreement over tactics.

As an aftermath of Kristallnacht, the National Conference of Christians and Jews designated November 20 as a nationwide interfaith day of prayer. In addition, the *Courier* reported on November 22 in Yiddish: "By prayer and the sounding of the Shofar Chicago Jews will join in the protest by the American people against the Nazi menace." It reported that thousands of Jews would gather at fourteen designated synagogues, all of which appeared to be Orthodox, to demonstrate their sorrow at Hitler's "blood-spilling hooligans." After describing in great detail the memorial services to be held in each synagogue, the Courier printed the following proclamation of the "Mercaz Harabbonim of Chicago":

> We are witness to the incomprehensible horrible tragedy which has befallen our people. Come join this evening in synagogues in every neighborhood of the city. Let our cry of woe be heard. Let us open the gates of mercy with our tears. Young and old, men and women, come to the synagogue this evening. Close up your businesses! Put aside every task! Let us plead with God for mercy! . . . No one must remain at home tonight. The Father of Mercy must hear our voice, our tears and rescue us from our misfortune.

Chicago Jewry reacted to the November crisis with an outpouring of money. The newspapers reported on the fund-raising activities of, among others, the Joint Distribution Committee, the Jewish National Fund, the United Palestine Appeal, ORT and Hadassah. Chicago Jews began a special two-million-dollar drive to aid European Jews. One newspaper reported that a group calling itself the International Jewish Colonization Society was organized under the leadership of an unidentified young Chicago industrialist with a program for resettling European Jewish refugees. Many of these drives would be coordinated at the end of 1938 with the founding of the United Jewish Appeal for Refugees and Overseas Needs.

The *Reform Advocate* carried a full-page ad on November 25 for a showing of the film "Inside Germany" at Orchestra Hall, proceeds to go to the Intergovernmental Committee for Political Refugees, headed by Myron C. Taylor, who was later appointed American Representative to the Vatican. On November 24 the *Courier* ran a long story on Kristallnacht from the *Jewish Telegraphic Agency Daily News Bulletin,* the main news source for the Jewish press. An adjoining column was headed "Agitation Combatted in Many Communities as Anti-Semitism Grows." This anti-Semitism was growing not in Europe but in the United States. There was a long report of a recent radio broadcast over Station WMCA in New York by Rev. Charles E. Coughlin of Royal Oak, Michigan, called the first anti-Semitic attack over a nationwide radio network in American history. Father Coughlin said that the Jews were suffering because Nazism "is a defense mechanism against communism," for which, he implied, Jews were responsible. The Chicago press denounced the broadcast and on December 11 Chicago's George Cardinal Mundelein declared that Coughlin spoke only as a private citizen and in no way represented the opinion of the Roman Catholic Church. Nevertheless, Coughlin had many local admirers, and his magazine *Social Justice* was widely available in Chicago, often being sold outside churches on Sundays.

The Chicago press frequently reported on meetings of the Silvershirts, the German-American Bund and other pro-Nazi groups active in the Chicago area, publicizing their "heiling of Hitler, denunciation of President Roosevelt and attacks on the Jews." The Jewish press, in particular, reported on the activities of these groups in various parts of the country. The American Jewish Year Book of 1938 said the "year witnessed an increase in activity on the part of anti-Jewish agitators. . . ." There were instances where Jews retaliated. On November 25, a free-for-all occurred at a tavern at 876 North Wells Street when 1,000 anti-Nazis waded into a Jew-baiting Silvershirts meeting. Six people were arrested. Several similar incidents occurred in New York after Kristallnacht.

The Jews who took on the Silvershirts on Wells Street most assuredly acted as most Chicago Jews would have liked to act toward the Nazis in 1938. But clearly, American Jews were powerless to change the country's political climate. Revisionist historians writing in the

1980s and not in the context of conditions as they existed fifty years ago, tended to distract from the Nazi's guilt by focusing on the so-called inaction of fellow Jews. By overlooking the realities of the times, they are rewriting history. It was perfectly sensible for American Jews to believe that only other governments, and particularly the United States, could stop Hitler. President Roosevelt certainly proved to be an implacable foe of Hitler, a president who was willing to speak out in a country where the majority of the people were still committed to isolationism and keeping America out of foreign wars.

These authors are understandably motivated by a desire to teach us that we must not repeat the passivity and failures of 1938 when it comes to our fellow Jews overseas. That is of course true. But they should realize that fifty years have passed since Kristallnacht. Isolationism disappeared with the Allied victory. America's immigration laws have changed, and the State of Israel has an open door policy for all Jewish refugees.

An examination of Chicago Jewry's reaction to Kristallnacht reinforces what is already evident. The guilt of Kristallnacht and its aftermath rests first and foremost on the Nazis and their European accomplices. Revisionist history, whether written by Gentiles or Jews, cannot detract one iota from that.

ROBERT ADLER PAPERS: REFUGEE AFFIDAVITS

———

WHEN THE NAZIS ROSE to power in 1933, many individual American Jews took extraordinary—and in hindsight, heroic—steps to help rescue their brethren from Germany, Austria and Czechoslovakia. These Jews could not don uniforms or hurl bombs at the Nazis, but they did the one thing they could do as individual American citizens: they saved fellow Jews by providing affidavits of support for them, crucial to their admission to America.

In 1933, the United States immigration laws were extremely restrictive. At the turn of the century, America's ports of entry had been wide open to immigrants, millions of whom entered, particularly from Eastern Europe. But after World War I, the Communist and anarchist scares and threats of an "invasion by Asian hordes" caused Congress to pass legislation effectively closing the doors to all but a limited number of immigrants each year.

The law enacted in 1924 limited immigration into the United States to 150,000 persons a year, apportioned among countries based on the national origins of the white population in the U.S. in 1920. The allocations were: about 75,000 from Great Britain, 25,000 from Germany, 1,500 from Austria, 2,800 from Czechoslovakia, 2,700 from Russia, 6,000 from Poland and 100 each from China and Japan. While later events made the number totally inadequate, the relatively large quota for Germany did provide an escape hatch for German Jews.

These quotas obviously hit hardest those people whose places of origin were Eastern and Southern Europe and Asia.

The quotas were further restricted by a 1930 order from President Herbert Hoover to American consuls resulting in the denial of visas to anyone who might become a candidate for public assistance unless each person had an "Affidavit of Support" from an American. Rules governing these affidavits varied somewhat from consulate to consulate, but basically the American citizen had to promise under oath to be responsible for the immigrant, and to furnish a financial statement, preferably accompanied by a copy of his latest income tax return, along with two letters of verification from an individual or a banking or accounting firm, certifying the net worth of the affiant. After Kristallnacht in November, 1938, when American consulates were flooded with applications for visas, some consuls—notably in Vienna and Berlin—enacted rules requiring the deposit of surety bonds or cash by the American citizen to support his affidavit.

From the beginning it was obvious that American Jewish organizations could not furnish the necessary affidavits. In the first place, the law provided that only an individual could be the affiant. Secondly, the Jewish organizations undoubtedly felt that, given the prevailing American mood of isolationism and nativism with outbursts of anti-Semitism, they could not appear to take an active role in anything that would result in an increase of immigration to a country in the desperate throes of the Great Depression. And how could an organization choose from among so many deserving applicants? Consequently, individual Americans were the refugees' only hope. One Chicago family in particular, the Max and Robert S. Adler family, furnished hundreds of these affidavits to prospective immigrants. The Adler family in turn was a local satellite of a much more substantial rescue effort financed by the children of the Chicago industrialist and philanthropist Julius Rosenwald, through an office set up in New York City for that specific purpose.

We know something of the Adler effort because after the deaths of Robert S. Adler and his wife, Helen Loewenstein Adler, Robert's longtime secretary, Eve Levin, received permission from the Adler family to deliver files containing his correspondence on these immigration affidavits to the Chicago Jewish Historical Society. Papers like these are extremely difficult to locate because the original affidavits were mailed to the American consulates, not to the immigrants, and, so far as can be determined, the files of those consulates have been destroyed.

These Adler files start with a copy of a Memorandum of Agreement prepared by a Chicago law firm, dated June 29, 1936, between Max Adler and his wife, Sophie Rosenwald Adler, on the one hand, and Lessing J. Rosenwald, Edith A. Stern, Adele R. Levy, Marion R. Stern and William Rosenwald on the other, the five children of Julius Rosenwald, who had died on January 6, 1932.

The Adler-Rosenwald agreement states that the Rosenwald children had previously agreed among themselves to provide a fund to assist in the immigration of individuals, primarily their relatives, from Germany, and the Adlers now agreed to provide ten percent of any amounts expended by the Rosenwald children in any one year, not to exceed $7,000 a year. The agreement was to last at least ten years. The Rosenwald children, through William Rosenwald, opened an office, hired a social worker and ran a basically private rescue effort to assist the refugees. The office provided affidavits, paid for transportation when necessary, arranged for living quarters and found jobs for the immigrants, many with suppliers of Sears, Roebuck & Company.

Max S. Perlman, a South Side resident who later became a longtime public relations executive of the Chicago Jewish Federation, headed this office in New York from 1936 to 1941. A number of immigrants now living in Chicago still remember Max Perlman's valiant efforts to rescue them from Germany and to find jobs for them in America. Among German immigrants to Chicago assisted by the Rosenwald office and Max Perlman were the Lorsch, Reissner and Plaut families.

Robert S. Adler was born in Chicago on August 21, 1900, the son of Sophie and Max Adler. Sophie was Julius Rosenwald's sister and Max, vice-president and general merchandise manager of Sears, was a noted concert violinist, who had studied music at the Royal Conservatory in Berlin. Initially employed in Sears' music department, he continued his interest in music and at one time gave weekly recitals in his impressive house at 4939 South Greenwood Avenue. In 1928, at the time Max Adler donated America's first planetarium to Chicago, he retired from Sears and began to spend much of his time in California at his home in Beverly Hills. His son Robert moved to Highland Park from the South Side and, choosing not to work for Sears, had become a partner in an investment firm. It was at his office in downtown Chicago that Robert undertook his extended efforts on behalf of the immigrants. Max Adler was particularly helpful in aiding refugee musicians, one of them being Isaac Stern, whose career Max supported in many ways.

Unlike the Rosenwalds, Robert Adler did not have a staff, apart from his secretary. All the correspondence in the files is signed by him on behalf of himself or his father. His correspondence appears unrelated to the Rosenwald efforts, though at times there are references to Perlman and requests for his assistance. Also, while the Rosenwalds primarily helped relatives of either Julius Rosenwald or his wife, Adler's affidavits went in nearly every instance to relative strangers. The files start in about 1937 and continue through 1942, when Adler joined the army. There is some correspondence after the war with immigrants who had come to the United States earlier, but most of the letters were written to people in Germany, Austria, Czechoslovakia and, in several instances, to families in Shanghai, where they had fled, often with Adler's assistance.

One file commences with a letter from Vienna dated November 27, 1938, two weeks after Kristallnacht:

Dear Mr. Adler: Excuse us very much for bother you. We got your address from the book: Jewish Charities of Chicago 1930, which was blissful to find between father's books. We are hurrying to write to you and asking you so much to help us. A young man and a lady, 33 and 28 years old, married. We hope you don't mind it Mr. Adler that we are writing you and that it will be possible for you to send us an affidavit what we need badly to go on from here to a better and free country. We are living in Vienna and what it means is awfully to say. It is much worther than it was in Germany and all what they've done there in five six month. You really would do real good work When you would be kind and send an affidavit. All what the newspapers write is nothing what we really have to suffre. We promise not to bother or to be in the wunderfull free country. Our name is Krausz Eugene born Dec. 6th 1905 in Vienna wife's our: Krausz Berta born Bruckner Fehr. 22nd 1910 Deutsch Kreutz, German Austria. My profession is fitter for gas and water-fittings, electrical engineer, and expert in the cornbusiness. My wife is a dressmaker seamstress for underclothes and an excellent sewer. If you need some information how to get an affidavit for us: the Hebrew Sheltering and Immigrant Aid Society of America (HIAS) or the Cunard Line will tell you all about and what kind of papers are necessary to get an affidavit. But please be kind and send the affidavit directly to us. We hope that our prayer don't be in vain and that we succeed and get soon same good news from you. We have got an order of expulsion and we must to be away from here by December 30th 1938. Every day living here means one year to every Jew here. If it is impossible for you so maybe you will have some good friends, who will be kind to help us. We remain with many, many thanks for all the troubles. We are making to you don't mind it. Gratefully and faithfully yours, Kraus Eugen.

On December 19, 1938, Robert Adler replied:

On November 27th you wrote to my father, Mr. Max Adler, and asked him to send you an affidavit which would aid you and your wife in obtaining a visa which would permit you to come to the United States. Since my father is not in Chicago just now and will not be here for some months, I am writing to let you know that we will make an affidavit for you and submit it as soon as we can. In order however, to complete it, it will be necessary for you to send me some additional information.

We will have to have the name, date and place of birth of your Father and Mother and the same information for your wife's Fa-

ther and Mother. Do you have any relatives in the United States, if
so their names and addresses, also the names and addresses of any
persons in Germany or Vienna who can give a letter of recommendation about you and your wife.

If you will send me the above information, printed so that it is
easily read, I will see that some papers are prepared for you. I would
suggest that you make application immediately for a visa so that
you will be at least assigned a number. We understand here that
applications are so many that it will require many, many months, if
not a year or more before a visa can be granted and the numbers
will be taken in proper succession.

Please advise me of your condition when you send me the information above request.

On January 31, 1939, barely two months after the original request, Adler sent this affidavit, accompanied by letters of recommendation, to the American consul in Vienna. Thanks to Adler, Berta and
Eugen Krausz were able to leave Austria and arrive in the United
States later that year. On November 14, Eugen wrote Adler again,
this time pleading for an affidavit for his parents who were still in
Vienna: "My dear parents wouldn't be to trouble you, never." On
February 26, 1941, Adler received a letter from a Chicago family friend
of the Krausz's, a Mr. Strasser, saying that the parents were about to
be deported to the Lublin ghetto if they could not show that they
could get an American visa. But a simple affidavit would not be enough;
it would have to be accompanied by a deposit of $8,000 in a U.S.
bank in the Krausz parents' name. On March 29, 1941, Robert Adler
wrote to Eugen (now Eugene):

Naturally I realize fully the keen desire which you have to bring
your dear parents to the United States. On the other hand, I am
sure that you recognize the fact that I have only a limited power to
help people in distress and that this power should be applied to
those cases which are most likely to produce the greatest benefits
for the people involved. I have, as I told Mr. Strasser, a large num-

ber of people who are looking to me for help, and of course I should like to help all of them. This is not possible, however, and I must, therefore, use my help in the way which I feel is best. Frankly, I believe it will be much better to help bring to the United States young people, such as yourself, who have a life ahead of them and who can get along once they are here. You can see that your parents, being older people, would find it very difficult, to say nothing of the added burden which would be placed upon you to find means to support them.

The Krausz correspondence exemplifies the Adler rescue effort. Adler replied instantly to a letter from a perfect stranger pleading for help. But he did not feel that he should honor the arbitrary demand for a substantial cash deposit. Eight thousand dollars was a very large amount at that time. In addition, Adler could not have known about the dreadful fate that awaited Jews who were "deported." The American quota law coupled with the consuls' restrictive policy, made things very difficult. The tragedy of elderly parents recurs constantly in the Adler correspondence.

In wrenching correspondence with a George Zoellner, then living in Berlin, Adler wrote on April 14, 1941, that he could send an affidavit for the son but not for the father and mother, since transportation and cash deposits were required:

I do hope that you will understand our feeling and that you will not think that we do not recognize how difficult your position is at the moment. We do, but there are so many problems that it is only possible to solve them a little at a time. If in the meantime the affidavit which I have just sent you is of some help to you, so much the better. When and if your son is here and is able to establish himself, then I shall again be in a position to help your children help you.

To the Zoellner daughter, Gerda, who was already in New York through an earlier Adler affidavit, Adler wrote encouragingly on April 9, 1941:

One other word to you personally. I have been giving considerable thought to the manner in which you have forced yourself to get along during the last year or so. I realize that it is difficult for you to wish to do anything which might afford you pleasure and entertainment, but, as I told you, I do not believe that you should continue in this way all the time. It will be very important to you that you be in an optimistic frame of mind when your brother arrives, and this you cannot be if you do not, as I put it, "look up and not look down." I, therefore, want you to devote a little time each week to your own entertainment. You should go to a movie occasionally, should make an effort to meet other people through those whom you now know and through the opportunities which are afforded by the various groups which exist in New York. I am sending you herewith my check which I want you to use for this particular purpose during the next few weeks, and I hope you will write and tell me what you are doing.

There is extensive correspondence in the Adler files with Dr. Emil and Marie Liefman of Frankfurt-on-Main, who received an affidavit from Robert Adler. On April 17, 1939, Adler received a letter from the National Council of Jewish Women telling him that the Liefmans had arrived in New York. In subsequent correspondence, Liefman requests and receives a loan for $300 and then one for $700 from Adler. Liefman eventually went to Albany for accreditation and became a licensed American physician.

There is a large file on a young artist named Madeline who lived in Berlin with her Russian-born father. Adler provided an affidavit and Madeline and her father managed to flee to Shanghai as the war started. When Adler helped them with another affidavit, Madeline was able to immigrate to the United States in 1941. She seems to be one of the few immigrants who actually came to Chicago to visit the Adlers, and she stayed in touch with Robert and Max Adler. In 1989, when she was in her seventies, she owned an art gallery in New York. She never forgot that the Adlers had saved her life as well as the lives of many others.

As the number of requests grew, Robert Adler's frustration with the American consuls understandably increased. The files contain correspondence between Adler and Wilbur Klebinger, the American consul general in Hamburg. One arbitrary consul rule was that an affidavit, once supplied to the American consul, was valid for only six months. The German national who had applied for a visa number had no way of knowing exactly when his number would be called. If it was called after the affidavit had expired, he would be passed over.

Adler wrote Klebinger on December 16, 1938, asking if this was really his policy. On January 14, 1939, the American consul replied that it was, adding that it would be up to the applicant to keep the affidavit current by filing statements of renewal signed by the American affiant. Adler wrote back on February 19, to pose two further questions: (1) Does the possession of an affidavit by a prospective immigrant help this person while awaiting his turn, and (2) Should Adler send such an affidavit to the person even though he may have to wait over two years for his visa. On March 6, Klebinger answered that he could not answer the first question, and could not make any recommendation on the second.

When Robert Adler joined the army in May, 1942, these rescue efforts ceased. After the war he was active for many years in the Chicago Jewish community and served as a trustee of the Adler Planetarium Trust endowed by his father.

There were, of course, a great many Chicago Jews who, like Robert Adler, worked to provide the affidavits needed to bring relatives, friends and, most impressive of all, strangers to America. This generosity in difficult times has frequently been overlooked amidst the despair and guilt of the Holocaust. The Adler papers will help future generations to recall the heroic efforts of such individuals on behalf of those who needed their help in desperate times.

III
CHICAGO JEWS AND ZIONISM:
LOCAL IDEALISTS

REVEREND WILLIAM BLACKSTONE:
METHODIST MINISTER

———

EVERYONE DISCUSSED BY H. L. Meites in his monumental history of the Jews in Chicago, was Jewish, except for the Reverend William E. Blackstone, a Methodist minister who lived in Chicago in the late nineteenth and early twentieth centuries. Reverend Blackstone was indeed an unusual man who played an interesting role in local Jewish history. His book *Jesus Is Coming*, written under the initials "W.E.B," has sold millions of copies since its first publication in Chicago in 1878, is still in print and on the evangelical best-seller list and has been translated into many languages, including both Hebrew and Yiddish. In Hebrew the book is called *Hofaat Ha Mashiash Ha-Shnia:The Second Appearance of the Messiah*. Blackstone stored many copies of the book in Petra, Jordan, for use by Jews who he believed would go there at the "time of Jacob's trouble," read the book, convert to Christianity, and thus save themselves from destruction. But Meites obviously did not include Blackstone in his book on Chicago Jews because of the Reverend's conversion activities; he did it because of Blackstone's role as an early Christian Zionist.

In 1888, Blackstone, then a resident of Oak Park, visited Palestine with his daughter Flora. He was forty-seven years old and a well-known evangelist and missionary. Revival meetings were at their height in America, and Blackstone, while not a household name like Billy Sunday, achieved fame as a lecturer and organizer, preparing his people

for the Second Coming of Christ. He was closely identified with Dwight
Moody, another Chicagoan. Both Blackstone and Moody were successful businessmen who had left the life of commerce to devote themselves to their religious missions.

Blackstone became close to Jews not only in Chicago but across
the U.S. He became a Zionist before Theodore Herzl called the First
Zionist Conference. Blackstone went to Palestine in 1888, ten years
before Herzl's arrival there. Like Herzl, Blackstone saw Palestine as
"a land without a people and a people without a land." He was impressed by the new Jewish settlements, which he believed signalled
great events to come. To him, as to many evangelical Christians today, the return of the Jews to the land was a fulfillment of Biblical
prophecies.

In November, 1890, Blackstone organized a Chicago conference
at the First Methodist Episcopal Church on the corner of Clark and
Washington Streets, to discuss the "past, present and future of Israel." Three leading Chicago Reform rabbis were among the participants: Emil G. Hirsch of Sinai Congregation; Bernhard Felsenthal,
the retired rabbi of Zion Congregation; and Joseph Stolz of Zion
Congregation. The Christian participants were Protestant ministers,
professors and theologians. One minister defined the theme of the
conference: that there could be no doubt "about the restoration of
Israel."

Rabbi Hirsch responded: "We modern Jews do not wish to be
restored to Palestine . . . We say the country wherein we live is our
Palestine, and the city wherein we dwell is our Jerusalem. We will not
go back . . . to form again a nationality of our own. . . ."

Rabbi Felsenthal, on the other hand, supported the return to Palestine—not for American but for Russian Jews, who in 1890 were
suffering from increasing anti-Semitism in the Russian Empire and
migrating to America in large numbers. Accordingly, the conference
unanimously called upon world leaders to help Russian Jews. The
rabbis did not respond well to the ministers' accompanying call for
the conversion of the Jews, believed by evangelicals to be necessary to
bring about the Second Coming.

The conference attracted a good deal of press attention. The Zionist proposal stimulated discussion among people of all religions in the city. Chicago Jews were to debate the question for more than two generations. After that, Blackstone organized a drive for a petition on behalf of the Jews, to be presented to President Benjamin Harrison. The petition, known as the Blackstone Memorial, completed in 1891, calls for the restoration of Palestine to the Jews, and asks the president to help convene a congress of European powers to give Palestine to the Jews and thus make it possible for Russian Jews, with Russia's and Turkey's consent, to settle there. The similarity to Herzl's writings a few years later is startling: it is highly unlikely that Herzl saw it before he wrote *Der Judenstaat* in 1896.

More than 413 prominent Americans signed the petition, among them J. P. Morgan, Cyrus Field, John D. Rockefeller, future president William McKinley; the Speaker of the U.S. House of Representatives, the Chief Justice of the U.S. Supreme Court; Chicago businessmen Potter Palmer, Philip Armour, Emmanuel Mandel and John Shedd; well-known newspaper and book publishers, and clergymen of all faiths including Roman Catholic archbishops. President Harrison expressed sympathy for the plight of Russian Jews, but never referred publicly to the Memorial itself.

A number of Chicago rabbis and laymen signed the Memorial, although they objected to the statement that Jews had not been farmers in the Diaspora because they felt themselves to be "sojourners" in strange lands until their return to Zion. They believed that Jews could indeed be farmers if only they were given the opportunity by society.

The Memorial brought Blackstone to the attention of U.S. Zionist leaders with whom he met frequently in succeeding years. He wrote to President Grover Cleveland in 1894 reminding him of the Memorial petition. In 1903, the Chicago Methodist Preachers meeting endorsed the petition, sent it to President Theodore Roosevelt and called for an "International Conference of the Powers" to "consider the conditions of the Jews and their right to a home in Palestine."

After Blackstone's wife died in 1908, he went to China to join his son in missionary work. Returning to Chicago in 1914, he again took up his Zionist work. The First World War had broken out, and the Turkish Empire was in shambles. Blackstone saw this as the opportune time to renew the drive for the Jewish homeland, and a new petition was prepared for presentation to President Woodrow Wilson.

The 75-year-old Blackstone worked closely with American Zionist leaders, with Nathan Straus in particular. The 1916 Petition, like the 1891 Memorial, asked the president to call for an international conference to deal with the question of a Jewish homeland. It was adopted in 1916 by the General Assembly of the Presbyterian Church and presented to President Wilson. Zionist leaders, including Rabbi Stephen Wise, Jacob De Haas and Supreme Court Justice Louis D. Brandeis, welcomed Blackstone's efforts, and kept in close touch with him. There is little evidence that Blackstone had much influence on Woodrow Wilson, or on the Balfour Declaration which came a year later.

Blackstone moved to Los Angeles and continued his efforts for Zion. He continued to write letters to succeeding presidents, but eventually faded into obscurity and died in 1935 at the age of 94. He was a staunch friend of Zionism at a time when many Jewish leaders openly denounced it. His activism undoubtedly helped to influence the American public to be receptive to the idea of a Jewish homeland. But the Jews instinctively recoiled from Blackstone's mission of conversion: he wanted to settle Jews in Palestine to fulfill the prophecy that after their return they would experience the "time of Jacob's trouble" in which two-thirds of them would die because they would not accept the Messiah, and the remainder (estimated then at 144,000) would survive because they would accept the true faith. Until the millennium, efforts at conversion of the Jews would continue.

American Zionist leaders who embraced Blackstone were not concerned that in the end Blackstone's evangelism offered no legitimacy to the Jewish religion nor hope for survival for its people. Meites, also willing to overlook the Reverend's conversion attempts, concluded: "Whatever may have been Blackstone's quixotic expectations as to the 'fulfillment of prophecy' through his efforts, his Memorial had a direct effect in the repeal by Russia of the expulsion edicts that had driven hundreds of thousands of Russian Jewish refugees to America and elsewhere. And it also started the first Zionist efforts in Chicago and in the United States."

Following is the text of Blackstone's 1891 petition, anticipating the ideas and even the language in Theodore Herzl's 1896 *Der Judenstaat*, which first outlined Zionist goals:

MEMORIAL PRESENTED TO PRESIDENT HARRISON MARCH 5TH, 1891

What shall be done for the Russian Jews? It is both unwise and useless to undertake to dictate to Russia concerning her internal affairs. The Jews have lived as foreigners in her dominions for centuries, and she fully believes that they are a burden upon her resources and prejudicial to the welfare of her peasant population, and will not allow them to remain. She is determined that they must go. Hence, like the Shepardim of Spain, these Ashkenazim must emigrate. But where shall 2,000,000 of such poor people go? Europe is crowded and has no room for more peasant population. Shall they come to America? This will be a tremendous expense and require years.

Why not give Palestine back to them again? According to God's distribution of nations it is their home—an inalienable possession from which they were expelled by force. Under their cultivation it was a remarkably fruitful land, sustaining millions of Israelites, who industriously tilled its hillsides and valleys. They were agriculturists and producers as well as a nation of great commercial importance—the center of civilization and religion.

Why shall not the powers which under the treaty of Berlin, in 1878, gave Bulgaria to the Bulgarians and Servia to the Servians now give Palestine back to the Jews? These provinces, as well as Roumania, Montenegro, and Greece, were wrested from the Turks and given to their natural owners. Does not Palestine rightfully belong to the Jews? It is said that rains are increasing and there are many evidences that the land is recovering its ancient fertility. If they could have autonomy in government, the Jews of the world would rally to transport and establish their suffering brethren in their time-honored habitation. For over seventeen centuries they have patiently waited for such a privileged opportunity. They have not become agriculturists elsewhere because they believed they were mere sojourners in the various nations, and were yet to return to Palestine and till their own land. Whatever vested rights, by possession, may have accrued to Turkey can be easily compensated, possibly by the Jews assuming an equitable portion of the national debt.

We believe this is an appropriate time for all nations, and especially the Christian nations of Europe, to show kindness to Israel. A million of exiles, by their terrible sufferings, are piteously appealing to our sympathy, justice, and humanity. Let us now restore to them the land of which they were so cruelly despoiled by our Roman ancestors.

To this end we respectfully petition His Excellency Benjamin Harrison, President of the United States, and the Honorable James G. Blaine, Secretary of State, to use their good offices and influence with the Governments of their Imperial Majesties—

Alexander III, Czar of Russia;

Victoria, Queen of Great Britain and Empress of India;

William II, Emperor of Germany;

Francis Joseph, Emperor of Austro-Hungary;

Abdul Hamid II, Sultan of Turkey;

His Royal Majesty Humbert, King of Italy;

Her Royal Majesty Marie Christiana, Queen Regent of Spain; and the Government of the Republic of France and with the Governments of Belgium, Holland, Denmark, Sweden, Portugal, Roumania, Servia, Bulgaria, and Greece, to secure the holding, at an early date, of an international conference to consider the condition of the Israelites and their claims to Palestine as their ancient home, and to promote, in all other just and proper ways, the alleviation of their suffering condition.

[There followed the signatures of 413 prominent and mostly Gentile Americans.]

RABBI BERNHARD FELSENTHAL: ZIONIST PIONEER

IN 1896, BERNARD HORWICH and some of his colleagues held a meeting in response to Theodore Herzl's call for a modern Jewish state. Most of the people who came that night were East European, the most recent immigrants to America, who looked to a national homeland as a haven for their persecuted brethren in the Old World. On the other hand, most Reform Jews, with their roots in Germany, opposed Zionism and were primarily concerned with their own integration into American society. The single exception at the meeting was 74-year-old Bernhard Felsenthal, the first rabbi of the Reform Chicago Sinai Congregation, who had been born in Bavaria. This was hardly the first time that Felsenthal had taken a conscientious minority stand against most of his community, but Bernard Horwich thought it noteworthy enough to merit mention in his 1939 autobiography, *My First Eighty Years*:

> Then and there was formed the first organized Zionist group in America, of which I was the president. It was called the Chicago Zionist Organization, No. 1 . . . A lone member of the German-Jewish group was present—Dr. Bernhard Felsenthal, who spoke in German. He encouraged us, and told us even though he was an old man and would not live to see the fruits of the vast undertaking, he would do everything he could, until his last day on earth, and in the world to come, to further the cause of Zionism. His words

were very impressive, and he inspired the new members with enthusiasm for their work.

Bernhard Felsenthal, one of the founders of the Zionist movement in Chicago, deserves to be remembered as a true pioneer. He
was born on January 2, 1822 in a Northern Bavarian village, into a
family well-versed in Jewish and German scholarship. As a young
child, he was introduced to rabbinic and Talmudic literature, and that
became a passion throughout his life. He developed an interest in
Jewish genealogy and history, and would eventually become one of
the first historians of the Chicago Jewish community.

Felsenthal had originally wanted to join the Bavarian civil service,
but he soon found that as a Jew he would have no future there, so he
took up teaching instead and graduated from a teachers' seminary in
1843. With the defeat of the revolutionary uprisings sweeping Bavaria in the late 1840s, he and other family members decided to leave
Germany. He emigrated to America in 1854, worked as a tutor for
two years in Lawrenceburg, Indiana, and undertook his first ministe-
rial duties in Madison, Indiana, in 1856. Two years later, in April
1858, he came to Chicago and obtained a position as a clerk in a
banking house owned by a relative, Henry Greenebaum, an early
Chicago settler. Legend has it that Felsenthal spent most of his time
studying the Talmud.

In 1859, while secretary of *Judische Reform Verein*, the Jewish
Reform Group he had founded, he published *Kol Kore Bamidbar*, "A
Voice in the Desert," a pamphlet that did much to promote the Reform movement in Chicago and that brought Felsenthal national attention. Felsenthal wrote prolifically in German on the objectives of
the American Reform movement. In one of these "theses," as he called
them, he wrote:

> We are deeply convinced that Israel has been called by God to be
> the Messiah of the nations and to spread truth and virtue on earth.
> In order to fulfill this high mission, Israel has to undergo a process
> of purification in its own midst. This object will best be accom-

plished in Israel and a free blessed America where no material forces check spiritual progress. The special mission of American Israel, therefore, is to place Judaism before the world, purified in doctrines and conduct, and so becoming a shining example for Israelites the world over.

In 1861, the Reform Verein formed the Chicago Sinai Congregation, destined to become one of the leading Reform congregations in America. Although Felsenthal was not ordained, the congregation persuaded him to become its first rabbi. Felsenthal quickly became known for his anti-slavery views and his liberal position on traditional Jewish ritual. Three years later, in a dispute with the congregation over his desire for a firm contract, he left Sinai. Within a few months he was asked to head the newly organized Reform Zion Congregation—today the Oak Park Temple B'nai Abraham Zion—a position he held until his retirement in 1886. He was an active writer throughout his years as a congregational leader and published many pamphlets, usually in German, achieving recognition as a leading intellectual of the American Reform movement. He, like many American Reform leaders, decried Zionism and other forms of Jewish nationalism. The Reform movement's objectives were messianic, humanistic, and universal, and had no room for Zionism's materialistic nationalism.

But Felsenthal's attitude underwent a subtle change after 1881, as East European immigrants began to stream into Chicago. The Felsenthal family lived on Desplaines Avenue, on the near West Side, where many of these new Jewish immigrants settled. Unlike many of his colleagues, he did not move to the South Side, but stayed and developed personal ties with this Yiddish-speaking community. Emma Felsenthal, in her 1924 biography of her father, *Teacher in Israel*, wrote:

Every Jew, wherever and whatever he was, was his brother. And now that Jewish refugees were crowding into Twelfth Street, naturally the problems of Twelfth Street absorbed him, mind and heart.

He consulted with others concerning the immediate economic welfare of the unfortunate people; he assisted in organizing evening
schools; he made friends of their rabbis and leaders. He made frequent visits to the school established by the B'nai B'rith in 1888,
and took deep personal interest in the progress of individual students. In recognition, they called a society which grew out of this
school, "The Felsenthal Educational Society."

He could not accustom himself to the Yiddish spoken by the new
immigrants, but studied and wrote in Hebrew, and was one of the
founders in Chicago of *Keren Or (Ray of Light)*, a Hebrew monthly.
Starting to question some of the early tenets of Reform Judaism, its
messianic nature and the exclusion of political and social issues from
its mission, he began moving slowly toward Zionism, then only a
whisper in the East European Jewish community.

In 1891, when Reverend William Blackstone, the Christian
millenarian, submitted his basically Zionist Memorandum to President Harrison, nearly all Reform leaders opposed it, but Felsenthal
and Liebman Adler (the retired rabbi of K.A.M., another leading Reform congregation) agreed to sign it along with more than 400 other
prominent American intellectuals, business leaders, newspapers, and
organizations, including the *Chicago Tribune's* Joseph Medill and
Victor Lawson of the *Daily News*. Rabbi Emil Hirsch, Felsenthal's
successor at Sinai and a leader of the radical Reform movement, vigorously opposed the Blackstone initiative, and he and Felsenthal exchanged angry letters about it. Hirsch declared, "We modern Jews do
not wish to be restored to Palestine. We will not go back to form a
nationality of our own." To which Felsenthal replied, "I vote for colonization. . . . The Jewish colonies in Palestine . . . hail to them! May
they increase rapidly and vastly! May they flourish! May they bring
happiness to those who dwell in them."

When the first Zionist Congress met in Basel, Switzerland, in
August, 1897, Felsenthal was a natural choice to represent Chicago.
Various ailments stemming from his advanced age prevented him from
attending, however, and Leon Zolotkoff, a writer, Hebraist, and long-

time leader of the early Chicago Zionists, went in his place. Felsenthal was able to throw his still considerable energies into Zionist endeavors. His daughter Emma noted, "After 1897 my father could scarcely write of any subject other than Zionism. . . . My father could not understand how others could remain from the movement."

Felsenthal was a close friend of Wolf Schur of 216 Maxwell Street, publisher of a Hebrew periodical, *Ha-Tehivyah*, *Regeneration*. Felsenthal was the only contributor to the periodical who was not Russian or Lithuanian. On January 5, 1899, *Regeneration* reported: "The Zionist Federation of Chicago, comprising five societies spread over the whole city, staged a meeting on New Year's day. The Hall was packed. The Editor of *Ha-Tehivyah* introduced to the audience the President of the Federation, Rabbi Dr. B. Felsenthal. He opened the meeting with a fiery address on the Love of Zion."

Felsenthal, a founder of the American Jewish Historical Society, continued to writing extensively on Chicago and American Jewish history. He was also a founder of the Jewish Publication Society and wrote for it as well.

In 1903, during the bitter divisions within the Zionist movement over the possibility of settling Jews in Uganda, Felsenthal sought a way to reconcile the two camps, saying that he was willing to accept Uganda "as a temporary place of refuge but not as the final aim of the Zionist movement. . . . The Zionist movement cannot cease and shall not cease until Israel dwells again, a fit people in its own land." In 1905 he received an honorary degree from the Jewish Theological Seminary in New York, the school of the Conservative movement headed by Dr. Solomon Schechter. By that time Felsenthal had repudiated the central Reform tenet: the idea of the special mission of Israel, and believed that the positions taken by Emil Hirsch and other Reform leaders were a form of "euthanasia" for Judaism. He wrote that "this extreme Reform we have in America will lead gradually to the extinction of Israel and its religion. Do you not agree with me that our Reform friends are preparing a beautiful death for Judaism?"

In the last years of his life, Felsenthal, confined to his home, carried on a lively correspondence with friends and family in Chicago and Germany. He frequently wrote in German to a young niece in Frankfurt. The letters, reproduced in his daughter's biography, reveal his kindness and good will.

On Sunday, October 15, 1905, Felsenthal, 83, visited Sinai for services honoring the twenty-fifth anniversary of Rabbi Hirsch's rabbinate. That same day he suffered a severe stroke and was hospitalized for nearly two months. Weakened, he was ill for the remaining two years of his life, but became even more convinced that only Zionism could save Judaism. In a letter written in March, 1907, he again expressed his conviction that the fruits of radical Reform "will lead gradually to the extinction of Israel and its religion." In late 1907, he contracted pneumonia and died on January 12, 1908.

In a tribute to his personal ecumenism, both Reform and Zionist groups held memorial services for him—separately. The Chicago Rabbinical Association issued a statement that read in part: "Of a peaceful disposition, he was a true disciple of Aaron, the High-Priest, seeking and pursuing peace. He proclaimed the truth as he saw it, though this may have been contrary to commonly accepted notions. Thus, too, he espoused the cause of Zionism, though that was not popular."

Anita Libman Lebeson wrote in her 1958 article "Zionism Comes to Chicago": "Bernhard Felsenthal, whom his daughter calls 'Teacher in Israel,' continues to amaze and astound the student of history. He was an anomaly . . . whose personality shines through intervening years with undiminished radiance." His life is a symbol of the historic contribution of German Jewry to the foundation and development of modern Zionism. Although his voice was largely ignored by the Sinai Congregation he helped to found, and by the anti-Zionist leaders of the American Reform movement, Felsenthal's piety and vision have outlived them all. His views and writings after 1881 represent what have become, today, the major ideologies of the American Reform movement. Never afraid to take a controversial stand on his own, Felsenthal in the end led countless American Jews in a new direction.

LEON ZOLOTKOFF:

CHICAGOAN AT THE FIRST ZIONIST CONGRESS

———

IT HAS BEEN MORE than a century since the First Zionist Congress, almost singlehandedly organized by Theodore Herzl, was held in Basel, Switzerland, on August 29-31, 1897, in the Stadt Casino, a concert and dance hall adjacent to the local historical museum. Apart from many interested spectators, the Congress was attended by approximately 200 delegates from fourteen countries: Russia, Germany, Austria-Hungary, Romania, Bulgaria, Holland, Belgium, France, Switzerland, Sweden, England, the United States, Algeria and Palestine. As Jacob de Haas, a leading disciple of Herzl, wrote of the gathering, "This was not a mere assembly of dreamers; the inward note was that of a gathering of brothers meeting after a long Diaspora." It was their collective vision that created the modern state of Israel.

One person, Leon Zolotkoff, attended as the official Chicago representative. Although almost completely forgotten today, Zolotkoff proved to be a dynamic and controversial leader in ways beyond his signal contribution to the city's Zionism. As one of the first Russian-born Jews to gain local political prominence, as a leading journalist, and as a gadfly of the first order, he played a key role in turn-of-the-century Chicago Jewish life. For all of his early success, however, he remained dogged by controversy, choosing eventually to leave Chicago and become a writer. His legacy is a mixed one, filled with both remarkable accomplishments and obvious shortcomings.

Zolotkoff was not forgotten by those who knew him. In his 1939 autobiography, Bernard Horwich, the leading Zionist and Chicago community leader, called Zolotkoff one of the "Russian Intelligentsia . . . a man of high caliber, a brilliant writer, linguist and Hebraist." H.L. Meites too mentions Zolotkoff his *History of the Jews of Chicago*. Zolotkoff's birth date is inscribed on his tombstone as May 14, 1863; Meites lists it as May 15, 1867. In any case, he was born in Vilna, Russia, now Lithuania, the son of Judah Z. and Rebecca Ostrichner Zolotkoff. He received a classic secular and traditional Jewish education in the Vilna schools, showing in early childhood the literary talent that was to make him for a time one of the leading Yiddish journalists and writers in the United States. When he was thirteen, his Hebrew articles were already appearing in a St. Petersburg weekly. At the age of seventeen, he went to live in Paris, studying at the Sorbonne while continuing to write for Russian periodicals. He returned to St. Petersburg for two years, and in 1886 made his way to London where he became involved in the Jewish labor movement and collaborated in writing a Passover "Socialist Haggadah" in Yiddish. During this time he was also a frequent contributor of short stories, plays and critical essays to Jewish periodicals, most of them in Hebrew or Yiddish.

In August, 1887, he moved to Chicago. Within a few months, in early 1888, using type fonts and accessories which he had brought with him from Europe, he founded the *Jewish Courier*, destined to be Chicago's leading Yiddish newspaper for many decades. A prodigious worker and writer, he also briefly published the unsuccessful Hebrew periodical *Keren Or* (*Ray of Light*)—while he went on writing Yiddish plays, stories and non-fiction. His humorous sketches, which ran under his pen-name "Zakoff-Gadol," were very popular with Jewish immigrants. Several of his plays, *Samson, The Heroes of Zion*, and *Zalman Troubedor*, were staged with considerable success.

On December 18, 1892, Zolotkoff married Fannie Ogus. He enrolled in law school at Lake Forest University in 1893, earning his degree three years later. He and Fannie had five children: Dina, who died in 1919; Sydney, Hyman J., Albert Herzl and Julia.

Meites says, "He occupied a unique place in the community, for his profound intellectual attainments were blended with a charm of manner and utterance that placed him in great demand at all public functions. Practically every movement that was launched and every important meeting, whatever the cause, called upon him to act in the capacity of spokesman or chairman."

Not everyone admired Zolotkoff. Bernard Horwich describes a shouting match between Zolotkoff and Sinai Rabbi Dr. Emil Hirsch, spokesman for the wealthy and elitist Chicago German Jews. Zolotkoff apparently remarked that Hirsch knew almost no Hebrew, to which Hirsch replied that Zolotkoff was a "greenhorn west-sider" who didn't know English. Zolotkoff answered that Hirsch didn't know Russian. When Dr. Hirsch responded that Zolotkoff didn't know French and German, Zolotkoff shouted that he did know French and German, and that Hirsch didn't know Polish, and that he didn't know Hebrew or the Talmud either. Things seemed to have calmed down before blows were exchanged, but Horwich says that a few days later a long article appeared in the *Jewish Courier* in which Zolotkoff "bitingly attacked the German Jews and Dr. Hirsch as only he could."

By 1895, Zolotkoff was the intellectual luminary of the recent Russian immigrants, a brilliant writer in English, Yiddish and Hebrew, a gifted orator, publisher of the leading local Yiddish newspaper, an active labor supporter and a lawyer to boot. He now brought his influence to bear on Zionism which, during the last decade of the nineteenth century—the time of the Dreyfus affair in France and rampant anti-Semitism and pogroms in Russia—was attracting the attention of Chicago Jewry, particularly of immigrants from Eastern Europe. Zolotkoff joined Bernard Horwich and others to organize a Zionist movement: Chicago Zionist Organization No.1, which Horwich claims was the "first organized Zionist group in America," a New York group not being formed until six months later.

In the summer of 1897, the new Chicago group learned of Theodore Herzl's call for a Zionist Congress to be held in August, 1897. Herzl had originally planned to hold it in Munich, but decided on Basel because of objections from some Munich rabbis. Zolotkoff was chosen by the Chicago group to be its delegate. Since the group was not yet an accredited member of the European-based Zionist organization, Zolotkoff probably went to Basel as a representative rather than as an accredited delegate. After an arduous fund-raising campaign, the Chicago group was able to pay Zolotkoff's traveling expenses. In Basel he had his first opportunity to meet Theodore Herzl and other legendary Zionist leaders, like Max Nordau and Jacob de Haas. In the ten short years before the conference, Theodore Herzl had used his charisma, arrogance, diplomacy, political and writing talent to form a cohesive Zionist movement in Europe from many fragmented and diverse Jewish groups. The Congress marked the peak of the accomplishments he would live to see.

After Herzl received a tumultuous reception, his first words to the assembly set forth the purpose of the conference: "We want to lay the foundation stone of the house which is to shelter the Jewish nation." The Basel Program, which became the official platform of the Zionist movement, was adopted: "Zionism seeks to obtain for the Jewish people a publicly recognized, legally secured homeland in Palestine." In addition, the main points of a Constitution for the newly created Zionist Organization were set forth: the creation of a bank and a national fund for the purchase of land in Palestine. In three days, the historic conference was over, and Zolotkoff went to New York to report on it to Bernard Horwich. On his return to Vienna, Herzl wrote in his diary on September 3, 1887: "Were I to sum up the Basel Congress in words—which I shall carefully refrain from uttering in public—it would be this: In Basel I founded the Jewish state. If I were to say this out loud today, everybody would laugh at me. In five years, perhaps, but certainly in fifty everybody will agree." It actually took six months longer than Herzl predicted: Israel declared its independence on May 14, 1948.

Inspired by Herzl's call to action, Zolotkoff helped in 1898 to organize the Knights of Zion, a successor to the Zionist group organized a year earlier. He became its first Grand Recorder and later served as Grand Master at different times. In a letter written in 1899, the original of which is in the Zionist archives in Jerusalem, Zolotkoff wrote to Herzl that the clubs which constituted the Chicago Knights of Zion were patterned after fraternal lodges like the Masons, and that these Zionist lodges (called "Gates") were working to present the Zionist case. Zolotkoff was a Chicago delegate to the third, fifth, sixth and seventh Zionist Congresses, held annually in Western Europe, and continued his association with Herzl until the latter's death in 1904. Throughout those years, the era of his most impressive accomplishments, Zolotkoff remained contentious and blunt. Horwich recalled a bitter argument the two had during this period over political policy questions. Zolotkoff accused Horwich of being irresponsible.

Zolotkoff was an assistant state's attorney in Chicago from 1904 to 1910, a considerable accomplishment for a relatively young Jewish immigrant. In March 1908, he became embroiled in the Lazarus Averbuch affair, leading to accusations by some writers that he had not done enough as assistant state's attorney to clear the name of Averbuch, a young Jewish immigrant accused of having attempted to assassinate Chicago's chief of police, who had shot and killed him.

In 1911, Zolotkoff sold the *Courier* to the owners of the New York City, *Tageblatt* and moved his family to New York where he edited the *Tageblatt*. In 1915 he returned to Chicago, once more to edit the *Courier*. He also became the executive director of the Federated Zionist Societies in the Middle West, a position he held until 1920.

He appears to have moved during this time between Chicago, New York, England and Palestine, where he spent a considerable amount of time in Jerusalem establishing the Jerusalem Printing Press, the first press in Palestine to print books in Hebrew for world-wide distribution.

He returned to New York in 1924, resuming his career as a writer, and wrote many novels, both in Yiddish and English. One, *From Vilna to Hollywood*, was translated from Yiddish to English and serialized in 1932 in New York's *Morgen Journal*. The book was said to be autobiographical, but it reads more like *What Makes Sammy Run*, a later novel by Budd Schulberg dealing with the impact of American materialism on Jewish immigrants striving for quick fame and wealth.

After the first two decades of the last century, Zolotkoff was no longer in an official leadership position in the Zionist movement. There are a number of possible reasons for this. Many American Zionists caught in internal disputes in the American Zionist organizations were displaced or resigned during this period, and this may have affected Zolotkoff. It is also possible that financial setbacks in his attempts to establish his own publishing house in New York or Jerusalem caused his withdrawal from public life.

His health began to fail in the mid-1930s, and he died in New York on July 31 or August 1, 1938. A funeral service was held in New York the day after his death, and his body was brought back to Chicago and taken from the LaSalle Street Station to the Jewish People's Institute on Chicago's West Side where, for the first time in its history, the main auditorium was converted into a funeral chapel to accommodate thousands of people who had come to pay their last respects.

Benjamin J. Daskal of Congregation Rodfei Zedek conducted the religious services with Cantor Joseph Giblichman. Bernard Horwich, Zolotkoff's old Zionist friend, presided over the ceremonies, and Zolotkoff was eulogized as a Zionist by Hyman Steinberg; as a lawyer by Peter Sissman, partner of Clarence Darrow whose daughter was married to Zolotkoff's second son; as a journalist by Dr. Mordecai Katz, and as a scholar by Dr. Abraham Levinson, his physician. From the JPI, the funeral party proceeded to the B'nai B'rith Cemetery for the interment next to his wife, who had died two years earlier, and his daughter Dina, who had died in 1919. Thus the community marked the passing of Leon Zolotkoff, Chicago's only representative to the historic First Zionist Conference.

JULIUS ROSENWALD MEETS AARON AARONSOHN

—

IT IS OFTEN SAID THAT American Zionism was born in Chicago. In 1891, the Reverend William G. Blackstone circulated his petition addressed to President Benjamin Harrison and Secretary of State James S. Blaine, urging them to convene an international conference for the purpose of creating a Jewish state in Palestine, to relieve the suffering of Jews in Russia. In 1897, Leon Zolotkoff, the Chicago writer and attorney, became the first American delegate to the founding conference of the Zionist Organization in Basel, Switzerland. H. L. Meites claimed to be "member number one" of the American Zionist organization.

Most Chicago rabbis and community leaders, however, were either neutral or opposed to Zionism; and often included among those opposed is Julius Rosenwald, the prominent Chicago philanthropist, who is closely identified with his mentor, Chicago Sinai Rabbi Emil G. Hirsch, an outspoken opponent of the Zionists. For Hirsch, Chicago was Jerusalem: "Let those who favor a return to Jerusalem go there if they will." Rosenwald was a Sinai congregant, but contrary to popular belief, he did not oppose Zionism but was in fact involved in early Zionist activities in America.

Among the Julius Rosenwald papers in the Special Collections at the University of Chicago Regenstein Library, is a folio containing correspondence between Rosenwald and Aaron Aaronsohn, an early

Zionist activist from Palestine. The letters show that Rosenwald had close contacts with Aaronsohn when the latter visited Chicago on different occasions in the early part of the century. Through Aaronsohn, Rosenwald and his good friend and fellow Sinai member, Illinois Appellate Judge Julian Mack, became involved with early Jewish agriculture and settlement activities in Palestine.

In 1882, Aaron Aaronsohn's brilliant and unusual family came from Romania to settle in Zichron Yaakov near Haifa. Aaronsohn was a gifted scholar—a botanist, agronomist, geologist, and geographer—who achieved international fame through his discovery in 1906 in Palestine, of Wild Emmer Wheat, the earliest known prototype of bread-producing grain, a discovery that was to prove of great importance not only for the settlers in Palestine but for the rest of the world as well. The U.S. Department of Agriculture published his pamphlet on wild wheat and in 1909 invited him to this country. In Chicago, he was taken by Judge Mack to meet the Rosenwalds, where he spent the day talking about Palestine and its agricultural possibilities.

Aaronsohn left for a conference on dry farming in Billings, Montana, but soon returned to Chicago, where Rosenwald and Judge Mack took him to dinner with a group of botanists and others from the University of Chicago, among whom was Roscoe Pound, a noted law professor, who had once been a state botanist and was an authority on the subject. Aaronsohn gave a lecture to the botanists the next day, which Rosenwald attended with great interest. The probable result was Rosenwald's decision to help finance Aaronsohn's work in Palestine. Aaronsohn had wanted for a long time to set up an agricultural research institute there, and now Rosenwald, Mack, and a group of East Coast Jewish leaders, including Louis Marshall and Augusta Rosenwald's friend Henrietta Szold became interested in the project. The Jewish Agricultural Experiment Station was incorporated in 1910 with Rosenwald as president and Aaronsohn as managing director.

It was located in Athlit, at the foot of Mount Carmel between Zichron Yaacov and Haifa, on land belonging to Baron de Hirsch's Jewish Colonization Association. Aaronsohn wanted to demonstrate the potential of supposedly barren and exhausted soil. Using scientific methods, he and his associates produced more wheat, barley, and oats than their neighbors; and also carried on valuable experiments with date and vine culture, which were later adapted for use in U.S. deserts. Aaronsohn set up a health bureau, and for farmers, published agricultural bulletins and gave lectures, both in Hebrew.

The Rosenwald archives include Aaronsohn's 1910 Department of Agriculture booklet, "Agricultural and Botanical Explorations in Palestine," giving details about varieties of cereals and fruits culti-vated in Palestine which could be grown in America, particularly in California. In addition to wild wheat, he discusses apricots, quinces, olives, figs, dates, and Jaffa oranges.

When Aaronsohn returned to the United States in the spring of 1913 to raise additional funds for his station, he visited the Rosenwalds frequently. It was then, apparently, that he persuaded them to visit Palestine. He wrote Rosenwald's wife Augusta from Washington on June 12, 1913: "Will your Palestinian trip make you a Zionist, you ask. Not necessarily. Zionism is becoming to a certain extent a for-mula; and dry formulas may be very helpful for masses, for meek individuals, but are like chains for individualities. But I have no doubt whatsoever that your Jewish self-consciousness will find reconfort [sic], tonicity in such a trip. What action will result? Let the future take care of himself."

The Rosenwalds did visit Palestine in February, 1914. They spent time at Aaronsohn's agricultural station, accompanied by Baron Edmond de Rothschild, and were apparently pleased with what they saw. Both of them were treated like "visiting nobility" by the local settlers, who welcomed them with fireworks and music. Rosenwald returned home well disposed toward Zionism and certainly toward Aaronsohn, but still unconvinced that Palestine could support a large Jewish population.

When war broke out in 1914, Aaronsohn worked with the British against the Turks for the liberation of Palestine. Rosenwald is said to have been annoyed by this because he believed it was Aaronsohn's duty to remain at his agricultural station and continue the important work which had consumed so much effort. When the Experiment

Station was occupied by the Turks in October, 1917, Aaronsohn's specimens and twenty thousand books and pamphlets had already been packed up by his aged father and hidden by the American consul. But the Turks found most of the boxes and carted many of them away. They also destroyed the station's mineralogical museum and chemical laboratory.

Rosenwald probably did not know that Aaronsohn and his family were part of a Jewish spy ring in Palestine, known as "Nili," that supplied British intelligence with vital information before General Allenby's conquest of the country. Aaronsohn's sister Sarah was captured by the Turks and cruelly tortured. She committed suicide in a Turkish prison.

Aaronsohn visited the U.S. briefly in December, 1917, and was irritated with Rosenwald's lack of support for Zionism. A month earlier, the Balfour Declaration, promising a Jewish homeland in Palestine, had been published. Aaronsohn wrote bluntly to Rosenwald from Washington on December 21, 1917:

> In my letter . . . I started to point out to you what wrong you were doing yourself, your posterity, your race in failing to respond to the call of the race, especially now, when the British Declaration and the conquest of Jerusalem have thrilled the souls, quickened the blood, stirred the hearts of millions and tens of millions of both Jews and non-Jews. . . .
>
> Unfortunately you have reached the stage when you are afraid of being pickpocketed whenever anybody approaches you. It must be a very uncomfortable state of mind. But I can assure you of one thing: We Zionists are not after your money. Not I at least. It is the salvation of your soul we are interested in . . . I am afraid you will find a good deal of "Hutzpa" in my letter. There very likely is. The time for persuasion is over. Every Jew who cares for himself or his children to remain Jews must join. They cannot escape it. Mrs. Rosenwald feels already this way. It is up to you now.
>
> The train is leaving and I have hardly time to thank you and Mrs. Rosenwald for your kind hospitality. Cordially, Aaron

Despite this, a friendly correspondence continued between Rosenwald and Aaronsohn. In an August 18, 1918, letter to Augusta Rosenwald from London, Aaronsohn mentions meeting Julius for dinner at the Savoy Hotel, when Rosenwald was on his way to Paris on a presidential mission in connection with the war. Aaronsohn writes warmly about Rosenwald's continued interest in Palestine and his desire to help improve the water supply in Jerusalem. The Savoy dinner was probably the last meeting between Rosenwald and Aaronsohn.

With the war's end, Julius Rosenwald returned to Chicago while his close friend Judge Mack went to Paris to represent Jewish interests in Palestine at the Versailles peace conference. In 1919, Aaronsohn joined the American delegation in Paris as an advisor. He left for London and on May 15 boarded a plane to fly back to Paris where Judge Mack was waiting for him at the airport. But Aaronsohn's plane crashed into the English Channel. His body was never recovered.

His death at age fifty-three brought an abrupt end to a career as important to the Zionist movement as the work of David Ben Gurion and Chaim Weizmann. It has been suggested that if Aaronsohn had lived, he might have become the movement's leader. In 1930, William C. Bullitt, the American diplomat who met Aaronsohn in Paris in 1919, remembered him as "the greatest man I have ever known. He was the quintessence of life, of life when it runs torrential, prodigal and joyous."

However, unfortunately at the time of his death, Aaronsohn and his family were embroiled in bitter disputes with Zionist leaders on, among other things, matters of priority, and the use of Arab labor, which the Aaronsohns favored. To make matters worse, his agricultural experimental station, virtually destroyed by the Turks, was deeply in debt. Julius Rosenwald came to the rescue once again, and by 1926 the debts and claims were settled. The archives include a wrenching letter dated May 20, 1927, in which Aaron's brother Alexander, writes with great bitterness about the treatment of his brother's memory by the Zionist leadership in Palestine. Rosenwald replied on June 27 that he disagreed with the policies of the Zionist leaders but added, "I am very careful, however, not to do or say anything publicly which would in any way hinder their program."

The Aaronsohn folio ends with a March 18, 1929, letter to Rosenwald from Knowles A. Ryerson, Senior Horticulturist of the U.S. Department of Agriculture, praising Aaronsohn for his agricultural contributions to the world, particularly to Palestine and concluding, "The part you played in encouraging or supporting Aaronsohn and making it possible for the future agricultural leaders of Palestine to secure thorough training is not known to many . . . if and when a sound rural life develops in the plains and hills of Palestine, it will have been due in large measure to your foresighted comprehension of the problems and your quiet but vital support of its rational solution."

Julius Rosenwald died in 1932, a great benefactor of good causes, and particularly those of benefit to Jews, and later to African Americans. As Ryerson noted, little is known or remembered of his early contributions to the settling of Jewish Palestine, but these were material and important, and, it should be remembered, resulted in no small part from his meetings with Aaron Aaronsohn in Chicago.

ZIONIST CONVENTION IN CHICAGO

—

IN SEPTEMBER, 1919, when Chicago was the site of the Twenty-Second Annual Convention of the Zionist Organization of America, Nathan D. Kaplan, a local attorney, wrote a poem praising his city as "renowned for achieving" and exclaiming, "Oh! Judah! Your exiles' duration/ is measured, God be with thee!" With the Zionist movement in America gaining strength from Britain's recent Balfour Declaration, the time of the "exile" really did seem "measured." Chicago, the "city renowned for achieving," made sense as the place to bring together a newly unified Zionist organization that seemed on the brink of achieving what had seemed the impossible dream of a Jewish homeland.

Held at the Auditorium Theater and presided over by Judge Julian Mack, the convention provided a brief moment of harmony in the history of American Zionism. It was one of the first truly comprehensive American Zionist meetings since the movement's earliest days and it also proved to be the highwater mark of participation by German Jews. By providing a platform for several of the country's leading Zionists, and making possible the election of several new leaders, the convention helped produce a new brand of American Zionism.

Called "the twenty-second" because the first Zionist conference had been held in Basle twenty-one years earlier, this 1919 convention was in fact the first time the New York-based Federation of American

Zionists and the Chicago Knights of Zion had come together since the two groups had become affiliated at a Pittsburgh conference in 1918. This harking back to the founding of political Zionism was an effort to smooth over real differences that could surface at the slightest provocation. There had been bitter struggles, many based on petty jurisdictional disputes, between the Chicago Knights of Zion, founded in 1913 as the first American Zionist organization, and the New York Federation. And there were conflicts within the Chicago Zionist community itself, not the least being those between German and Eastern European Jews.

The Chicago Zionists dominated the convention, presided over by Judge Julian M. Mack, national president of the ZOA as well as of the American Jewish Congress. Chicago organizers included journalist, publisher and former assistant states attorney Leon Zolotkoff; Judges Hugo Pam, Harry M. Fisher and Joseph B. Fisher; and Max Shulman and Nathan B. Kaplan, both of whom were lawyers.

The fullest record of the proceedings comes from a report by Meyer Weisgal in the December, 1919, issue of *The Maccabean*, the official ZOA organ. The convention opened on Sunday afternoon, September 14, with an audience of over 700 delegates and hundreds of guests. Judge Mack in his opening address recalled three auspicious events of 1918: first, President Woodrow Wilson's New Year's letter to Dr. Stephen Wise, Vice President of the ZOA giving public "adhesion to and approval of" the Balfour Declaration and Zionist work and aims in Palestine. Second, the American Jewish Congress meeting in Philadelphia where Zionism had a presence, although in an aside Mack expressed regret that some dissident forces, among them the American Jewish Committee and certain Orthodox groups, had not gone to Philadelphia. He called upon them "to awaken and join hands in the work." Thirdly, the judge expressed the hope that at the Paris Peace Conference then in progress, the Balfour Declaration would be officially mandated, along with resolutions guaranteeing Jewish rights in Poland and Russia: "But with the pledged word of Great Britain, endorsed by France, endorsed by President Wilson, endorsed by all other nations, and with the express personal assurances of all of the leading allied statesmen of the world, I say we look forward with the absolute confidence that in due course, the mandate, represented by our representatives last February in the hearing granted to them by the Conference, will issue."

Mack then turned to the thorny question of dual loyalty, a question that had arisen particuarly because Louis Brandeis, formerly president of the Federation of American Zionists and now honorary vice president of the ZOA, had recently been appointed to the U.S. Supreme Court. In the Senate, his nomination had evoked a bitter debate often tinged with anti-Semitism. Mack pledged that the American Jew "is and will be, now and forever, a true and loyal citizen of the land, owing and granting it full and complete political allegiance. But we will be a kin to the Jewish people re-established in Palestine. They will be his brethren, children of a common stock . . ."

Mack went on to outline the work of the ZOA for the coming year, placing great emphasis on medical needs in Palestine, especially the need to eradicate malaria, and concluded: "The future of Palestine rests with American Jewry. European Jewry is impoverished and will be for years to come." This comment pointed up another problem—a conflict between American and European Zionists centering around Louis Brandeis, who had just returned from a trip to Palestine and Paris with some of his colleagues, including Felix Frankfurter and Jacob De Haas. Both Brandeis and Mack believed in the efficacy of economic initiative and thought that the Balfour Declaration had made further political action unnecessary. Brandeis took the position that with scientific planning, intelligent investments and the benefits of free enterprise, Jews could be transferred every year from hostile environments to Palestine, which would have an increasingly absorptive economy. He disliked the idea of communal *kibbutzim*.

But for the European leadership of the World Zionist movement, headed by Chaim Weizmann and A. M. M. Ussishkin, the Balfour Declaration was only a stepping stone to further political action. They looked upon Zionism as a step toward the creative rebirth of the Jewish people everywhere, in which national forces would be harnessed to rebuild the homeland. To them, the pioneers were the spearhead and hope of Zionism, the expression of Jewish nationalism. Disputing Brandeis's emphasis on an economic process, they called for political action and mass settlement. After hearing Brandeis's opinions about the need for malaria control, Shmarya Levin, the Russian Zionist leader, was said to have remarked that Brandeis would favor mass Jewish settlement in Palestine only after the last mosquito was eradicated.

To the European Zionists, the divisions in American Zionism seemed deeper than the Americans would admit. Brandeis, in 1919 the hero of the Jewish masses, had been the undisputed leader of American Zionists. His family had come from Middle Europe, and were closely identified with German Jews like Mack. Chaim Weizmann was upset by Brandeis's acceptance of the Supreme Court nomination, which necessitated his resignation from the ZOA presidency, and his putting his commitment to his native country over the duty that Weizmann believed he owed to the Jewish homeland. These feelings were an undercurrent among the Zionist leaders at the meeting in Chicago, though many of the delegates would not become aware of that until a year later.

Mack's speech was followed by reports from the three ZOA secretaries: Jacob De Haas, former secretary to Theodore Herzl, Louis Lipsky, and Henrietta Szold, head of Hadassah, the ZOA women's organization, who spoke emphatically about the need for an intensive Jewish education in the Diaspora. The convention was then greeted in Hebrew by the Hebrew and Yiddish writer Reuben Brainin—probably the first time that language was heard in the Auditorium Theater. Brainin urged the assembly to begin an intensive study of Hebrew: the homeland, he said, could not be built without the Hebrew language. When in the course of his remarks he mentioned the name of Theodore Herzl, the audience rose and sang "Hatikvah." The first day ended with the election of Mack as chairman, and Wise and Lipsky as vicechairmen, and three secretaries to record the proceedings in English, Hebrew and Yiddish.

On Monday evening, the assembly heard a number of congratulatory messages from Zionist leaders throughout the world, among them a letter from Dr. Max Nordau, chosen by Herzl to be one of his successors, who wrote: "Palestine must be respected as an integral geographical individuality with its traditional frontier. Every pretension of mutilating it in the north or the south must be resisted with the utmost energy . . . You American Jews have behaved wonderfully during these horrible years of war and ruin . . . But money is not everything. We now ask of you, and expect from you, that you will make a new and far more decisive effort."

The next speaker was Harvard Professor Felix Frankfurter, who received a tremendous ovation as he rose to give a report on a trip he and Brandeis had recently made to Palestine. Frankfurter optimistically presented Brandeis' case on the need to build innovative commercial enterprises in Palestine. Stephen Wise, vice-chairman of the ZOA delegation to the Paris Peace Conference, reported on the proceedings there, adding that he was confident that the conference would ultimately endorse the Balfour Declaration.

On Tuesday morning Justice Brandeis presented resolutions for approval calling for the raising of "vast" sums of money for the purchase of land in Palestine, and for the campaign against malaria, and concluding that "all present differences of opinion against malaria and concerning the movement must be forgotten and all Jews of the world must participate in this great work." The Tuesday evening session began with eloquent personal tributes by his close friends Judge Mack and Henrietta Szold to the memory of the Palestinian activist Aaron Aaronsohn, who had recently died in a plane crash over the English Channel as he was returning to the Paris Peace Conference, where he was serving as an advisor to the American Jewish delegation. A copy of the resolution passed by the convention was later sent to Aaronsohn's family in Palestine. Another resolution was offered in praise of American Jews who had served in the Jewish Legion fighting with the British Army against the Turks. Robert Szold, a native of Streeter, Illinois, who had accompanied Brandeis to Palestine, gave a detailed report of the various agricultural and educational groups being established there; of the population of approximately 700,000, he said, 70,000 were Jews who lived in Jerusalem and Jaffa and some sixty settlements.

Szold was followed by Bernard A. Rosenblatt, head of the American Zionist Commonwealth which worked to acquire land in Palestine, who reported that it was Commonwealth policy to buy land whenever possible from absentee Turkish landlords, in order to avoid friction with local Arabs who would "gradually come to understand our good faith and purpose." He was happy to announce, he said, that the first hundred Jewish soldiers from the Jewish Legion in Palestine were ready to settle on newly acquired land in a settlement to be called Balfouria in honor of Lord Balfour, and the Commonwealth intended to raise five million dollars to acquire additional land for many more Jewish soldiers. He ended: "The third and permanent Jewish Commonwealth is dependent to a very large extent upon the support of the three million Jews of America."

On Wednesday, H.L. Meites, the Chicago editor and publisher, introduced a resolution calling for the publication of a Yiddish Zionist daily, a project that never came to fruition. The rest of the Wednesday sessions were filled with lengthy debates dealing with the election of members of the Executive Committee—one person's democracy being another's dictatorship. Stephen Wise argued for the preservation of the status quo in which members of the Executive Committee were elected by the central body and not by the membership at large. That evening an audience of four thousand heard the concluding speeches. After paying homage to Lord Balfour and President Wilson, Judge Mack turned to Jacob De Haas, who gave a "soul-stirring" picture of conditions in Palestine, a land of "indestructible beauty," damaged by the ravages of war, disease and neglect. He concluded: "If love for Zion makes Zion ours, we can truly make all of Palestine ours by loving, earnest, physical effort."

In the final speech, Rabbi Zvi Hirsch Masliansky, a popular Yiddish speaker, recalled for the audience forty years of Zionist activity starting with the early days in Russia when the young Weizmann was his pupil. When the rabbi pointed to Brandeis who was sitting on the platform, the entire audience stood and cheered, while Brandeis rose and bowed repeatedly. With the singing of the "Star Spangled Banner" and "Hatikvah," the meeting adjourned shortly before midnight.

Except for the passage of mandatory resolutions and the election of officers on the following day, the Twenty-Second Zionist Organization of America Conference was over. Julian Mack was reelected president and the other incumbents were reelected to their positions. The convention received wide coverage in the Jewish press and to some extent in Chicago dailies. The *Daily News* on November 16, 1919 carried a lengthy article about Zionist settlement activities, quoting Felix Frankfurter who had been an Assistant Secretary of State: "There can be no dissent; there will be no dissent. The Zionist cause has been accepted by the Peace Conference, not as a formality but as a spiritual finality."

Frankfurter was mistaken. The Peace Conference failed to implement the Jewish homeland and England retreated from the Balfour Declaration. Within a year all the convention's hopes and pleas for unity were ignored as the Weizmann forces, headed by Louis Lipsky, challenged Brandeis, Mack and De Haas for control of the ZOA. In the 1921 convention in Cleveland, the Weizmann forces were in the majority and Mack and his colleagues were turned out of office and Louis Lipsky became president. American Jews lost a large part of their American Zionist leadership. In the 1930s only Stephen Wise returned to the fold as the leader of the new American Jewish Congress and the ZOA.

Today, more than eighty years after the Chicago Convention, many of the Chicago delegates' dreams have been realized. There remain serious problems that had arisen for discussion in 1919, but despite all the failed promises and bitter disharmonies, the State of Israel exists in no small part due to the efforts of these early American Zionists.

MEMOIR: CAMP AVODAH SUMMER OF 1946

A FEW YEARS AGO, traveling through the beautiful rolling farmland of southwestern Michigan, we happened to stop at a small store on the shore of Clear Lake for some ice cream. Trying to make conversation with the elderly waitress, I told her that fifty years ago, I had spent two months at a camp on the other side of the lake. "Oh," she said at once, "You must be one of the Jewish boys from Chicago who camped there."

Indeed I was. In June 1946, after my junior year at Hyde Park High School on Chicago's South Side, I joined two of my classmates, Werner Frank and Eddie Rosen, for a summer at Camp Avodah at Clear Lake. Since it was a work-camp sponsored by the Chicago Board of Jewish Education, it cost very little. During the war the camp had been sponsored by Victory Farm Volunteers of America, a program created by the government to help alleviate the farm labor shortage. It was located during its first two years, 1943 and '44, in DesPlaines, Illinois, to help the war effort and bring young Jewish boys together in a spirit of comradeship. The camp was devoted almost exclusively to agricultural work at nearby farms. Now in 1946 the war was over, Camp Avodah was energized with a somewhat different purpose, although we were still participants in the nation's effort to recover from the labor shortage, and the camp received compensation for our work. Avodah had been given this beautiful piece of open land bordering Clear Lake.

When we arrived—I believe it was by bus—tents had been pitched for temporary shelter, and counselors close to our own age were building army-style barracks. There were about 100 campers, including about twenty-five from the Marks Nathan Home, a Jewish orphanage. The director was Sam Kaminker, who as the son of a West Side Orthodox Rabbi was steeped in Jewish learning and ritual. He was also an ardent Zionist and had been a member of Hashomer Hatzair, a leftist Zionist youth group.

From early morning through mid-afternoon we worked on the farms in the Buchanan area, hoeing, weeding and picking vegetables and fruit like raspberries and peaches. We were given a break for lunch and often ate with the itinerant farm workers. The labor was difficult at first. Even lunch was a problem. When we first went out to work we found to our consternation that the Jewish women who ran the kitchen had made lox sandwiches for us. They considered this a treat, but of course the salted salmon made us very thirsty as we worked under the broiling sun. Lox was eventually replaced by tuna.

Our afternoons were spent on clean-up, rest and swimming and other sports. There was also, as I now realize, a rather subtle inculcation of Jewish history, with an emphasis on Zionism. While we worked to build our khaki-colored permanent barracks, we were told that we were doing exactly what the Jews in Israel were doing as they built their kibbutzim.

The cultural programming was intense. For example, one night we were awakened, divided into three groups: Jews, British and Arabs, and taken through an exercise on how to bring Holocaust survivors illegally from Europe into Israel. On another night, in front of a roaring campfire, we went through a mock trial of Josephus, the Jewish general who in the great uprising against the Romans, after watching his men slay each other, betrayed them by surrendering himself to the Emperor Titus. We learned that Josephus had gone on to become a famous historian, preserving for his people an eyewitness account of the revolt and creating a lasting record of Jewish history. Was his contribution as a historian a vindication of his betrayal? What did we think? We split on this issue but the program was brilliant in its conception and execution.

In another program, we pretended to establish a kibbutz over-night just as had been done by Zionists in Palestine to outwit the British authorities.

The Sabbath was the highlight of the week, heralded by classical and Jewish music from loudspeakers Every Friday evening began with music from Grieg's Peer Gynt Suite, that still brings waves of nostalgia each time I hear it. The Sabbath service was basically secular, with readings from various Jewish sources, and material written by Ben Aronin, our poet in residence.

We had a camp newsletter for which I did some writing. I had encountered anti-Semitism from one of the farmers and wrote about it, naming the farmer. This raised a commotion. Sam Kaminker backed me, but warned about printing the name of the farmer, who had told me that the German prisoners of war who had worked for him the previous year were better workers than "Jew boys." There was a sign near his store that said only Christians were welcome.

Camp Avodah continued to prosper along with Camp Sharon, its smaller neighbor, established in 1946 by the Chicago Board of Jewish Education. Camp Sharon was coeducational, and concentrated on Hebrew language and literature studies.

By the 1960s, Camp Avodah had lost its appeal for Jewish boys, and was sold to a Christian evangelical church, which to this day uses it as a summer camp for its members.

Camp Avodah had ceased to exist to a large extent because the times had passed it by. In the 1940s, when the State of Israel had not yet been established, Sam Kaminker and his group had been able to convince the Board of Jewish Education and B'nai B'rith, which had helped raise funds for the camp, that tilling the soil was a worthwhile activity for young Jewish boys. In postwar 1946, Kaminker could include Zionist indoctrination in the camp's study program. The return to the land and the rescue of Holocaust victims made the establishment of a Jewish State a less controversial subject.

In the 1960s, the boys could participate in any of a growing number of travel-work-study programs in Israel. They could farm a real kibbutz and debate the character of Josephus while standing upon the actual site of the battle. But we "Men of Avodah 1946" will always remember the physical challenges, intense idealism and true comradeship of our summer in Michigan.

MEMOIR: ISRAEL INDEPENDENCE CELEBRATION

IN JUNE 1938, I CAME to Chicago with my family—refugees fleeing Hitler's Germany. My introduction to active Zionism came in 1946 when I attended Camp Avodah. At the University of Illinois at Chicago's Navy Pier, when I became an active member of the Intercollegiate Zionist Federation of America (IZFA), I attended two memorable programs celebrating the creation of the new State of Israel. The first, held on Sunday, December 21, 1947, at the Civic Opera House, hailed the adoption by the United Nations on November 29 of a resolution in favor of a Jewish state in a part of Palestine. Coincidentally, that was the fiftieth anniversary of the First Zionist Congress in Basle and the founding of the Chicago Zionist Organization in 1897. I remember how impressed I was with the December 21st celebration program, reminiscent of the popular earlier Chicago Chanukah festivals.

But even more impressive was the second program at the Chicago Stadium on Sunday May 16, 1948, in celebration of the actual establishment of the Jewish state a day earlier. Over 25,000 people attended, with many having to stand in the aisles. This was the largest assembly of Chicago Jewry since July 3, 1933, when Meyer Weisgal's pageant "The Romance of a People" was performed before an audience of 125,000 at Soldier Field.

For a young person like me, already grateful to have escaped Nazi Germany, all this seemed like a miracle. A giant portrait of Theodore Herzl hung from the stadium rafters; a banner strung beneath it was imprinted with Herzl's famous words: "IF YOU WILL IT, IT IS NO DREAM."

Of the many speakers that day, I especially remember two. The first was Bartley Crum, a noted liberal Republican attorney who had endeared himself to American Jews as a member of the Anglo-American Committee of Inquiry on Palestine, which, after much bitter debate, had urged the British to permit 100,000 Jewish refugees to enter Palestine. In a powerful speech, Crum emphasized the urgent need for a homeland for the Holocaust survivors languishing in Europe. The other memorable speaker was Reuven Dafni, a commander of the Haganah, the Israel Defense Force, who repeatedly enthralled the audience with descriptions of his experiences as a paratrooper during the Second World War, helping to rescue Jews in Yugoslavia. Dafni later became the Israeli Consul General in New York and other cities, but unfortunately not in Chicago. Fifty years after the event, I can still hear the words of this heroic man.

The evening ended with the lighting of candles for the *Shekheyanu* prayer, and the singing of "Hatikvah," the national anthem of the new state. Then came the spectacle of the bearded Old Patriarch, overcome by the passion of the moment, leaping to his feet in the aisles in an Hassidic dance. His picture was carried in the newspapers the next day. Years later we discovered that his name was Elisha Kite. His ecstatic dance of pure joy was unforgettable.

Of course, there have been other spectacular celebrations in Chicago since 1948. One was the huge gathering in Grant Park in 1967 after the Six-Day War. But none, I believe, can match the overwhelming happiness evinced fifty years ago when Israel declared its independence.

IV
CHICAGO JEWS AND ZIONISM:
RENOWNED VISITORS

SHMARYA LEVIN

———

SHMARYA LEVIN IS VIRTUALLY forgotten today, but his visit to Chicago in 1906 had an electrifying effect on the local Zionist organizations, boosting them to world-class status. As one of the twelve Jewish representatives to the Russian Duma, the short-lived parliament formed after the revolution of 1905, Levin enjoyed an international reputation as a clever politician and a passionate speaker. Many memoirs attest to the lasting effect of Levin's visit, when he met with, among others, Judge Julian Mack, Julius Rosenwald, Adolph Kraus, Rabbi Emil Hirsch, and Bernard Horwich.

Born in Russia in 1867, Levin was educated in both Jewish and secular schools. Like many Russian intellectuals of his time, he studied in Germany, at Heidelberg and Berlin, where he developed close ties with German and American Zionists. After receiving his doctorate, he returned to Russia and was appointed Rabbi of Grodno, Ekaterinoslav and Vilna by the Czar. He was a natural choice to be a Jewish representative to the newly formed Duma, and rapidly gained world fame when reports of his Duma speeches appeared in Yiddish and Hebrew newspapers. When the Czar disbanded the Duma in 1906, Levin fled to Berlin and embarked on the lecture tour that would eventually take him to Chicago, where he had a number of discussions about Zionism with Julius Rosenwald, whose house guest he may have been.

Rosenwald would eventually help Levin found a publishing house in Tel Aviv, and would also contribute to the establishment of the

Jewish Institute of Technology in Haifa. How convinced a Zionist Rosenwald was before he met Levin is not clear. Louis Lipsky, in *A Gallery of Zionist Profiles*, notes that at that time Rosenwald gave the name Tel Aviv to his country house in Highland Park. He was certainly influenced by the agronomist Aaron Aaronsohn, but he did not meet Aaronsohn until 1909. In fact, it was Augusta Rosenwald who was said to have become attracted to Zionism because of Levin, who is supposed to have told Rosenwald, "I could convert one member of your family to the cause of Zionism, but I would first have to remove your wife from her husband's influence."

Bernard Horwich called Levin's visit "electrifying," but he records a number of troubling moments from the visit in his autobiography, *My First Eighty Years*. In one instance, when Horwich arranged for him to speak at Anshe Knesset Israel, then the largest Orthodox synagogue in Chicago, Levin addressed the largely European audience in Hebrew, a language almost nobody there could understand, and, to make matters worse, ended his incomprehensible speech in just fifteen minutes, irritating, among others, Horwich, who wrote:

> All in all his visit here was not a happy one. Of the true Russian intelligentsia, he was of a highly nervous temperament and like most men of that type, was rather self-centered and felt himself superior to the average person. He did not like the well-to-do Jews of the South Side, nor did he have much use for the poor Orthodox Jews of the West Side. What he had expected was to encounter here a group of Russian intelligentsia like himself, and that he did not find. However, he infused new life into the Zionist movement, which gained heavily by his presence.

Levin did have one success: a meeting at the Standard Club, where he spoke in German, a language the South Side audience could understand The meeting was chaired by Adolph Kraus, and Rabbi Emil Hirsch, a noted opponent of Zionism, was also present. In *Hadassah* magazine in 1933, twenty-seven years later, an anonymous essay, in

Yiddish and English, presented the visit through the eyes of the poor West Side Jews; demonstrating the tension that existed between the West Side and South Side Jewish communities:

> The first time that a reformed temple of the Chicago German Jews opened its portals to a Zionist conference was in 1907 when the late Shmarya Levin visited Chicago for the first time.
>
> This transpired at the Isaiah Temple. The President there was the late Adolph Kraus, grandmaster of the B'nai B'rith, who hails from Bohemia. It was necessary to think up a resourceful pretext in order that the temple be obtained to house a Zionist mass meeting. It was performed thus: Adolph Kraus was approached and told that into Chicago comes a grand man, a Russian of the Mosaic faith. Pray, Herr Kraus, and contribute to the expenses incurred by the visit of the guest. Interrogates the Herr Kraus: Who might the illustrious Jew be? So he is informed: The great Jew is Dr. Shmarya Levin, a member of the imperial Duma. He flows the German language like water. Berlin is 'his meat,' and the Czar causing the dissolution of the Duma leads to the doctor's escape to Chicago.
>
> Thus parleyed a Zionist committee with the old Sire Kraus of Bohemia and led him to understand that the doctor, the fleeing congressman, need be provided with a lodging place and a table to feed at. It was not fair to dispatch such a great man and a martyr, to boot, to the sheltering house? Herr Kraus telephoned the Auditorium Hotel and ordered a suitable suite of rooms for the guest. With this alone, the transaction has not yet ended.
>
> The interest just began and a new chapter commenced in the Temple crisis in behalf of Zionism. It started out with a banquet in honor of Dr. Shmarya Levin at the Standard Club where there were over two hundred men and women of the foremost Yehudic aristocracy assembled. Herr Kraus invited them himself and he himself was the toastmaster, too. And even Dr. Emil Hirsch, reformed Rabbi of Sinai Temple (the most antagonizing anti-Zionist of that day), was also present at the banquet and, what's more, the chief speaker

in the audience. Not, Providence forbid, did he speak to the good
of Zion, this Rabbi, but speak he did and this alone was accounted
as a big victory, a very big victory, indeed.

Chaim Weizmann, in his autobiography *Trial and Error*, says that
Levin held "first place" among the Zionist propagandists of the day.
Much impressed by the older man's drive and occasional audacity,
Weizmann tells a classic Levin story. On one occasion Levin had at-
tended a speech by Jacob Schiff of New York, a close friend of Julius
Rosenwald and a well-known philanthropist, in which Schiff said in
his heavy German accent, "I am divided into three parts: I am an
American, I am a German, and I am a Jew." When Schiff finished,
Levin rose immediately and asked whether Schiff divided himself hori-
zontally or vertically: if horizontally, exactly which part had he left
for the Jewish people?

Levin returned to Chicago a number of times, and although no
subsequent trip would duplicate the excitement of his 1906 visit, the
first by a world-class Zionist, he continued to be in demand as a
speaker. To those Chicagoans who remembered him, he was a giant.
Louis Lipsky wrote, "They remembered him as he stood there, looking remarkably like Lenin . . . They remembered the lather of excitement in which he was immersed. They remembered the tone of exal-
tation which rang in his voice, the sarcasm, the rebuke. He appeared
like Mephisto in reverse, speaking like any Prophet of God."

Rufus Learsi wrote, in *The Jews in America: A History*, "With his
first appearance in America in 1906, Levin left his audiences dazzled
and astonished. He was one of the most potent forces in the progress
of Zionism in America, a rare synthesis of the teacher and orator,
standing before his audiences like an ancient Hebrew prophet, casti-
gating them and uplifting them at the same time."

Ironically, Levin's memory was virtually eclipsed by the fame of
several of his followers, including Chaim Weizmann, Ahad Ha'am
and Chaim Nachman Bialik.

NACHUM SOKOLOW

———

THERE IS A GROUP PHOTOGRAPH in H.L. Meites's *History of the Jews of Chicago* of "Nachum Sokolow and a Group of Chicago Zionists Taken on the Zionist Leader's First Visit Here, April 1912." Sokolow's visit to Chicago actually took place a year later, in April, 1913, but that is a minor error. What is interesting is that this is a photograph of fourteen prominent Chicago Zionists early in the last century. Sitting between Bernard Horwich and Max Shulman is Nachum Sokolow, who followed the tradition set by early Zionist leaders like Aaron Aaronsohn and Shmarya Levin, of visiting U.S. Jewish communities to plead their cause and receive much-needed assistance for their impoverished brethren in Palestine.

The *Chicago Tribune* on Monday, April 14, 1913, under front page headline "Jews Cheer Plea of Noted Zionist" reported: "Nachum Sokolow of Warsaw, Poland, a leader of the Zionist movement, spoke to an audience of nearly 1,000 yesterday at the American Music Hall. When he was introduced by Max Shulman, chairman, the audience arose, waved hats, handkerchiefs and canes, and cheered for two minutes before Judge Hugo Pam obtained silence for Dr. Sokolow to speak." Sokolow was well-known to his audience. He and Chaim Weizmann became elder statesman of the Zionist Movement after the death of Theodore Herzl in 1904.

Nachum Sokolow was born in 1860 in Poland. Like his colleague Vladimir Ze'ev Jabotinsky, he was proficient in Yiddish, Polish, English and German, and a pioneer in modern Hebrew journalism. As a young man he had been the managing editor of *Ha-Tzephirah* in Warsaw. But unlike Jabotinsky, Sokolow was not an ideologue; his political views were moderate, and with his impeccable manners and dress, he was said to have given the impression that he might be a Polish nobleman. Like Weizmann, Sokolow loved to travel, always in style, staying at the finest hotels or clubs, much like a foreign diplomat. He was considered a perfect emissary for the Jews, like a *Shtadtlan*—a spokesman with the authorities for his fellow Jews in medieval Europe.

Sokolow talked to the heads of European states, and to the Pope, but his vacillation on issues and his middle-of-the road positions irritated many of his Zionist colleagues, who said he lacked passion. But they could not deny his talents as a writer and scholar or his genuine love for missions that involved travel. He made his home in Europe: first Warsaw, then Cologne, Germany, and, after World War I, London, where his devoted wife awaited his brief returns.

It was during his first trip to the United States in 1912–1913 that Sokolow came to Chicago, on a mission to explain Zionism as he saw it to the Jews in the New World and to seek their aid for settlements in Palestine. His moderation quickly became apparent to his Chicago audience. He saw Zionism as a movement that "looks after the welfare of the Jew as a Jew, whatever the country in which he abides," unlike many Russian Zionist leaders who spoke of all Jews returning to Palestine. Sokolow said that a Zionist should put the welfare of the Jew first: "Judaism, as well as Zionism, requires knowledge of Jewish history, traditions and literature."

Two of Sokolow's Chicago speeches in 1913 were reported by the *Chicago Sentinel*. In one, on April 11, he stressed the need for colonization in Palestine and the encouragement of Jewish education there, but he also reassured American Jews that Zionists did not oppose the immigration of Russian Jews to America. There was "no competition," he said, "between this country and Palestine in that regard." The descendants of American Jews might some day, with their background in democratic institutions, become valuable settlers in Palestine. Almost a week later, when Sokolow was the guest of honor at a luncheon at the LaSalle Hotel given by Jacob M. Loeb, president of the Chicago Hebrew Institute, he made a few remarks about the need to support impoverished Jewish settlers from Eastern Europe who had no place to immigrate but to Palestine, then under Turkish rule: "Nearly 100,000 of our people are living there now—not as Talmudic students, but as workers in trades of all kinds" and those with "sufficient funds" could be successful. "The land is adaptable to the growth of fruit and will yield large profits to the investor, but it takes time for the trees to bear fruit, and here lies the present difficulty. We need financial assistance. It is for our brethren in America, in Europe and elsewhere to lend their financial support to this work."

During World War I, Sokolow remained in London, working closely with Weizmann and other European leaders to obtain a commitment for a Jewish homeland in Palestine, although his relations with Weizmann were not without tension and conflict. Weizmann's resolute singlemindedness was in sharp contrast to Sokolow's moderation.

In 1933, Sokolow briefly succeeded Weizmann as president of the World Zionist Organization and the Jewish Agency for Palestine. When Weizmann resumed the offices in 1935, Sokolow was elected Honorary President and president of the *Keren Hayesod,* the Jewish National Fund. He had by then also become a respected scholar, historian and diplomat. He died on May 17, 1936.

Blessed with a photographic memory and a soothing manner—unusual for a Zionist leader, to say the least—he helped to persuade many Jews to accept Zionism because he asked for their help while making it clear that they should continue to go on living in America. This position clashed with the beliefs of other Zionists of his day and later with those of some Israelis like David Ben-Gurion, but today increasing numbers of Zionists see no conflict between encouragement of Jewish education and culture in the United States and support of a Jewish homeland in the State of Israel.

EINSTEIN AND WEIZMANN: A ZIONIST ODD COUPLE

———

MANY OF EUROPE'S MOST prominent Zionists visited Chicago in the early decades of the last century, but possibly the most unusual pair were Albert Einstein and Chaim Weizmann. When Aaron Aaronsohn, Shmarya Levin, Vladimir Jabotinsky, and Chaim Weizmann came to Chicago, each was a seasoned public figure whose political positions were familiar to most in their audiences. Einstein, on the other hand, was the most famous scientist in the world, but was only just beginning to speak publicly about Zionism when he came to Chicago with Weizmann in 1921.

Weizmann was a popular speaker beloved by Zionists—he would eventually become the first president of the State of Israel—but it was Einstein who drew large crowds during the pair's Chicago stay. From his publication of the general theory of relativity in 1905, Einstein had made a series of significant contributions to theoretical physics and in 1921 was awarded the Nobel Prize in Physics. Still a young man, he was widely considered to have taken the most significant step forward in physics since Newton.

The visit of Einstein and Weizmann marks another chapter in the story of Zionism in Chicago. The unlikely pair came here together, but with different agendas and motives. Einstein came to raise funds for the new Hebrew University in Jerusalem, while Weizmann was working to inaugurate the Jewish National Fund, *Keren Hayesod,* for the purpose of "redeeming the Land of Israel" by the purchase and development of land in Palestine.

Both men shared an interest in Jewish culture, and both were scientists. Weizmann was a chemist whose development of a potent explosive useful to the British during World War I had played a role in the Balfour Declaration of November 2, 1917, in which the British declared their support for a Jewish national home in Palestine. Unlike Einstein, Weizmann had devoted his energies to politics, becoming the leader of the European Zionist Movement. By 1921, he was deeply involved in the struggle for the overall leadership of the Zionist Organization of America.

A Zionist mission to the U.S. was an unlikely one for Einstein; he was extremely naive politically, a pacifist, an anti-nationalist, and a non-observant Jew. Weizmann had not known Einstein personally before the two began discussing a trip to America, but he soon became aware of the possible benefits to his mission if someone of Einstein's stature joined him. Einstein had impressed Weizmann with his stand against German anti-Semitism and his support for the Hebrew University in Palestine

Einstein was born in Ulm, Germany in 1879. His early school years were spent in Munich and Zurich, and he graduated in 1900 from the Federal Institute of Technology in Zurich. In 1902 he became a Swiss citizen while working in the patent office in Bern, and in 1905 received his doctorate from the University of Zurich. In 1910 he became a full professor in the German University in Prague, and in 1912 returned to Zurich to accept a chair in Theoretical Physics at the Federal Institute of Technology. By 1913 he had achieved international fame for his work on the theory of relativity, and was appointed Director of Theoretical Physics at Kaiser Wilhelm Institute in Berlin.

Although he became a German citizen, his pacifist opinions brought him into conflict with German militancy during World War I and he was upset by the resurgent waves of anti-Semitism both during and after the war. Seeing first-hand the oppression of East European Jews, he became convinced that a national home was the only solution for their plight, although he was importuned by his Jewish colleagues to resist Zionist overtures. They argued, as would many in the United States, that Zionism made assimilation more difficult, that it gave credence to the accusation that Jews had divided loyalties and were different from other people in the countries in which they lived.

Although Einstein did not immediately declare himself a Zionist, he made clear his distaste for such arguments. On April 3, 1920, he sent his now famous letter to the Central Association of German Citizens of the Mosaic Faith, decrying Jewish self-hatred: "I am a Jew and glad to belong to the Jewish people, even if I do not consider them in any way God's elect. Let us calmly leave anti-Semitism to the non-Jews and retain our love for people of our kind." Later he wrote to another German Jewish group: "The German Jew who works for the Jewish people and for the Jewish home in Palestine no more ceases to be a German than the Jew who becomes baptized and changes his name ceases to be a Jew."

Einstein's views soon reached the headquarters of Chaim Weizmann in London, where he functioned as the *de facto* leader of European Zionism. At that time, in 1920, Weizmann was planning his fund-raising trip to the United States, and he urged Einstein to come along; Einstein would focus on raising funds for the Hebrew University and Weizmann for the National Fund. To everyone's surprise, Einstein quickly accepted Weizmann's offer. He may well have had no idea of what he was getting into. He knew little about Zionist "realpolitic," or that Weizmann was "overbearing and politically ruthless." He did not know that Weizmann was locked in a political struggle with Justice Louis Brandeis and his group for control of the Zionist Organization of America. The Brandeis group disapproved of the *Keren Hayesod* and Weizmann's fund-raising efforts in America. On March 21, 1921, Einstein left Berlin for Holland, accompanied by his second wife (and first cousin) Elsa. Chaim Weizmann and his wife joined them there and together they sailed on the liner *Rotterdam* for New York. During the voyage, Weizmann wryly wrote, "Einstein explained his theory of relativity to me every day and on my arrival I was fully convinced that he understood it."

The two couples received a tremendous reception in New York. "What the crowds saw at the top of the gangway was Weizmann, smiling but stiff, almost a model of Lenin in physical features as in single mindedness, and beside him the shorter features of Einstein. Einstein wore a faded gray overcoat and a black hat. He looked like an artist, a musician," wrote one reporter. "He is of medium height with strong . . . shoulders, but with no air of fragility and self-effacement. Under a broad, high forehead the large and luminous eyes were almost childlike in their simplicity and unworldliness." From New York they went to Washington, where Einstein visited President Harding with a group from the National Academy of Sciences, at whose annual dinner Einstein spoke.

On May 2, 1921, Weizmann and Einstein arrived in Chicago, where they quickly went their separate ways. Weizmann and his chief lieutenant, A. M. M. Ussishkin, went to the West Side immigrant community where speeches were given, and there were parades and demonstrations. Einstein chose the quiet intellectual world of the University of Chicago, where he lectured to academic audiences. The *Chicago Tribune* under the headline, "Dr. Einstein Here Today to Explain His Relativity," reported that Einstein was to give one-hour lectures for the next three days at the University of Chicago's Mandel Hall. "Dr. Einstein, who is in Chicago in the interest of a drive for funds for the Hebrew University in Jerusalem, now being erected on the Mount of Olives, maintains that a conception of relativity cannot be properly expounded in less than three hours, and has steadfastly refused to undertake treatment of the subject in less time."

The *Sentinel*, Chicago's Jewish-English weekly, largely ignored Weizmann to cover Einstein in great detail, noting that a committee of fifteen university people had met him at the railroad station, and that a group of "Hadassah girls headed by Miss Shulman presented a bouquet of flowers to Mrs. Einstein." In an interview with the *Sentinel* at the Auditorium Hotel, Einstein said, "If the Chicago Jews will respond to my appeal on behalf of the University, I will be the happiest man on earth," adding that he was pleasantly surprised at the generosity of American Jews. "They are liberal minded and generous and take a deep interest in the life of our people abroad." The strongly Zionist Yiddish-language *Courier*, unlike the *Sentinel*, gave short shrift to Einstein and concentrated on Weizmann and Ussishkin with wide coverage and strong editorial support. Both Chicago Mayor Thompson and Illinois Governor Small issued messages of welcome to the visitors.

On May 3, the *Tribune's* headline read, "Audience Sinks Into Einstein Relativity Sea." It ran a large picture of Einstein and his wife under the banner, "World's Smartest Man?" and reported that the audience listened to Einstein explain the "The Theory of Relativity . . . The scientists looked, listened and partly understood. The rest of the audience just looked and listened." Einstein spoke in simple German, but the audience was soon lost.

After three days, Einstein left Chicago to lecture for a week at Princeton before returning to Germany. His first mission to America was called a success even though his fund-raising had been disappointing. Two years later, Einstein visited Palestine with great fanfare, but this visit was not successful either: he came into conflict with political problems in the Zionist movement and did not undertake an active role at the Hebrew University. In 1933, when the Nazis came to power, Einstein was a visiting professor at the California Institute of Technology and did not return to Germany. He joined the Princeton faculty, and became an American citizen in 1940.

An interesting final footnote to the Einstein-Weizmann mission came in 1948, when the Israeli Knesset, seeking a person with international eminence, asked Einstein if he would accept the largely ceremonial position of president of Israel. Flattered, Einstein nevertheless declined the honor. The Knesset's second choice was Weizmann.

CHAIM NACHMAN BIALIK: HEBREW POET

———

IN ITS APRIL 9, 1926 issue, the weekly *Sentinel* announcing the forth-coming visit of Chaim Nachman Bialik, commented that although he was the first, and indeed the greatest, modern Hebrew poet, there was "a marked lack of real enthusiasm which the arrival of such a man should arouse." While he was to be welcomed by local Zionists and a small Hebrew-speaking society, there were no plans for the kind of mass meeting and parades that had greeted the earlier visits of Zionist leaders like Chaim Weizmann, Albert Einstein and Shmarya Levin.

Bialik, who had left Russia for Berlin in 1921, and two years later settled in the new city of Tel Aviv, had come to the U.S. in March on a mission for the United Palestine Appeal to raise money for Jewish settlements. As the *Sentinel* had predicted, when he arrived in Chicago on April 15, he received only a modest welcome, but a dinner was given for him at the Palmer House with 400 guests, among whom were Rabbis Saul Silber and Solomon Goldman, Judges Henry Horner, Julian Mack and Hugo Pam, and leading Zionist citizens like Julius Rosenwald, S.B. Komaiko and Max Shulman. Bialik apparently addressed them in Yiddish, since he spoke little English at that time. Individual contributions totalled $30,000. Bialik also addressed the Chicago Rabbinical Association, in Hebrew.

In the *Reform Advocate*, the editor, Dr. Gerson B. Levi, rabbi of Temple Isaiah Israel, commented at length on Bialik's presence in Chicago, calling him "an unassuming genius" whose poems he had read and admired "long before the Zionists had sent him to Chicago on his mission to raise funds." The struggle between Reform Judaism and political Zionism was growing, and Levi, a leading Reform thinker, disapproved of Bialik's nationalist approach to Jewish history and culture; Jewish culture in the Diaspora should not, he said, be denigrated and the Zionists should "take their hands off" Jewish thinkers and stay with their "philanthropic needs": "Whoever wants to go to Palestine, let him go, but let him go without saying before he leaves that Judaism in the world has no chance."

It was not only Reform hostility that affected Bialik's visit. That same year, wealthy Chicago Jews were also called on to support efforts by the Joint Distribution Committee, among others, to raise large sums of money to build Jewish settlements in the Ukraine. At that time it was believed that Soviet leaders supported the plan, which was of course opposed by Zionist organizations as inimical to their efforts in Palestine. The Ukraine plan collapsed when it was learned that the Soviets had no intention of supporting it.

Bialik went from Chicago to Washington, where he had an audience with President Coolidge on May 10. In early June he returned to New York City for further fund-raising meetings, and to receive an honorary doctorate in Hebrew Literature from the Jewish Theological Seminary. He concluded his American tour with a speech at the 28th annual convention of the Zionist Organization of America in Buffalo, before over one thousand delegates, including many from Chicago. American Jews, he said, were the sole hope of the world who would restore and rebuild the Jewish homeland. In a letter to an American journalist after he returned home to Tel Aviv, Bialik said that Palestine was "the single and central location toward which G-d has pointed His finger, saying: This is the only place where you will find rest. There is no other."

Bialik's visit to Chicago came only two years after he had fled Odessa to settle in Palestine. Since his early life had been spent in Russia, he did not know much about Western Jews. In 1926, Chicagoans had a unique encounter with a fine poet and fervent nationalist who preached a Zionism that most American Jews were not prepared to accept.

The following are excerpts from two of Bialik's greatest poems:

EL HA-TZIPOR (The Bird)

A little bird, the first bird of Spring, alights upon the window sill. It must have just returned from southern climes. To Bialik, it appears as though the bird in its flight has visited Palestine, the land that to him means relief and hope. And he tenderly greets the little creature:

> *Bird on my window perching*
> *Returned from the land of the sun,*
> *Blessed by this thy coming,*
> *For now is the winter done.*

He eagerly speaks to it: Tell me, there in Eretz Yisrael, how fares it with my brethren? Hast thou brought me word of the swift Jordan, of the hills of Judea, of the vineyards of Carmel. And how about the palm trees and orange groves and the fresh breath of the meadows?

> *Is Hermon still covered with pearls*
> *When the dew of the morning distills?*
> *And what news of the waters of Jordan?*
> *What news of the ancient hills?*
> *Has the shadow departed*
> *And the cloud been lifted at last*
> *From the land where my youth was passed?*

BE-IR HA-HAREGAH (The City of Slaughter)

The pogrom is the climax of the bitterness of the exile. Bialik paints the scenes after the massacres in Kishinev with great pathos, not unlike Jewish liturgy. The wretched survivors, who have lost father and mother, wife and child, huddle together in cellars of the Shul beating themselves on the breast, uttering the *Ashamnu,* "We have sinned" prayer recited on the Day of Atonement, begging G-d to forgive their sins. G-d addresses the survivors:

> *They pray of Me forgiveness for their sin.*
> *Their sin? the sin of shadows on the wall,*
> *The sin of broken pots, of bruised worms!*
> *What will they? why stretch out their hands to Me?*
> *Has none a fist? and where's the thunderbolt*
> *To take revenge for all the generations,*
> *To blast the world and tear the heavens asunder*
> *And wreck the universe, My throne of glory?*

Translations and commentary from article, "Golus and Geulah," dedicated to Chaim Nachman Bialik, by Rabbi Philip A. Lang. The Sentinel, April 9, 1926

CLARENCE DARROW AND
STEPHEN S. WISE DEBATE ZIONISM

———

A CULTURAL HIGHLIGHT OF Chicago during the years following World War I was the annual series of lectures, debates, and discussions scheduled by S. D. Schwartz, executive director of Chicago Sinai Congregation, then located at 46th Street and South Parkway. In those days, before television brought the famous into everybody's living room, the annual Sinai Temple Forum, as the series was called, made it possible for Chicagoans, for a modest fee, to see and hear in person well-known artists, scientists, politicians, and other public figures. Stimulating discussions of broad general interest were held before diverse audiences and frequently reported on by Chicago newspapers. Other synagogues and churches presented similar series, but few, if any, achieved the quality or popularity of the Sinai Forum.

Of the many topics discussed, perhaps none was more stimulating than the debate held on October 24, 1927: "Is Zionism a Progressive Policy for Palestine and America?" Taking the affirmative was Dr. Stephen Wise of New York City, with Clarence Darrow of Chicago representing the negative. S. D. Schwartz acted as moderator. Both Wise and Darrow were well known in Chicago. Dr. Wise, 53, was a leading Reform rabbi and an articulate Zionist spokesman. Darrow, nearly 70, was probably the most famous trial attorney in the United States at that time, having recently been involved in the Leopold-Loeb murder case—the principals were from Sinai families—and the Scopes trial on the teaching of evolution.

They were debating a controversial subject of concern to many Americans. American Zionism had had its birth in Chicago in the 1880s and had always had strong supporters in the city, though perhaps not many among Sinai's membership. In 1924 the U.S. had closed its doors to Eastern European immigrants and there was consequently great pressure for the creation of another haven for them. While the Balfour Declaration had been issued by Great Britain in 1917, a great many American Jews were lukewarm to the idea of the establishment of a Jewish homeland in Palestine, and many were opposed, as were social and political liberals like Clarence Darrow.

Stephen Wise opened his argument with the obligatory witticism. He recalled that the atheist Robert Ingersoll, after a bitter debate with Rabbi Isaac Mayer Wise (no relation) had said: "Ladies and gentlemen, have you ever noticed things like this in your experience? The shortest, littlest man I ever knew was named Long. The thinnest man I ever knew was named Stout. And that rabbi from Cincinnati is named Wise." He continued, "The theme of this debate is, 'Is Zionism a Progressive Policy for Israel and America?' Ladies and gentlemen, within and without Sinai, Zionism is not a policy. It is a principle. It is a conviction. It is an ideal. It is one of the inevitable movements that grow out of the history of a people. I dwell for a moment upon the term "policy" because, Brother Darrow, you will be interested, as a non-Jew, to learn that there are some Jews, alas, who are so ill-informed about Zionism that they think that a handful of Zionists, led by Herzl and Sokolow and Weizmann and Wolfson and Brandeis and Mack, just define Zionism as a policy when, in truth—perhaps you haven't heard, sir—Zionism began on that day in July, or in the month of Ab, we Jews say, in the year 70. In other words, 1,857 years ago, when Jews were exiled from Zion; and there has never been a hour since the year 70 that Jews have not deeply believed, ardently hoped, and passionately prayed for the restoration of the Jewish people to Zion, or Palestine.

"Is Zionism good for America? It is not a question of whether America is good enough for the Jews; Jews cannot come into America any longer; the various handful are granted the freedom of admittance; the rest must remain outside the doors of America and wait for years, decades, even for a generation, before they are granted admittance.

"Is Zionism a progressive force? Yes, of course. Zionism is a movement that aims to restore to the ancient land of the Jews, those Jews who are homeless and those Jews—not me—who will live a holy Jewish life from every point of view in the land of their Fathers . . . The cause of Zionism is to be found in the discovery of the Jews of the '70s, '80s and '90s in the last century, that a people which has no home of its own is welcome nowhere; that in order that a people may enter into the full advantage of life . . . it must have a home, it must have a center, it must have a country of its own; it must live and think and feel in the terms of freedom and self-determination, the things for which you and I bled and fought during the years of war."

Wise pressed his argument that Jewish nationalism was a progressive force. Like Herzl, he believed that Zionism had given Jews a sense of security, so that they could walk upright in their own land and in the world at large. "That is what Zionism has done for the Jews. Again, Zionism has not only given the Jews security and peace in the face of oppression, it has done something infinitely more. It has ended the confession of the Jews—the confession of the Jews that we are nothing more than a religion."

Standing at the pulpit recently held by Rabbi Emil G. Hirsch, who had opposed Zionism, Wise thundered: "Once more . . . we seek Jewish life to be reinvigorated, reinspired by keeping constant contact with the land, which, after all, is the land of the prophet and the psalmist, the land of the Decalogue, the land of the teachings by which the Western World lives 20, 30 hundred years after these teachings were promulgated. Once again we wish the Jew to enter into a heritage in which he shall be creative, spiritual and constructive." After his 30-minute opening, Wise took his seat, to great applause.

Darrow opened in his turn with a witticism. "Well," he said, "I see that all the Jews are not in Palestine anyway." He quickly moved to the central question: Is Zionism good for the Jews? "I think not. I think it is about the most abused enterprise that I know anything about." He deplored the new immigration laws that excluded Jews, or anybody else, from America: after all, most Americans were foreigners. His own people had come from Europe in the seventeenth century. He would prefer that all the energy and money used by Jews to promote Zionism be used instead "to try to civilize Americans" so that foreigners could continue to come to America.

He disagreed with Wise's definition of Zionism, saying that to him it had only a practical meaning: "It means taking the Jews from the four corners of the earth and landing them in Palestine where they can be happy ever after. It means gathering up the Jews and taking them back to Palestine, partly an industrial and partly a religious question." And as for Wise's idealistic vision of Zionism: the Jews had conquered land, held it for less than 500 years and then lost it in a war. "Of course, we lawyers know that the statute of limitations would run against any title like that. (Laughter). Utterly absurd to talk about it being the homeland of the Jews. When they went up from Egypt with manna in their hands it was acquired by someone else. They got it, as everybody gets everything else in the world, I am sorry to say, by fighting, and then lost it by fighting, and all of them moved away who could afford to. And nobody would be there now if they could walk home." (Laughter).

He had recently visited Palestine. "I have been there. I didn't stay long. It was a small country containing some 10,000 square miles, about one-sixteenth as big as Illinois. It can't be farmed because there is no soil there. Oh no, you won't till the soil. The Jews are not given to cultivating the soil, even if it is good land, but they are too smart to want to dig it there. Now, I love idealism. I am something of a dreamer myself, but there are some things that are not worth dreaming about, and this is one of them . . . Were you there? Well, now, I have been there. I walked up to the top of Mount Olive, I don't know how far it is anyway, maybe four miles, but it seemed further, up a narrow, dirty street, down a filthy, impossible land, which everybody tramped down; the poor, the ragged, the illiterate. The chief transportation is the ass. You could see Balaam riding down and the same old ass that stuck." (Laughter).

He had taken a trip to Jerusalem. "Well, as I got into the Jaffa Gate I heard somebody speak a strangely familiar language, not English, but American. I think he was a ballyhoo for Riverview Park, and I heard him say, 'Right this way to the Wailing Wall; wailing now.'" And what did Darrow find at the Wailing Wall? "A lot of old, dirty, decrepit men and women standing holding a tin cup in their hand saying 'Baksheesh' or something like that, picking up pennies, and little children with sore eyes, the worst, most base-looking people I ever encountered, and I have seen beggars everywhere, even outside of Chicago . . . I am willing to concede right off that the Jews have not been fairly treated. What of it? Nobody else has." (Laughter).

Darrow turned his attention to one of his favorite targets: religion. "You cannot attack this: the foundation of this movement is a religious movement, to bring back Zion. Of course, there is another Zion up north of Evanston. How is it that in this Zion, only ten to fifteen percent are Jews? There are ten percent Christians and all the rest are Arabs. All were living in this desolate Holy Land.

"Who is going anyway? . . . Why, one of the leaders is Louis Marshall, partner of Sam Untermeyer. Is the firm of Untermeyer and Marshall going to open a law office in Jerusalem? Not they. There is my friend Greenebaum; is he going there with his bank? Hope not . . . Is Rosenwald going to have his store there? Why, even my friend [Stephen Wise] would not want to establish a church there; there would be nobody to listen to him. (Laughter). And to revitalize the land? How much would it cost? Why, all the Jews in the world haven't got enough money to do it—and for what? Do you suppose there is any one of them would ever think of it as a business proposition, connected with anything else but a religious movement?"

With three minutes remaining for the opening argument, Darrow reached another of his main points. "What about the Jews?" He did not believe in races, he said; there were differences among people caused by climate and geography, but otherwise people were all alike. "Jews are a commercial people. They may have been farmers once, but they got over it. They are traders. They have no mission except to live like all other people."

Darrow finished, and Wise began his response by asking Darrow when he had been in Palestine. "About three or four years ago," replied Darrow, "in October." Wise said that he himself had been there first in 1913 and then again in 1922, and the transformation that had taken place was a miracle. "Did you go to the Emek?" asked Wise. Darrow said he had not. "Well, I wish you had," Wise said. "In 1913 it was just desolation itself. In 1922, the Valley of the Emek, as we lovingly style it, had been transformed into one of the most fruitful valleys on earth."

Wise attacked Darrow for a remark "not worthy of him—that 'Jews have not been fairly treated. What of it?' Is it fair, Brother Darrow, to speak of the hell of Russia, to speak of the foul and fiendish treatment of my people for nineteen hundred Christian years as if they had not been fairly treated? You speak about working against nature. It is not done and it ought to be done. Brother Darrow, Brother Darrow, were you in Dayton, Tennessee [at the Scopes trial]? (Laughter). Why, you sound as if you had become a disciple at the feet of the late William Jennings Bryan [Darrow's adversary at the trial]." (Laughter).

Darrow responded very seriously: "I have many friends who are Zionists. I think a great deal of them. I love the idealist. I cannot help being a dreamer myself. Neither can I help waking up. It would be all right to dream if you were not obliged to wake up . . . But, for a proposition that is absolutely impossible, a proposition which goes against space and time and the laws of nature, I tell you, you cannot do it, and many of you will be bound to regret that you ever undertook such a foolish thing." (Applause).

In his closing argument, Wise said he believed that one half of the fifteen million Jews then living in the world would go to Palestine if they could. At the moment, he, Wise, supported the British limit on immigration to Palestine because economic facilities "had to be prepared." He asked Darrow at what time of the year he had been in Palestine. "October," replied Darrow; "it was cold." Wise replied that the previous winter a friend of his from Berlin had visited Chicago and was dead in three days. "Yet I don't say that Chicago is unfit to live in. I don't know what this man saw in Palestine, but I tell you what I saw: such sunshine as I have never looked upon; the gleaming of such stars as I have never beheld; the iridescence as well as the richness and beauty of the soil is incomparable."

Wise urged Darrow to join the Jews in their new endeavors instead of mocking them. He addressed the audience: "I tell you, I shall not live to see it, but you and your children and your children's children will bless and bless over again the day that saw Jews, forgetful of their personal, physical, material advantage, take up the march again and go to Palestine, to rebuild a great life, and once again to become moral leaders and spiritual benefactors of the human race." Wise concluded, noting that he had taken five minutes more than he should have, and offering Darrow the same amount of extra time.

Darrow, too, was gracious in his closing argument. He knew, he said, that the Jews had not had a fair deal in history. He also knew that "Jews do more for their class than any other class that I know of, but all I am insisting on, is that their charity and their helpfulness would do a great deal more good, and accomplish more permanent benefit to their people and to the world [in ways other] than the way that my friend thinks it ought to be diverted . . ."

Clarence Darrow retired from legal practice soon after the debate. He became an early outspoken foe of Hitler's Germany and often spoke out on behalf of the Jewish victims of the Nazis before his death in 1938. Stephen Wise became a rallying force of American Jewry against Hitler in the 1930s and the prime American Jewish leader of the hopeless struggle to rescue European Jewry from the Nazis. An active Zionist for the rest of his life, he died in 1949, shortly after Israel became a state.

Times have changed, but elements of the Darrow-Wise debate held in Chicago in 1927 remain with us today. Although Darrow's comments about the soil of Palestine were proven wrong, problems with Zionism do still exist. Zionist idealism, however, is as vital as it was for Stephen Wise over seventy-five years ago.

PETER BERGSON, THE IRGUN AND CHICAGO

———

PETER BERGSON, WHOSE REAL name was Hillel Kook, died on August 18, 2001 at his home in Kfar Shmaryahu, Israel. During World War II he campaigned for the formation of a Jewish army and for the deliverance of the European Jews. He came to the United States in 1940 and often traveled to Chicago, where his most memorable achievement was his financial support of the pageant "We Will Never Die," at the Chicago Stadium in 1943.

Bergson, born in Lithuania in 1915, was ten years old when his family fled to Palestine, where his uncle Avraham Yitzhak Kook was the country's first Ashkenazi Chief Rabbi. Young Bergson soon joined the Irgun, a faction that in 1931 split from the Haganah, the Jewish Agency's defense organization. Dissatisfied with what they perceived as the Haganah's tepid response to both attacks by the Arabs and the repressive policies of the British Mandate, the Irgun set out on a more militant path. Thus began a long tortuous conflict between the Irgun, allied with a new political party called the Revisionists, and the Haganah, whose leaders, David Ben Gurion and others, headed the powerful Labor parties. Bergson had changed his name from Kook because he did not want to embarrass his family, and especially his uncle, by his actions.

At the beginning of World War II, the Irgun was acting as the military arm of the Revisionists, led by Vladimir Ze'ev Jabotinsky. In 1939 Jabotinsky came to the United States to agitate for the formation of a Jewish army in Palestine to fight alongside the British forces against the Nazis, and a year later Bergson and several others joined Jabotinsky in New York. When Jabotinsky died suddenly of a heart attack, it fell to Bergson to lead the Irgun's American campaign.

Bergson opened a small office in New York and began to make contacts. His main argument was that a Jewish army of 200,000 volunteers from Palestine, Europe and the United States could help stop the German army under General Rommel in North Africa. He argued that Jews, motivated to avenge their murdered brethren in Europe, would follow the precedent set by the Jewish Legion which had fought in World War I. The British were opposed to this idea because they believed it would endanger their relationship with the Arabs. With no budget, Bergson set out to campaign for that army.

He enlisted the help of journalist, novelist and playwright Ben Hecht, a former Chicagoan who had previously distanced himself from Jewish organizations, but who had been galvanized by the Nazi onslaught to write a number of articles calling attention to the horrors in Europe. Bergson brought his message effectively to Washington, where a number of legislators gave him their support, as did Adlai Stevenson of Illinois, then Assistant Secretary of the Navy under Frank Knox.

In Chicago Bergson received donations from Ernest Byfield, an influential Jewish businessman not otherwise identified with Zionist causes, and bought a full-page ad headlined "Jews Fight for 'The Right to Fight,'" in the *Chicago Sun* on January 18, 1942. But the efforts to raise money and influence public opinion to pressure the British aroused the antagonism of other groups. The mainstream Zionist organizations denounced Bergson's Jewish Army Committee as Irgunists and Revisionists—terms which for them were synonymous with "terrorists" and "fascists." By the end of 1942, Bergson's group had made no progress in its efforts to pressure the British to organize a Jewish army.

It was now becoming known that two million Jews had been massacred by the Nazis in Europe and millions more were threatened with annihilation. Rabbi Stephen S. Wise, president of the American Jewish

Congress, publicly confirmed this and met with President Roosevelt to call for government action. A National Day of Mourning was held on December 2, 1942. Bergson's group, looking, like other Jewish organizations, for new courses of action, hit upon the idea of a pageant to dramatize the plight of the Jews to the American public. The idea of a Jewish army was now set aside; instead there would be a dramatic call for the rescue of the remnants of European Jewry.

Ben Hecht was commissioned to write the pageant that Bergson's American League for a Free Palestine would finance and produce. Hecht wanted a unified Jewish community to sponsor the pageant, but that did not happen. The political divisions among the organizations were too wide; the American Jewish Committee, for example, refused to have anything to do with the enterprise. Hecht had expected the same kind of community cooperation which had made "The Romance of A People" successful ten years earlier. But as the date for the first performance approached—March 10, 1943, in New York's Madison Square Garden—Rabbi Wise became increasingly hostile, demanding the pageant's cancellation even though it was already in rehearsal, and announcing that on March 1st, his organizations would hold an anti-Nazi rally called "Stop Hitler Now," also at the Garden. The American Jewish Congress and other Jewish organizations did indeed hold their rally on March 1, but it did not affect ticket sales for the Hecht-Bergson production. New York Governor Dewey declared March 9 an official day of mourning, and "We Will Never Die" was performed on schedule on March 10. The demand for tickets was so great that a second performance was added on the same night.

The pageant then moved to Washington, Philadelphia and Chicago, where it was performed at the Stadium on May 19, with Sydney Lumet in a starring role. But an extensive campaign was organized against the pageant and the Bergsonites in the city. They had engendered hostility by running a full page advertisement in national newspapers, urging acceptance of an alleged offer from the Nazis to release thousands of Jews in exchange for money. Other Zionist organizations correctly called the offer fraudulent.

Bergson's group ran ads and wrote articles attacking the results of the Bermuda Conference held in the summer of 1943, which had been called by the United States to see what steps could be taken to provide a haven for Jewish refugees—preferably by other countries. Nothing came of the conference, but Senator Scott Lucas of Illinois and Congressman Sol Bloom of New York, delegates to the conference, were infuriated by the Bergson attacks. Rabbi Wise and Dr. Nahum Goldmann of the Jewish Agency also bitterly attacked Bergson, who believed that the two, working with Bloom and Lucas, were instrumental in calling a Congressional hearing to investigate his activities; the FBI, he thought, was tapping his phone lines. According to Goldmann, Rabbi Wise "regarded Bergson equally as great an enemy of the Jews as Hitler for the reason that his activities could only lead to increased anti-Semitism."

Bergson said later that his organization deserved credit for prodding the Roosevelt Administration to organize the War Refugee Board which helped to rescue some Jews in 1944, and that Wise and Goldman had done everything in their power to hinder his efforts. Nothing, apparently, came of the Congressional hearings. Public pressure—that Bergson claimed to have organized—forced the Committee to drop its efforts to deport him as an unregistered alien. Three volumes of records of the hearings were on Bergson's library shelves.

In 1948, Bergson returned to Israel and was elected to the first Knesset. But he was opposed to many of the policies of the new state, and in 1951 he came back to the United States, and went into business, a venture that was successful but not without controversy. In 1970 he returned once more to Israel. To Peter Bergson's admirers his struggle in America during World War II was a heroic attempt to assist European Jewry at a desperate time. To others his actions served only to create bitter divisions within the Zionist movement itself.

BEN HECHT PAGEANT I: WE WILL NEVER DIE

IN THE TEN YEARS BETWEEN the presentation of "The Romance of A People" in 1933, and Ben Hecht's pageant "We Will Never Die," there was a dramatic change in the Jewish situation. Where 1933 had been a hopeful year, 1943 marked the darkest time imaginable. Two million European Jews had already been murdered, while four million more stood on the brink of extinction. The enthusiastic Zionist groups that had united in producing the first pageant were stunned, unable to come up with any rescue plans. Into this depressing situation stepped a previously silent group whose anger and outrage shook American Zionism, culminating in the production of "We Will Never Die."

Ben Hecht was then at the height of his fame. After years as a Chicago journalist and fiction writer, he had gone to Hollywood, where he wrote many successful screenplays, including *Scarface*, *Twentieth Century* and *Wuthering Heights*. With Charles MacArthur, he had written one of the biggest hits ever produced on the America stage, *The Front Page*, also a successful film.

Some time in the mid-1930s, Hecht, enraged by the Nazi persecution of Jews, had begun to write articles and plays and place advertisements attacking Nazism and calling for action. In early 1943 he joined the American League for a Free Palestine and started writing the script for a pageant to arouse American Jews to demand, among other things, the formation of a Jewish army. But while Hecht was working on this pageant, opposition to its production was growing from mainstream Jewish organizations. The Bergson group was anathema to the American Jewish leadership.

On December 2, 1942, a nationwide day of mourning was proclaimed by these mainstream organizations: a day of fasting and prayer, and a ten-minute work stoppage. A week later, a delegation of Jewish leaders met with President Franklin D. Roosevelt at the White House, but the only result was a statement by F.D.R. condemning the Nazis. By then, specific details of the horrifying slaughter in Eastern Europe were becoming known to American Jews. Working with Dr. Hayim Greenberg, editor of the Labor Zionist journal *Jewish Frontier*, Hecht began to write vivid descriptions of these Nazi atrocities. One of these articles appeared in the January 1943 issue of the *American Mercury*. He also completed the script for "We Will Never Die."

The pageant, which took place in New York's Madison Square Garden on March 9, 1943, featured an impressive lineup of talent: Kurt Weill wrote the musical score, Moss Hart directed it, Billy Rose produced it, and the New York cast, headed by Paul Muni, included Edward G. Robinson, Luther Adler, Jacob Ben-Ami, Claude Raines, Burgess Meredith and John Garfield. But to groups like the American Jewish Congress, led by Rabbi Wise, the pageant was a perversion of Zionism. Wise had been offended at the outset by the Irgun's full-page newspaper ads calling for the payment of ransom to the Romanian government for the rescue of Jews, and later by Irgun's plan to raise a Jewish army to fight the Nazis. The mainstream organizations' opposition proved surprisingly ineffective, however. The pageant was performed twice on the same day in Madison Square Garden to sold-out houses of 40,000 people.

After the pageant was performed in New York and several other East Coast cities, the rights to it were acquired by the Chicago Committee for a Jewish Army and on the evening of May 19, "We Will Never Die" was performed at the Chicago Stadium, drawing a capacity crowd of 20,000. Film stars John Garfield and Burgess Meredith, who had been in the original cast, and the great actor of the Yiddish stage, Jacob Ben-Ami, were the narrators. Leo Kopp of the Chicago Civic Opera Company conducted the orchestra. Avrum Matthews, a well-known Chicago cantor, who had led the cantorial singing in "The Romance" ten years earlier, was the featured singer once more.

The stage held two towering Tablets of the Ten Commandments. As Matthews finished chanting the Kol Nidre, Ben-Ami, in white robes as the Rabbi, stepped onstage and, as the audience stood with heads bowed in prayer, intoned: "We are here to say our prayers for the two million who have been killed in Europe because they bear the names of Jews. We are not to weep for them, although our hearts are burdened with their fate. We are here to honor them and to proclaim the victory of their dying. For in our Testament are written the words of Habakkuk, Prophet of Israel: 'They Shall Never Die.'"

Garfield and Meredith began their narrative against a background of soft music from a hidden chorus. Alternately, the two actors spoke of the contributions of Jews to the welfare of humanity. One hundred and fifty black-robed women, each carrying a lighted candle, filed onto the stage, one by one, as Garfield and Meredith called the roll of famous Jews: "Moses . . . David . . . Solomon . . . the Prophets . . . Spinoza . . . Maimonides . . . Montaigne . . . Mendelssohn . . . Disraeli . . . Zangwill . . . Proust . . . Heine . . . Brandeis . . . Freud . . . Einstein . . . We summon this fame not to boast, but to give strength to hearts that have forgotten in their sorrow the shield, the sword, the valor and the indestructability of their people."

As the lights dimmed, a "Table of Judgment" appeared on the stage with the Axis leaders on one side and on the other, the delegates of the victorious United Nations, there to pass judgment on the defeated enemy. From between these gigantic tablets came a long procession of slaughtered Jews—men, women and children chanting "Remember us. . . . Remember us—we are the children of Freiberg, hanged and left dangling from our kitchen windows. Remember us—we are from the town of Szcuccin in Poland—all of us were killed before sundown. Remember us—in Lublin, five hundred of our women and children were led to the marketplace, put against the wall and machine gunned."

The procession of these living corpses continued, until the pageant ended with "Jews in the War," a sequence in which the dead victims were replaced by U.S. soldiers, sailors and marines marching onto the stage; Garfield and Meredith wore Amrican military uniforms.The narrators read accounts of Jewish war heroes: Irving Strobing, a 22-year-old prisoner of war from Brooklyn who had telegraphed the final message from Corregidor; Maurice Levy, a tall, lean Chicago soldier, nicknamed "The Blue Crane," who killed twenty-five Japanese before he was felled by a sniper's bullet. The narrator quoted the Nazis: "'The Jews cannot fight,' . . . Wait until Barney Ross gets to Berlin." Ross, the world middleweight boxing champion, raised in Chicago's Maxwell Street area, became a war hero. As two soldiers blew Reveille, the orchestra played "The Star Spangled Banner" to the cheers of the audience.

The narrator went on: "Every Jew who fights today is not only a soldier, but also an avenger. They fight on all fronts, but we feel the stateless Jews have a right to form an army of their own and to strike back at Hitler under their own banner—the Star of David. The corpse of a people lies on the steps of civilization. But we here tonight have a voice. Let us raise it. Perhaps the dying will hear and find hope. Perhaps the four freedoms will hear it, and find tongue. It is the voice of prayer."

"Hatikvah" was sung as the entire cast gathered on the blazingly lighted stage with the American flag and the Star of David banner side by side. Cantor Avrum Matthews then led the audience in a recitation of the Kaddish, and the narration concluded: "They shall never die though they were slaughtered with no weapons in their hands. Though they fill the dark land of Europe with the smoke of their massacre, they shall never die. For they are part of something greater, higher and stronger then the dreams of their executioners."

As a one-night performance, "We Will Never Die" was a great success, and received wide sympathetic coverage from the Chicago press: the *Tribune, Times, Daily News* and other papers carried warmly supportive lead stories on the event. The Jewish press, however, gave it scant attention: the *Sentinel* in its May 27, 1943 issue, ran a short article by Rabbi Dr. G. George Fox, saying that the pageant was full of historical errors, but was "nevertheless . . . a fine spectacle," and calling on Ernest Byfield and his committee to repeat the performance for non-Jews so they could "really see what has been done to the Jews in Europe. We know; they don't."

From Chicago, "We Will Never Die" moved for its last performance to the Hollywood Bowl, where many more movie stars performed before a mass audience. Splendidly written and produced, with famous actors, its central theme was criticized by mainstream Jewish organizations as a call for "foolhardy" Jewish action. Thus it cannot be compared to the 1933 "Romance of a People," which was simply a pageant of Jewish history and the emergence of Jewish nationalism in Palestine, and elicited no controversy because it made no direct demands on its audience. Hitler had just come to power in 1933, but certainly few imagined that he would adopt a policy of mass extermination. By 1943, that policy was a fact. Yet American Jewish leadership felt powerless to help and the Jewish communities appeared bewildered by the situation. The pageant presented at the Chicago Stadium on the evening of May 19, 1943, should be remembered. But unlike the feeling of good fellowship and pride that was the legacy of "The Romance of a People," the memory of "We Will Never Die" evokes only uncertainty and dismay.

BEN HECHT PAGEANT II: A FLAG IS BORN

———

"A FLAG IS BORN," Ben Hecht's second pageant-play dramatizing the plight of world Jewry, opened in New York in the summer of 1946 for a successful run of over a month. On January 6, 1947, with a different cast, it opened in Chicago at a sold-out Studebaker Theater, 418 South Michigan Avenue. The pageant's sponsor was the American League for a Free Palestine, which had also sponsored Hecht's earlier pageant "We Will Never Die." Now, over three years later, six million Jews had been annihilated and the focus was on the rejuvenation of the remnant of European Jewry and the struggle for a Jewish state in Palestine. And again as in 1943, Peter Bergson, Hecht, and the rest of the league were at odds with mainstream Jewish organizations.

The league distributed pamphlets announcing what it called "The Three Rs": *Repatriation* of a million and a half Jews to Palestine with or without the consent of Jewish mainstream organizations accused by the league of foot-dragging; *Recognition* of the Hebrew nation; and, finally, support of *Resistance* to the British in Palestine. The Zionist establishment argued that while the Haganah was struggling to bring thousands of Jews into Palestine and fighting the British with all its resources, the diversionary activities of the league amounted to propaganda for the Irgun's terrorist tactics in Palestine. Ben Hecht, however, was not daunted. His solution to the problem of raising money to rescue the Jewish survivors in Europe was to stage another pageant in his usual aggressive fashion, this time to raise millions of dollars for the Three R's.

Kurt Weill, who had written the score for "We Will Never Die," wrote the music for "A Flag is Born." The lead role of Tevya was played by Jacob Ben-Ami, a prominent actor of the Yiddish and English stage. In New York this role had been played with great success by Paul Muni. Celia Adler, the "First Lady of the Yiddish Stage," the daughter of celebrated actors Jacob and Sara Adler, was Tevya's wife Zelda. David, the young survivor, was played by Sidney Lumet, who had just resumed his acting career after two years in the army. In New York this part had been taken by another actor soon to achieve his own fame: Marlon Brando. The role of the singer went to Avrum Matthews, the well-known Chicago cantor who had, in the words of the Studebaker playbill, "created a sensation" in the Chicago production of "The Romance of a People" and had also appeared in "We Will Never Die." Other well-known actors appeared in secondary roles, and local Chicago talent was recruited for the parts of guards, attendants, soldiers, ladies-in-waiting and choristers.

The plot revolves around Tevya and Zelda, survivors of Treblinka, who are seeking a new life. It is Friday and they decide to sit and rest in a Jewish cemetery, where they meet David, a young Jewish man, like them a survivor, but one who has lost faith in God. Zelda and Tevya have lost their children in the war but are still religious Jews. Realizing that it is Friday night, they light candles on a tombstone. As Tevya begins to pray, the three are magically transported to his hometown synagogue.

The cantor sings the Sabbath service as a robed choir of eight men circle the bimah. Suddenly a trumpet sounds and King Saul and his captains appear dressed for battle. Men of Biblical Jabesh Gilead appear, pleading for Saul's help to save them from the Ammonites. Here Hecht satirically introduces the town's representatives who have come to see Saul—the Old One, the Middle-Aged One and the Young One. While the Old One cries for mercy, the Young One is bitter about the cowards who want to surrender to the enemy; and he especially singles out the Middle-Aged One—a rich man who aims to please and to present a moderate viewpoint, saying, "Who knows, perhaps we can make friends with the Ammonite—do nothing to anger him—show him how learned and law-abiding we are—woo him by turning a kindly face to him."

King Saul, rejecting the Middle-Aged One's advice, decides on a fight to the death—and wins the battle. Saul notices Tevya, asking, "Is that Tevya from Dubinsky?" and tells Tevya that all the heroes and prophets "are alive together in the dream of Israel." Tevya realizes that all the Jewish heroes of the past are in his blood. "Then what am I worried about?" Saul, pointing to the sky, tells Tevya that he must cross a bridge in order to find Israel. King David appears above them on a cloud, playing his harp and repeating the 23rd Psalm: "The Lord is my Shepherd, I shall not want . . ." and fades away. At the cemetery, Zelda begins her Sabbath meal talking as if her dead children are with her: "How nice everyone looks! What are you doing, Rochel? Enough *lokshn*! Leave some room for the fish! Yosele, Yosele, use a napkin! Don't wipe your hands on the tablecloth! Esterl, you are not eating. Stop sitting in a dream and eat." The scene ends as she sings the lullaby "Almonds and Raisins."

David, who has been observing the scene, bursts out in anger:

> Where were you, Jews? Where were you when the killing was going on? . . . You Jews of America! You Jews of England! Strong Jews, rich Jews, high-up Jews . . . A curse on your silence! That frightened silence of Jews that made the Germans laugh as they slaughtered. You with your Jewish hearts hidden under your American boots . . . you let six million die—rather than make the faux-pas of seeming Jewish. We heard your silence—in the gas chambers. And now, now you speak a little. Your hearts speak—and you have a dollar for the Jews of Europe. Thank you. Thank you.

The scene shifts to another vision: King Solomon and his royal entourage in front of the pillars of Solomon's Temple. His maidens dance as he reads from the "Song of Songs." Solomon asks Tevya what he is complaining about and Tevya answers, "The world."

Solomon replies, "Then go to the world." In the next scene, a group
of delegates from the world's nations have come to hear Tevya plead
the case for a Jewish homeland in Palestine. The English delegate is
ridiculed as the new "German" enemy. The Russian delegate does not
know of any anti-Semitism in the world and the American delegate is
highly ambivalent. Tevya addresses the world:

> And Tevya says to everybody, to the whole world here, under all its
> fine flags—the Jews are tired of building a sickness in the souls of
> others. Be tired with us. You couldn't swallow us. And who wants
> to swallow you? Let us go and become a nation instead of a sick-
> ness in strangers' lands. Let us go and build a land of our own. Let
> us go and become part of the world—an arm, a hand, a finger of
> the world—instead of a fever in alien veins. Tevya says open one
> little door for the Jews who have opened so many big doors for
> everybody else. Open one little door to Palestine, to Eretz Yisrael.

In response to Tevya's pleas, all the statesmen show their approval
and there is a mighty "yes" from the chorus of nations. But almost
immediately the British statesman moves that the matter be put on
"tomorrow's agenda"—and the American statesman agrees. Tevya is
stunned—his pleas have fallen on deaf ears. He looks down at the
ground where Zelda is lying motionless. She is dead. David tells Tevya
that they will continue their journey to Palestine without Zelda, but
Tevya, replying that he has seen the Angel of Death, sinks to the ground
beside his wife. David speaks bitter words, "Better to be dirt than to
be a Jew," and raises a knife as if to plunge it into his own heart.

At this point, against the swelling strains of "Hatikvah," three
soldiers in the uniform of the Jewish army of Palestine, appear and
urge David to join them in the battle against the new enemy, the British. "We promise you a battlefront of Jews that will stand and die and
stand until a Hebrew nation arises out of the Hebrew soul. Come,
David, and fight for Palestine." David stoops to remove the tallis from
Tevya's body. He takes a blue star from his pocket and puts it on the
tallis, which he fastens to a branch, creating a Jewish flag. Then he

joins the soldiers walking toward a distant bridge to Palestine, from which can be heard the strains of "Hatikvah," the sound of joyous singing and the roar of guns. With this melodramatic ending, the curtain falls.

The play ran for over a month in Chicago to generally favorable reviews from both the *Sun* and the *Tribune*, where Claudia Cassidy called it both passionate and compassionate. Between ticket sales and additional contributions, the league raised a great deal of money for its campaign of agitation against the British.

From Chicago, the play moved to Detroit and then to Philadelphia, where it was picketed by Jews. After successful runs in Baltimore and Boston, it went on to South America. Meanwhile, the millions of dollars raised by the pageant were sent, at least in part, to purchase a ship for transporting Jews from Europe to Palestine. Unlike the rescue activities of the Haganah, which were conducted in secrecy, the league's venture with the ship, renamed the *S.S. Ben Hecht*, was well publicized at every step, so that when the boat with its human cargo approached the shores of Palestine, it was seized by the British and its passengers interned in Cyprus. The league responded with a propaganda blast including full-page ads, many written by Hecht, viciously attacking the British in major American newspapers.

Soon after, on April 16, 1947, the British hanged four Irgun soldiers in the Acre prison. Their leader, Dov Bela Gruner, became the central figure in Hecht's last pageant, *The Terrorist*. Hecht let loose a blast in the media, comparing the British to the Nazis and saying that he "had a holiday in his heart" whenever he heard that a British soldier had been killed in Palestine. These diatribes caused the British movie industry to declare a boycott of all movies with which Hecht had any connection. Although he had written scores of screenplays for some of Hollywood's biggest successes, he was blacklisted by the American film industry, and his career collapsed. He began to distance himself from his Irgun friends and to grow increasingly bitter toward Zionist leaders in general.

Among his papers at the Newberry Library in Chicago is a letter signed by "Ben-David," the underground alias of Menachem Begin, then the Irgun commander in Palestine. Written in the summer of 1947 after the hanging of Dov and his men by the British, the letter calls on Hecht to use his "brilliant pen" to write a spectacle to memorialize Dov. The letter, dated Tammuz, 5707, concludes: "Permit me to take this opportunity of shaking your hand for all you have done for us . . . You have taken your stand at our side without fear or compromise, and have moreover drawn your readiness to take the stone hurled at you from all sides . . . We shall not forget it."

The State of Israel declared its independence in May, 1948. Menachem Begin apparently believed that "A Flag is Born" had helped to bring that about. But to many others, Ben Hecht's outcry against the world became lost in a war of words with his fellow Jews. Nevertheless, Hecht's words in "A Flag is Born" still resound with the passion of the age-old Jewish longing for justice and a national homeland.

V
CHICAGO JEWS AND THE ARTS:
THE PAGE AND THE STAGE

ROSA SONNENSCHEIN:
JOURNALIST, FEMINIST, ZIONIST

—

DURING THE LAST FOUR years of the nineteenth century, Rosa Sonnenschein of Chicago became one of the world's leading Zionist feminists: she published what she described as the first magazine dedicated to the interests of Jewish women; was a delegate to the First Zionist Conference; a friend of Theodore Herzl, and a divorced woman active in the male world. Her roles as publisher of a magazine with international distribution and an outspoken public figure added to Chicago's reputation as a center of Jewish feminism. Although less prominent than Hannah Solomon, the founder of the National Conference of Jewish Women, who was also a Chicagoan, Rosa Sonnenschein in the prime of life seemed destined to maintain her leadership role. Then, as the twentieth century began, she all but vanished from the public scene.

She was born in the Austro-Hungarian Empire on March 12, 1847. Her father, Hirsch Baer-Fassel, was a wealthy rabbi in Moravia, accomplished orator and scientist who introduced many religious reforms to his congregants, and who preached in German rather than the customary Yiddish. He owned impressive homes in various places, maintained an extensive library and a salon frequented by intellectuals and professional and business leaders. Rosa's mother died when the child was very young, and the rabbi married a woman with several older children. As his youngest child, Rosa received the lion's share of her father's attention and was exposed to the stimulating discussions at her parents' salon. As historian Jack N. Porter put it: "By the time she was in her teens, she had absorbed the education that in those days would have been remarkable for a male twice her age."

Apparently, Rabbi Baer-Fassel indulged his beloved daughter further. Instead of choosing a husband for her as was the custom, he permitted her to reject her first two marriage proposals when she was sixteen, although he insisted that she accept the third. Years later, Rosa called this choice a disaster. The man was Solomon Sonnenschein, a bright, handsome young rabbi from a neighboring village who had risen to prominence from an impoverished background. He soon became a radical Reform rabbi in Prague, but earned a reputation as a drunk and a womanizer.

The couple left for America with their three children in 1869 when Solomon was offered a pulpit in New York. But that assignment ended abruptly when he was caught having an affair with the young daughter of a prominent businessman. Despite this, he was soon offered a pulpit in St. Louis, a rather provincial place for an aspiring young Reform rabbi. The move to St. Louis coincided with Rosa's emergence as a public figure in her own right. She had married at seventeen, and given birth to three children in Europe and a fourth in America. Now, witty, sophisticated, and remarkably beautiful, she began a career as a journalist. Her combination of brains and beauty unsettled the mostly male circles in which she had begun to travel. Rabbi Jacob Rader Marcus, the late dean of American Jewish historians, reports hearing from a participant at the Philadelphia Conference of Reform Rabbis in 1869 that when Rosa "strode in the assembly room, full of rabbis, in all her extravagance, looking like nothing so much as a Jewish Carmen, all eyes turned to her and conversation stopped." Rosa seems to have liked the effect she produced: she reportedly exercised every morning to keep trim and smoked little Between the Acts cigars, popular with young men at the time.

Her public profile rose even higher after she published a series of articles about the Paris Exposition of 1878. She was invited to address a press conference at Chicago's 1893 World's Columbian Exposition. Her theme was the need for a literary magazine to cover the broad spectrum of topics interesting to women. During that visit to Chicago, she attended the World Parliament of Religions and witnessed the founding of the National Conference of Jewish Women. By that time, Rosa had decided to divorce her philandering husband, and to remain in Chicago. After the divorce, she set out to raise money to establish the magazine she had talked about in 1893. The result was the monthly *American Jewess*, launched in Chicago in April, 1895.

For her first issues, Rosa managed to attract well-known contributors, both men and women. From the articles and the general makeup of the magazine, it is clear that her prospective audience were middle- and upper-class German Jewish women. She lived—at least during 1896—at 3756 South Ellis Avenue in an established German Jewish neighborhood.

In her early days as an editor, Rosa traveled to Europe to write about the case of Alfred Dreyfus, the French army captain who was the victim of a false accusation of treason prompted by anti-Semitism. Hers were among the earliest American reports on the Dreyfus affair. During that trip abroad, she met Theodore Herzl, who was covering the affair for a Viennese newspaper for which Rosa's nephew also worked. Herzl, outraged at the treatment of Dreyfus, had became convinced that Jews would continue to suffer from anti-Semitism until they could establish their own state. When Rosa returned to Chicago, she published a moving appeal by Dreyfus's wife calling on the pope to intervene in this miscarriage of justice. Because of her association with Herzl, Rosa also became a strong champion of Zionism, a position violently opposed by most American Reform rabbis, including her former husband.

Rosa was at the height of her career as a journalist in the summer of 1897 when Herzl issued his historic call for the First Zionist Congress to be held in Basel, Switzerland. She was one of thirteen women participants, and is featured in a famous poster of the 1897 delegates, a copy of which is reproduced in the *Encyclopedia Judaica*. As might be expected, the pictures of all the women delegates were relegated to the bottom row of the poster. Rosa's participation may have received little public attention, but she was clearly noticed by Herzl. She is the only American participant mentioned in his diary: he writes that Rosa told him on the eve of the first meeting of the Congress, "They'll crucify you and I'll be your Magdalene."

When Rosa returned from Basel, she wrote with enthusiasm about Herzl, his associate Max Nordau, and the conference as a whole, but she did have a number of complaints. She was upset that the conference had been completely secular, without even an opening prayer. And women had not been allowed to vote on any issues, because, she wrote, the Zionist leadership had kowtowed to East European Jews who treated women as inferiors, in religious matters at least.

The *American Jewess* prospered for two years more, publishing articles titled "The Successful Businesswoman," "Single Women," "Cycling as an Exercise for Women," and "Women and the Law." In addition, Rosa herself wrote many editorials, urging women to lobby for equality in education and to work to improve their communities. At the same time she said women should remember their obligations to the family, should be "saintly" mothers and wives, and serve as the "keeper of religious tradition, a bulwark against anti-Semitism, and the conscience of synagogue and Jewish community life." She opposed the Reform movement for Sunday Sabbath observance, and criticized the National Council of Jewish Women for its policy of non-observance of the Jewish Sabbath.

Repeatedly calling for equality for women in Chicago synagogues, Rosa enlisted the support of Rabbi Emil G. Hirsch of Sinai Congregation, the foremost Reform leader in the city, urging him to permit single women to become members of Reform congregations. She called as well for women to be allowed to speak from the pulpit, something Hirsch apparently also supported. It is hard to know what role Rosa's efforts played, but Temple Isaiah, another leading Chicago Reform congregation, announced in 1898 that it had agreed to admit women to full independent membership for ten dollars a year.

Throughout the run of the *American Jewess,* Rosa embraced an eclectic range of positions. She was a Reform Jew who championed

Zionism; an advocate of feminism who also believed that a woman's first priority was the family, and a liberal advocate for Jewish rights who did not broaden her vision to protest discrimination against blacks. But above all, Rosa was a dynamic and dramatic figure in Jewish life, not only in Chicago, but in the world. When the *American Jewess* folded in 1899 because of dwindling circulation and her backers' inability to raise more money, Rosa was fifty-two years old and in apparent good health. She would live thirty-three more years, for most of them a silent, forgotten figure. She returned to St. Louis to live quietly until her death on March 5, 1932. She is buried in the Har Sinai cemetery there.

Until recently, Rosa's eclipse was puzzling. But in the middle 1980s, her grandson, David Loth, divulged that when he recorded her oral history, she told him that she had begun to lose her hearing even at the peak of her journalistic career, and that within a few years of the magazine's collapse, she had become completely deaf. As a consequence, "her pen ran dry." She did apparently travel often to Europe to be with her friends and family, but she could no longer take part in public affairs. One of the most brilliant women of her era, she was unable to investigate and report on world events.

Once out of the public eye, she was soon forgotten. When H.L. Meites compiled his encyclopedic *History of the Jews of Chicago* in 1924, Rosa Sonnenschein did not merit a single mention, and little has been written about her in the last century. Her decline into silence is tragic, but her contributions to world Judaism and to Chicago as a capital of Jewish thought make her someone who should be remembered.

LEFT: Ben Hect, 1924

BELOW: The University of Chicago, circa 1908

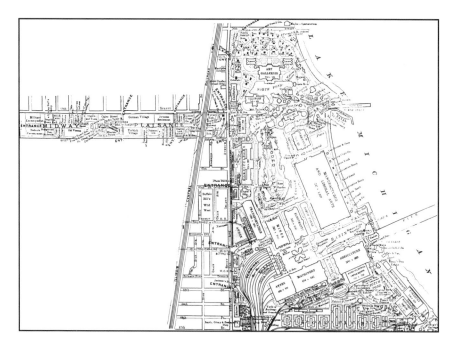

ABOVE: World's Columbian Exhibition map *(Chicago Historical Society)*
BELOW: Moorish Palace *(Chicago Historical Society)*

LEFT: Algerian Dancer
(Chicago Historical Society)

RIGHT: Turkish Vendor
(Chicago Historical Society)

LEFT: 1933 *Romance of a People* "Dudele" Dancer Nathan Vizonsky

BELOW: Maxwell Street Scene: the view looking north from the intersection of Halsted and Maxwell Streets early in the 20th century.

CLOCKWISE FROM TOP LEFT:
Bernard Felsenthal; Leon
Zolotkoff; Elisha Kite
dancing at the State of
Israel Independence
celebration.

Camp Avodah 1944
(ABOVE) and 1946 (LEFT)

TOP: Reception committee for Nahum Sokolow's visit to Chicago. *Seated from left*: H. Steinberg, H. Weiss, Bernard Horwich, Nahum Sokolow, Max Shulman, Samuel Ginzburg, Benjamin Perlstein. *Standing*: B.A. Antonow, H.L. Meites, D.B. Pollack, Bernard Shulman, Meyer Abrams, Harris Horwich, Jacob Miller, Jonah Fisher

CENTER: Weizmann Einstein Group, April 2, 1921. *From left*: M.M. Ussishkin, Chaim Weizmann, Vera Weizmann, Albert Einstein, Elsa Einstein, Ben Zion Mossinsohn

RIGHT: Bialik Stamp

"WE WILL NEVER DIE"
A Dramatic Pageant
Chicago Stadium • May 19, 1943

LEFT: Ben Hecht Pageant I, Program Cover: Art by Arthur Szyk

BELOW: Ben Hect Pageant I, *We Will Never Die*, 1943

LEFT: Rosa Sonnenschein
(Helaine Victoria Press)

ABOVE: Sol Bloom's
"Hoochy-Kootchy" music

RIGHT: Sol Bloom

LEFT: Jacob Loeb
BELOW: Foodless
Banquet

RIGHT: Edna Ferber
BELOW: Maxwell Bodenheim

ABOVE: Meyer Levin
LEFT: Shmarya Levin

LEFT: Dora Feldman McDonald

BELOW: McDonald Trial Montage. *Clockwise from top left*: Webster S. Guerin, Judge Theodore Brentano, Detective Clifton R. Wooldridge, Col. James Hamilton Lewis and P.H. O'Donnell, Michael C. McDonald, Dora McDonald, Sam Berkeley, Assistant State's Attorneys Edwin S. Day and William A. Rittenhouse

LEFT: "Nails" Morton

BELOW: Young Davey Miller at the racetrack

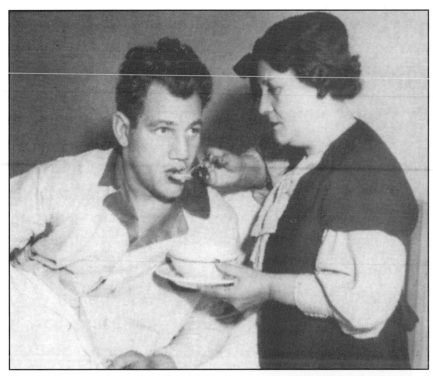

ABOVE: Boxer
"Kingfish" Levinsky
and his sister
"Leapin' Lena"

RIGHT:
Al "Wallpaper"
Wolff

Moe Berg

SOL BLOOM, THE MUSIC MAN

———

THE WORLD'S COLUMBIAN Exposition of 1893, held in Jackson Park on Chicago's South Side, was called "the most stupendous, interesting and significant show ever spread out for the public." It drew an estimated twenty-seven million people, making it the greatest tourist attraction up to that time. Its central feature was the White City, designed by prominent architects under the direction of Daniel Burnham: a circle of colossal buildings and statuary in Romanesque and Renaissance styles, filled with displays of impressive achievements in the 400 years since Columbus's voyage to America.

But the fair had another feature: the Midway Plaisance. Located outside the exhibition proper on the undeveloped one-mile strip of land connecting Jackson and Washington Parks, the Midway housed an enticing world of displays and amusements provided by private vendors, many from foreign countries. This section—the first of its kind at a world's exposition—became the great crowd pleaser, earning most of the fair's income. "Midway" became the generic word for the sideshow area of a carnival or circus. All but forgotten today is the fact that Sol Bloom, then only twenty-two years old, was the leading planner and organizer of the Midway Plaisance.

Bloom, born in 1870 in Pekin, Illinois, was an infant when his pious Polish Jewish immigrant family moved to San Francisco. In his 1948 *Autobiography of Sol Bloom*, he tells of getting his first chance in show business when he was about eleven years old, working in a brush factory. He had attended public school for only one day, because he had no money to buy the schoolbooks that were required: "One day on my way home from the factory, as I stood gaping at the new playbill outside the Baldwin Theater, a man called to me from inside the lobby. He was the son of a Jewish family named Belasco who lived a few blocks from my own home." This was David Belasco, then working as call boy, someone who called the actors when it was time to go on stage, and who was to become one of the world's most noted theatrical producers and dramatists, the author of *Madame Butterfly* and *Girl of the Golden West*, both later adapted into operas by Giacomo Puccini. Bloom notes that Belasco even then had an air of distinction, and was treated with deference.

David Belasco introduced young Sol to show business: Bloom took small parts in theatrical productions, and worked as an usher, candy vendor, hat checker, and seller of violets, took orders for tickets, and learned all he could about the business side of theater. This led to a job as box-office manager of the new Alcazar Theater, owned by Mike de Young, who, through his ownership of the *Chronicle*, was one of San Francisco's most powerful figures. The Alcazar had a gymnasium on the second floor; many theaters had art galleries, or were combined with hotels, like the Auditorium in Chicago.

Bloom writes that in the 1880s, boxing had the same sort of appeal to young college men that football has today. He had, he says, a measure of success as an amateur lightweight, perhaps because his instructor was James "Gentleman Jim" Corbett, who was to become the world's heavyweight champion. Bloom staged boxing matches at the Alcazar gym; one of the most exciting was a 28-round bout between Corbett and a Jewish San Franciscan, Joe Choynski.

In 1889, seeking spectacular new shows à la Barnum, he sailed for New York, and went on to Europe to visit the Paris International Exposition, where he was most fascinated by the spectacular French colonial exhibits. Bloom's favorite was the Algerian Village, although he doubted that anything like it had ever been seen in Algeria. In fact, nothing like these dancers, acrobats, glass-eaters and scorpion-swallowers had ever been seen in the Western Hemisphere. Bloom decided that "a fellow from Arabia who could swallow a sword exhibited a culture on a higher plane than that of a Swiss peasant who passed his days making cheese and milk chocolate." He was sure he could make a fortune with them in the United States. Before leaving Paris, he negotiated an exclusive two-year contract to exhibit the Algerian Village in North and South America.

Hearing, when he got back to New York, about plans for the Columbian Exposition, Bloom hurried to Chicago to try to set up the Algerian Village there. Plans were going slowly, so he returned to San Francisco to manage a boxing match between Corbett and John L. Sullivan. When he went back to Chicago he found that progress was being made in construction of the principal buildings under Burnham's direction, but work on the Midway Plaisance was still poorly organized. He was surprised to learn that a Harvard professor of Ethnology, Frederic Putnam, had been put in charge of the Midway. The area had originally been planned for exhibits of historical and cultural interest, also including "the rare human exotic"—like the French colonial troupes that had been so popular at the Paris Exposition—but Putnam wanted to keep it "dignified and decorous."

Bloom comments: "To have made this unfortunate gentleman responsible for the establishment of a successful venture in the field of entertainment was about as intelligent a decision as it would be today to make Albert Einstein manager of the Ringling Brothers and Barnum and Bailey Circus." On the recommendation of his mentor Mike de Young, who had been appointed one of the commissioners of the exposition, the twenty-two-year-old Bloom was named manager of amusement concessions and superintendent of construction of the Midway Plaisance, with the full confidence of Daniel Burnham.

Bloom introduced the central feature of the Midway: the Ferris Wheel, the popularity of which rivaled the Eiffel Tower at the Paris Exposition. The Algerian and Tunisian Village, as Bloom's production was called in Chicago, became a great money-maker. The dancing girls gave performances in a 1000-seat hall. Their great specialty was the *danse du ventre*. When the public learned that this meant "belly dance," they concluded with delight that it must be salacious and immoral, and paying crowds poured in. Bloom writes that the dance, "while sensuous and exciting, was a masterpiece of rhythm and beauty." Almost immediately imitated in amusement parks around the country, however it was debased into the crude, suggestive "Hootchy-Kootchy."

Bloom admits that he helped to corrupt the *danse du ventre* by coming up with the "hootchy-kootchy" melody. Shortly before the fair opened, he says, he was invited to present a preview dance performance for the Press Club of Chicago. To give an idea of the rhythm to a pianist who had been hired for the occasion, Bloom says he hummed a tune and then picked it out on the piano. From this improvisation a score was later arranged, and the music became better known than the dance itself. Bloom says regretfully that his "failure to [copyright the music] cost me at least a couple of hundred thousand dollars in royalties."

After the fair, Bloom decided to remain in Chicago. A successful showman, he got to know many Chicago politicians, particularly "Bathhouse John" Coughlin and Michael "Hinky Dink" Kenna of the First Ward, and made important contacts within the Democratic party, nationally as well as locally. Bloom's political career had started almost as soon as he came to Chicago in the spring of 1893 during the successful mayoral campaign of Carter Henry Harrison, who had strong support from the First Ward. Harrison was a strong booster of the Columbian Exposition, and apparently of Bloom and his ideas. Bloom got an education in practical politics: the affiliation of corrupt First Ward politicians with a powerful mayor, a formula somewhat new to Chicago but already in full force in New York, with Boss Tweed and Tammany Hall. Bloom notes: "If this seems somewhat sordid, I can only remark that every great accomplishment outside the realm of pure art has been brought about through compromise."

Bloom quickly found employment as the Chicago branch manager of M. Witmark & Sons, then the biggest publisher of popular music in America. By 1896 he had left Witmark to establish his own firm at the corner of Wabash Avenue and Jackson Boulevard. His business prospered, with many of his publications becoming hits. On

June 22, 1897, he married Evelyn Hechheimer. At their engagement party at the Wellington Hotel, composer Paul Dresser sang his song "On the Banks of the Wabash" and Charles K. Harris played his composition, "After the Ball." The new couple had an apartment at 4736 South Prairie Avenue, near Washington Park and Lake Michigan, then a very fashionable area. In addition to the music publishing business, Bloom was managing the music department of Rothschild's department store. Ever an innovator, he introduced a piano player and singer who performed the songs to encourage sales of the sheet music.

Bloom broadened his reputation by organizing the "World's Musical Library." He enlivened the appeal of his sheet music by the innovation of printing photographs on the covers. In a big newspaper ad, he proclaimed: "Sol Bloom, the Music Man" had secured "Copyright Number One for the Twentieth Century" on January 2, 1900 for "I Wish I Was in Dixie Land Tonight" by Raymond A. Browne. Bloom's songs were published as a separate feature in William Randolph Hearst's Chicago newspapers. He also began to sell musical instruments. He commuted between Chicago and New York, and in 1903, deciding with great fanfare that it was time to move East, he became a New Yorker.

He invested in real estate and dabbled in the theater, opera, and nearly all types of music, some of which he composed himself. By 1910, he says, he owned more than seventy music departments in retail stores throughout the country, and had become involved in the new recording industry by opening a store in New York selling Victor Talking Machines. By 1920 when he was fifty years old and financially secure, he felt in need of a new stimulus. He had continued his political activities as a staunch Democrat and member of Tammany Hall, so when the U.S. representative of New York's 19th Congressional District died in November, 1922, and the Democratic Party called on him to run for the vacant seat, Bloom accepted the challenge. He won the normally Republican "silk stocking" district by 145 votes, a seat he kept for over twenty-five years until his death in 1949.

He directed the George Washington Bicentennial Exposition in 1932, and the Constitution Sesquicentennial Exposition in 1937. In

1938, he became chairman of the House Committee on Foreign Affairs. He was a U.S. delegate to the Anglo-American Conference on Refugee Problems in 1943 and a member of the delegation to the San Francisco conference that established the United Nations. Sol Bloom was a genius in the field of musical entertainment and a long-time Democratic politician, but his career essentially started in Chicago in 1893 at the World's Columbian Exposition, with his belly dancers and his "hootchy-kootchy" melody.

CARL SANDBURG'S LETTER TO JACOB LOEB

CARL SANDBURG (1878–1967), one of America's preeminent poets and the author of classic works on Abraham Lincoln, had his initial literary success in Chicago. In 1914, *Poetry* magazine published his poem "Chicago," with the famous lines characterizing the city: "Hog Butcher for the World/ Tool Maker, Stacker of Wheat . . ." In 1999, Ivan R. Dee published *Poems for the People*, a collection of 73 newly discovered poems from Sandburg's early years in Chicago, when he was deeply concerned with the plight of the working classes and the unemployed. One poem, first published in 1915, is in the form of a letter:

To Jacob M. Loeb:
You are one of the Jews sore at Georgia for the way they hanged
     Leo Frank and called him a damned Jew there in Atlanta.
And you're talking a lot about liberty and the rights of
     school children.
You came from Kovno in Russia and you ought to know
     something about liberty;
And how school boards, police boards, military boards and czars
     have gone on year after year
To choke the Jews from having societies, organizations,
     labor unions,
Shoving bayonets into the faces of the Jews and driving them
     to the ghettoes

You know what I mean. You know these European cities where
     they call the Jews a despised race;
And anybody who spits in a Jew's face is not touched by
     the police.
D'ye get me? I'm reminding you what you already know.
You're the man who is leading the school board fight on the
     Teachers' Federation.
And you forget, your memory slips, your heart doesn't picture
How you and your fathers were spit upon in the face.
And how the soldiers and police misused your women—
Just because they were Jews, and in Kovno
Anybody could get away with what they did to a Jew woman
     or a Jew girl;
And now you, a Jew stand up here in Chicago and act proud
Because you have in effect spit in the faces of Chicago women,
     accused them, belittled them.
First you tried to cut their wages, back here in May, a seven-and-
     a-half per cent cut,
And now you're going to make it a law that teachers can't have
     a labor union;
And they got to take what you and Rothmann and Myer Stein
     hand 'em.
I don't think you'll get away with it.
Sam Gompers, an English Jew, will speak tonight at the
     Auditorium,
And Jacob LeBosky and Sam Alschuler and other Jews in
     this town
Are against the game of shackling the teachers and repeating
     Kovno and Kiev and Odessa here in Chicago.
In fact, five hundred Jews are already in revolt at your Kovno trick
Of slamming the door on the free speech at the Hebrew Institute.
These five hundred are the real blood of the Jew race
That give it a clean flame of heroism.
You belong with the trash of history, the oppressors
     and the killjoys.

Jacob Loeb was born in Chicago on September 17, 1875. His mother and father, Johanna and Moritz, were born in Germany, and his mother was active in women's Jewish organizational work, counterparts to work by the B'nai B'rith for men. Jacob Loeb graduated from public school at sixteen and started in business, initially choosing insurance as his career, forming a company, Loeb & Coffee, in 1894. This became Eliel & Loeb in 1902, and in 1916 the partners incorporated their firm, which soon became one of the city's most prominent, with Jacob M. Loeb as its president.

At the same time, Johanna Loeb was working to establish an institution on Chicago's West Side, devoted to the education of the new wave of Eastern European immigrants. Under the leadership of Julius Rosenwald, who was also its principal benefactor, the Hebrew Institute was incorporated in 1908. Rosenwald became its first president and Jacob Loeb chairman of its committee on physical culture. In 1910, when Rosenwald retired as president, Loeb succeeded him, and the institute was officially named the Chicago Hebrew Institute. Jacob Loeb, well-known and respected as a community leader, was appointed to the Chicago Board of Education in January 1913, and on June 29, 1914, was elected its president.

At this time an effort was being made to unionize Chicago's teachers. On September 1, 1915, the Board of Education passed the "Loeb Rule" "prohibit[ing] teachers from belonging to organizations affiliated with organized labor or employing paid business representatives." As if this was not enough to infuriate labor organizers, Loeb, as president also of the Hebrew Institute, refused to allow it to sponsor a meeting organized by the Labor Defense League to raise money for "union men unjustly held in prison." The result was that about five hundred Institute students, mostly immigrant Russian Jews studying English, went on strike to "gain freedom of speech."

In his poem, Sandburg calls Loeb's attention to the lynching of Leo Frank, a Jew, at the hands of a mob in Atlanta on August 17, 1915. On that same day, Kovno, now in Lithuania, had fallen to the German army, and there were reports that Jews of the area had been massacred by the retreating Russians. Sandburg's assertion that Loeb came from Kovno, was obviously wrong—Loeb was born in Chicago—and was an emotional attempt to connect Loeb with Jewish persecutions in Europe. Sandburg's poem must be looked at as an unpleasant reflection of the class struggle between Chicago's immigrant community and its powerful establishment. The bitter Hart Schaffner & Marx strike a few years earlier had also been fought between Jewish labor and Jewish capitalist owners

Inevitably, this conflict over labor tore at the fabric of the Jewish West Side community. In its August 20, 1915 issue, the Jewish *Sentinel* rose to Loeb's defence:

> It is easy to condemn Jacob M. Loeb's summary action last week in refusing the use of the Chicago Hebrew Institute by a radical labor meeting, but various considerations have first to be taken into account before a proper judgment can be arrived at. If the action taken by Mr. Loeb were the result of a personal antagonism to I.W.W. efforts and leaders, if he acted primarily as a capitalist throughout the proceedings, his actions were an abuse of his power. But no one who has a bit of sanity left will believe for a moment that Mr. Loeb injected anti-labor venom into the proceedings. This is what the labor agitators and the weak-minded sentimentalists who they appeal to, always insist upon and this is what their crowd, if not they, really believe. Mr. Loeb had only one thought in mind, we believe. He sought to prevent anything taking place at the Institute which might be a reflection on the Jewish name or the basis for an unjust charge against the Jewish people. Anyone who knows the easy way in which such elements as sought to use the Institute last week, attack members of the government, outrage American sentiment and insult the American flag, realizes what inflammable stuff the Institute and Jews of Chicago and elsewhere were confronted with, Mr. Loeb had to act quickly, and he acted for the good of the Jewish people. This, after all, is the main point.

Jacob Loeb remained president of the Board of Education through June 17, 1917. He continued to be influential in Jewish philanthropic activities and was a leader in raising funds and food for Eastern European Jews after World War I, organizing the highly successful "Foodless Banquet" at the Drake Hotel on December 7, 1921. When 800 relief campaign workers arrived for dinner in the candlelit, crepe-hung ballroom, Loeb, chairman of the committee, delivered an impassioned address in which he told them that the banquet was foodless because the $3,500 that the dinner would have cost was going to be spent in a more meaningful way—helping the impoverished Jews of Europe. Loeb served as president of the Standard Club from 1923 to '24. He died on February 17, 1944.

"Sandburg to Loeb" was published in the newspaper *The Day Book* on September 8, 1915, but never included in any Sandburg collection before its publication in *Carl Sandburg—Poems for the People*, although it was reprinted twice by Robert Reid. The editors, George and Willene Hendricks, comment that the poem, admittedly difficult to read, reflects Sandburg's reaction to Loeb's effort "to break the Chicago Teachers' Federation, led by Margaret Haley, a friend of the poet's . . . *The Day Book* published many reports about Loeb and his vendetta against the teachers' union and against free speech." The editors say further that although "[t]here is no indication in Sandburg's life and work that he was anti-Semitic . . . this bold poem is likely to be misinterpreted." They included it in their collection, they say, "because it reflects an aspect of Sandburg's radicalism during his *Day Book* years." That newspaper reported extensively on what the Hendricks characterize as Loeb's "vendetta against the teachers union and against free speech." They explain that Sandburg's sympathies in this ugly poem "are with those fighting repression."

EDNA FERBER: NOVELIST AND PLAYWRIGHT

—

SHOW BOAT, WITH MUSIC by Jerome Kern and lyrics by Oscar Hammerstein II, one of the most popular musicals of the American stage, was performed in Chicago as recently as 1996. Few people remember that it was based on the novel *Show Boat* by Edna Ferber, who lived in Chicago in the first two decades of the twentieth century.

She was born August 15, 1887, in Kalamazoo, Michigan. Her father, Jacob Charles Ferber, was a Hungarian Jew, and her mother, Julia Neumann Ferber, came from a prosperous German Jewish family of merchants, bankers, writers, and teachers. In Ferber's 1939 autobiography *A Peculiar Treasure,* she says that in 1889 when his store failed, her father—whom she adored, while remaining aware of his weaknesses—moved the family from Kalamazoo to Chicago to live with the Neumanns in a four-story house on Calumet Avenue.

Ferber recalls in affectionate detail her grandparents' observation of Jewish traditions. She enjoyed not only the Neumanns' warmth, but their intellectual and artistic interests. They were well-to-do Jewish immigrants, largely assimilated into American secular culture. Her grandfather's cousin was a well-known playwright in Berlin. After only a year in Chicago, her father moved the family to Ottumwa, Iowa, still seeking the business success that had so far eluded him. The Ferbers lived in Ottumwa from 1890 until 1899, unhappy ones for the family. Jacob Ferber began to lose his eyesight and young Edna had to spend a great deal of her time helping her mother tend the family store. The business did not prosper and Julia Ferber eventually decided to move the family once again, this time to Appleton, Wisconsin.

Although Jacob Ferber died soon after they arrived in Appleton, life there was much improved for Edna. She came to love the Midwestern countryside, the flowers and rivers, and the hardy Americans, whom she later drew upon in her novels. She had a decided talent for writing and after graduating from high school became a reporter for the *Appleton Daily Crescent*, and then for the *Milwaukee Journal*.

It was while she was with the *Journal* that she began to hone her skills as a writer, producing a novel, *Dawn O'Hara*, set in Milwaukee. However, her most successful early work was a series of short stories featuring Emma McChesney, a delightful and witty travelling saleswoman, who became such a popular character that Ferber continued writing about her for years, and in fact made Emma the protagonist of four of her novels. It was said that Emma was based on Julia Ferber, a strong-willed woman whom Edna both feared and loved.

Her second novel, *Fanny Herself*, is based on Ferber's life in Appleton. The character of the old German rabbi is patterned after Rabbi Grechter whom she knew in Appleton, and the hard-working Jewish mother is based once again on Julia Ferber. She writes perceptively about Jewish life in a small Midwestern town, and about the Americanization of German-Jewish immigrant families. She also deals poignantly with the snobbery with which these assimilated Jews regarded the more recently arrived immigrants from Russia and Poland. Nevertheless, her portrait of Jewish life is a positive one.

She felt strongly that Jews should assimilate, and embraced the "melting pot" ideal for American Jews in her early works, believing that if Jews were allowed to flourish without persecution, they would disappear in two hundred years. Later, in the 1930s, she would lash out at Hitler and other anti-Semites, observing that the Nazi scourge was forcing American Jews to "become intensely racial."

In 1911 Julia Ferber, with her daughters Edna and Fannie, left Appleton for Chicago once again, moving into a three-story South

Side apartment building on Vincennes Avenue, near the Neumanns. It was there that Edna learned that *Dawn O'Hara* had been accepted for publication. Its first edition sold over 10,000 copies. "Chicago," she writes, "opened up before my eager receptive eyes. The slightest stimulus sent the imagination racing. First to be out on the Chicago streets, and their smoke-blackened apartment houses and their bedlam traffic; their musty green lakeside parks and windswept skyscrapers—strange mixture of provincial town and cosmopolitan city with the stench of the stockyard from the west side, and the fresh tang of Lake Michigan from the east side—this was to know adventure."

She published many short stories about life in Chicago: the concerts at Ravinia; Maxwell Street in the heart of the Jewish district on a Saturday night; the Loop during national conventions; the slaughter of pigs in the stock yards, and black South Side neighborhoods. And she met many of the authors who were part of Chicago's literary renaissance. "Carl Sandburg," she writes, "was writing his powerful lusty Chicago poems. Ben Hecht was living there, trying to be Rabelaisian, sliding his eyes around in a leer, trying to hide his warmhearted conventional soul; Maxwell Bodenheim striding along Michigan Avenue in beret and smock, looking like a Weber and Fields version of an artist. They were sometimes referred to as the Chicago School of Writers." Hecht and Bodenheim produced work that was cynical, acerbic and even cruel; Ferber, on the other hand, evinced a love of America and wholehearted sympathy for its struggling people. She never became close to this Chicago School, though she noted that "many of them were Jews like myself." She found them individually "exhilarating," but collectively "almost too heady."

On Sunday mornings, she went to the Reform Sinai Temple on Grand Boulevard to hear Rabbi Emil Hirsch. "Aquiline, acid, interpretive, bold—all these words crowd the mind when one tries to describe this great Jewish scholar. Courageous, too, and wise with a terrible wisdom, like the Prophets." She was deeply influenced by Hirsch's humanism and universalist interpretation of Judaism. Although she was not religious in any formal way, she wrote: "God is Good and Good is God." Among her women friends in Chicago, Edna admired Lillian Adler, a feminist active in the United Charities of Chicago and the Maxwell Street Settlement House.

She began to travel, to visit New York publishers and other writers. But Chicago, where she lived with her mother in Hyde Park, was her home base: "I wanted to picnic in the woods south of Chicago; I wanted to see the kids in Lillian Adler's dancing class at Maxwell Settlement; I wanted to bathe in Lake Michigan which seemed to be so accommodatingly at the foot of every west-east Chicago street."

She covered several Democratic and Republican national conventions in Chicago as a syndicated reporter, and worked with the editor William Allen White, who became her close confidant. At the Congress Hotel in 1912, she interviewed Theodore Roosevelt, then running for president on the Bull Moose ticket. Roosevelt's first comment to her was: "What are you going to do about Emma McChesney?" She was immensely flattered that Roosevelt had read her stories and taken aback when he suggested further adventures for Emma. In early 1914 she did publish a successful second collection of Emma McChesney stories, *Personality Plus*.

In 1914, she took her first trip to Europe, to Hamburg, Vienna, Budapest, Prague and Paris, experiencing the Old World and its cultural life before it vanished in the First World War. Her observations on this trip were perceptive, incisive, and refreshingly naive. Sailing back to America in August, 1914, she noticed that the German crew had suddenly become uncharacteristically inept. It was then that she learned that war had been declared, "but it was their war and none of our business. How grateful I am to have seen that Europe in 1914 just before it vanished, never to return. Gay, brilliant, beautiful, richly historic. And the madman who was to follow—he of the Charlie Chaplin mustache and the hysterical woman's voice—had not been thought of."

Back in the States, she stayed frequently in New York, and began work on her first play, *Our Mrs. McChesney*. It was ultimately produced starring Ethel Barrymore, but was not particularly successful. She returned to Chicago in the spring of 1920 to cover the Republican Convention, where she met Herbert Hoover, Frank Lowden, Hiram

Johnson and Senator Robert S. La Follette of Wisconsin. She also met the man the Republicans would nominate for President: Warren G. Harding. She listened to his speeches and thought: "Here is a living cartoon of the American Fourth of July stuffed shirt order."

She went to California to cover the Democratic Convention and began to write a new novel, *The Girls*, dedicated to her friend Lillian Adler, "who shies at butterflies but not at life." It received superb reviews. In 1923, she took her mother, who had been ill with pneumonia, to Europe. In Berlin, she noted the social upheavals: "They [the Nazis] killed Rathenau [the German Minister]," she observed. "Europe, an entire continent was doomed. This I shouted at the top of my voice when I returned to my country . . . Well, what if Europe is sick? It's none of our affair."

In the summer of 1923, Ferber returned to Chicago, to live with her mother at the Windermere Hotel, across from Jackson Park. In the next few years, in Chicago and New York, she wrote some of her best-known novels. Although she often spent only a few weeks in the places where the books are set, her research and literary skill enabled her, in *Cimarron*, to create a convincing picture of life in early Oklahoma: Sabra Cravat is its feminist heroine and Sol Levy, a peddler, is another character. She wrote also *American Beauty*, a historical novel set in Connecticut.

In 1925 she became the first Jewish writer to win a Pulitzer Prize, for *So Big*, a novel about a strong character named Selina DeJong, who spends her life working to support her son in a town near Chicago. *So Big* sold over 300,000 copies and was filmed three times, in 1925, 1932, and in 1953, when Jane Wyman played Selina. By the early 1930s Edna Ferber was both famous and rich, and had taken a luxury apartment at 50 Central Park West in New York City.

How *Show Boat* evolved is a tale in itself. George S. Kaufman had adapted one of Ferber's stories for the stage and she recalled later that Winthrop Ames, who produced that play, had said to her one evening during a tryout outside New York, "Some day let's all run away and join a show boat troupe on the Mississippi and forget there are things like Broadway and First Nights." Ferber asked, "What's a show boat?"

Ames told her about the theatricals and games staged on these river paddlewheelers, and the rest is history.

Ferber wrote the novel *Show Boat* about life on the Mississippi from the viewpoint of Magnolia Ravenal and her father Captain Andy, folding it into a story she had been writing about the Clark Street gambling district in Chicago near the notorious Levee. She worked on the book for more than a year, and when it was published by Doubleday, it was an immediate bestseller here and abroad. Her description of Chicago's "nether world" makes compelling reading even today. Later, she met Jerome Kern and Oscar Hammerstein, Jr., and as we have said, sold them the musical and dramatic rights, and in fact collaborated with them for many months on the adaptation.

One day, she recalls, Jerome Kern came to her apartment and sat down at the piano to play "Ol' Man River" for her. "The music mounted, and I give you my word my hair stood on end, the tears came to my eyes, I breathed like a heroine in a melodrama. This was great music. This was music that would outlast Jerome Kern's day and mine," she says. *Show Boat* was successfully filmed three times; in 1929, in 1936, with Irene Dunne as Magnolia and Paul Robeson as Joe, and again in 1951 with Ava Gardner as Julie.

Ferber was not only an important novelist, she was also a successful playwright. In time, her collaboration with George S. Kaufman produced such outstanding hits as *Dinner at Eight*, *The Royal Family*, *Stage Door*, and *The Land is Bright*. She was also part of the legendary group of writers who gathered at the Algonquin Hotel Round Table. As the noose began to tighten around German Jewry in the 1930s, she wrote a number of anti-Nazi diatribes. And she found time to write articles about American anti-Semitism.

In 1934 she traveled to Egypt and Palestine. She detested Egypt, the land of the Pharaohs. "I can't account for it," she wrote. "The fields seemed to me to be fertilized with old dried blood of centuries." Her feeling about Palestine was different. She recalled that the Jews were the "original farmers." She remembered Aaron Aaronsohn, the Palestinian agronomist and pioneer who had been to Chicago and who had developed a strain of wheat that would help to feed millions.

She loved Jerusalem. "I know why it was known as 'Jerusalem the Golden.' It is golden." In the faces of the young Jewish settlers, she saw hope for Jews everywhere. "I am not a Zionist," she said, "I only know this, with increasing assurance: that if suffering has for centuries been the badge of all our race it is high time to tear off the badge and to put in its place another—a new shiny one which says that Justice is the badge of all our race."

During World War II, she produced a number of novels. The highly successful *Saratoga Trunk*, published in 1942, and later a major movie, dealt with the gaudy life at the celebrated New York spa over fifty years earlier. When her old Chicago colleague Ben Hecht tried to enlist her for his Zionist Revisionist pageants and propaganda, she refused. In his autobiography, *A Child of the Century*, Hecht mentions Edna Ferber only once—to attack her for not helping him in these projects. After the war she became more of an American patriot than ever, and was increasingly alienated from Judaism, which seemed to her too legalistic to appeal to her emotionally.

In 1952 she wrote *Giant*, a story about Texas, its size and its crude materialism. It was highly successful and became an epic film co-starring Elizabeth Taylor and James Dean. After *Giant* was published, she visited the young State of Israel, and wrote in the second volume of her autobiography, *A Kind of Magic* (1963): "Israel was like a Jewish Texas without oil wells." She no longer admired the idealistic young Jewish pioneers she had written about on her visit in 1934. This time she saw the Israelis as "arrogant, ignorant of the world beyond the Israeli borders, and lacking in basic manners." In 1959 she engaged in a vitriolic exchange with Ben Gurion, disagreeing with the Israeli Prime Minister's suggestion that Diaspora Jewry should settle in Israel. Echoing the opinion of Rabbi Hirsch, she proclaimed that America was her Jerusalem.

Ferber's last novel, *Ice Palace*, about life in Alaska, was published in 1958, and of course made into a film. *A Kind of Magic* lacked the warmth of *A Peculiar Treasure*, possibly because she was seriously ill with cancer. A biography by her grandniece, Julie Goldsmith Gilkert, reveals the suffering and loneliness of her bitter last years. She died in

1968 in New York City, and did not have a Jewish funeral. The last words of *A Peculiar Treasure* provide a fitting epitaph: "It has been my privilege, then, to have been a human being on the planet Earth; and to have been an American, a writer, a Jew. A lovely life I have found it, and thank you, Sir."

MAXWELL BODENHEIM: DOOMED POET

MANY YOUNG WRITERS IN the Chicago Literary Renaissance in the first decades of the twentieth century became luminaries of American literature, among them Edgar Lee Masters, Sherwood Anderson, Theodore Dreiser, Carl Sandburg and Ben Hecht. But there was another: a fleeting comet named Max Bodenheim, a poet who met a tragic and horrible end. His work has come to epitomize the misery and degradation to be found in big American cities like Chicago.

In the autobiographical poem, "Introducing Irony," Bodenheim says he was born in 1892, though his family Bible (printed in Hebrew, with French translation) records the year as 1893:

> In 1892, when literature and art in America
> Presented a mildewed but decorous mien,
> He was born.
> During the first months of his life
> His sense had not yet learned to endure
> The majestic babble of old sterilities.

He was born in Hermanville, a small town in Mississippi, named after his mother's brother, M. B. Herman, a well-to-do merchant and surgeon. Bodenheim's parents were Alsatian immigrants. His father Solomon was a financial failure who had worked as a travelling whiskey salesman and clerked in a clothing store. He was dominated by Bodenheim's strong-willed mother, Carrie. Around 1902, the family moved to Chicago, to live in poverty and tension on the South Side. Bodenheim attended Hyde Park High School for a time until around 1908 he ran off to work at odd jobs in the South before enlisting in the army. Two years later he deserted, was caught, jailed and dishonorably discharged.

He returned to Chicago around 1912 and began to write poetry, which was published in Margaret Anderson's *Little Review* and Harriet Monroe's *Poetry* magazine. His biographer, Jack B. Moore, writes that during this period "Bodenheim wandered through Chicago's Literary Bohemia as the incarnate terrible child; sarcastic, sardonic, ironic; he behaved disgracefully but was recognized as a young talent in the heady, liberal, amorphous society. He was described as a golden-haired youth, with pale eyes and the looks of a pensive Christ."

It was at this time that he met Ben Hecht, then a newspaper reporter who wielded a sharp, sarcastic pen and who, like Max Bodenheim, had a self-hating view of traditional Jewish life. But while Hecht went on to gain fame and wealth as a writer of novels, plays and movies, ultimately embracing Jewish Nationalism as a means of fighting Nazism, Bodenheim could not make a successful transition.

In Chicago in their early years, Hecht and Bodenheim wrote and spent time together. Once they arranged a debate before a literary society: "Resolved, that people who attend literary debates are imbeciles." Hecht said that he endorsed the affirmative view and sat down, after which Bodenheim rose to announce that the audience's willingness to listen to a debate like that was conclusive proof that Hecht was correct, and no further debate was necessary. Hecht later founded an underground newspaper, *The Literary Times*; Bodenheim was the editor and principal writer. This biweekly publication satirized and ridiculed anyone and anything that Bodenheim and Hecht felt merited their attention.

Bodenheim also wrote plays and novels as well as poetry. In 1923, he published an autobiographical novel, *Blackguard*; the protagonist is Carl Felman, a young Jew living on the fringes of society, who returns to Chicago after serving in the army. He slips into his parents' apartment in a row of buildings that look "like factory boxes awaiting shipment, but never called for." The Felmans "are middle-aged Jews with starved imaginations and an anger at the respectable poverty of their lives." Felman's mother's family was wealthy, but his father hovers on the brink of financial ruin. Both parents want Carl to stop writing and "go out and get a regular job like a man."

Mrs. Felman is the typical Jewish mother—soon to become a standard character in American fiction—the frustrated woman trying to drive her son to "success." She blames her husband, of course, calling every failure the result of his weakness and softness, and tells her son, "All your wildness, Carl, has come from your father's side and not mine." Carl leaves home and enters the Chicago poetry scene, severing his ties with his parents and his lower-middle-class Jewish background. After an ill-fated love affair, Carl moves to Memphis to be with his wealthy uncle, the man so often held up to Carl's father as a symbol of success. But eventually Carl decides to return to Chicago to live as a poet—and a criminal. At the conclusion, he joins with one of Bodenheim's most admired creatures—a prostitute. They live together in bliss "without touching each other and each will be the monk and nun that they should have been."

> At twenty-four his flesh became tired,
> And to amuse his weariness
> His hands wrote poetry.
> He had done this before,
> But only as a gleeful reprimand
> to the speed of his limbs.
>   —"Simple Account of a Poet's Life"

Bodenheim socialized with the new literary lights; he was a "character," one of the avant-garde, giving readings of his work at Ben Reitman's Dill Pickle Club and Ben Hecht's Chicago Players Workshop. He went East and met Eugene O'Neill; in Europe he and his wife Minna met T. S. Eliot and stayed with other prominent English and French poets and writers. He had dedicated his first volume of poems, *Minna and Myself*, to his wife: poems about nature, city life, old age and death.

Time and ghostly coffins
Display their shameful greys and reds
Against the passive vividness of morning.
No illusion of hope exists now,
No dreamed of place of escape.
Afternoon has fallen on this street.
Like an imbecilic organ-grinder
Grinning over his discords . . .
Real men and women spin
Their miracles of motion
Upon the greyness of this street.
—"North Clark Street"

In 1923, his supposed friend Ben Hecht, in his novel *Count Bruga,* drew a caricature of a "Poet" modelled on Bodenheim. It was a vicious, mean-spirited attack that incorporated the many rumors circulating about Bodenheim's Bohemian lifestyle. Bodenheim's response was more moderate:

Your head is steel cut in drooping lines
They make a mask satirically meek.
Your face is like a tired devil weak
From many vapid, unsought wines.
The sullen skepticism of your eyes
Forever trying to transcend itself
is often entered by a wistful elf
Who sits naively unperturbed and wise.
—"To a Friend," from the book "Advice."

Bodenheim left Chicago in 1923 for New York, though he returned at various times, the last time apparently in 1952 when he was arrested for vagrancy. The novel that contributed most to his reputation as a rogue and libertine was *Replenishing Jessica,* published in 1925. Jessica sleeps with many men, and Bodenheim's description of her sex life would be considered mild today, but in 1925 he and his publisher were indicted for distributing an obscene and pornographic book. Although he was never called to the trial, Bodenheim was described by witnesses as a Don Juan and lecher, a member of the Greenwich Village "Greta Garbo Social Club," the avowed purpose of which was the seduction of young innocents. Both writer and publisher were acquitted, and sales of the book increased—it sold better than any of his novels—but Bodenheim's reputation was ruined. He continued to write poetry and novels, but no one would publish them. He drifted into the dives of Greenwich Village and Manhattan's Lower East Side, associating with social outcasts.

For a short time in the early 1940s, he seems to have joined Hecht's propaganda efforts on behalf of Zionism and Jewish Revisionism. Little of the material that he wrote in his attempt to regain his Jewish identity is extant. Ben Hecht in *Letters from Bohemia,* includes a sonnet written by Bodenheim during this period:

> The scapegoats of the centuries have shaped
> A slow enduring miracle from pain.
> Their spirits, tortured, vilified and raped,
> Now climb, embattled, fused in growing gain.
> They claim as glory, exaltation, might.
> Plain hearts and brains with ordinary faults,
> They move with common Gentiles seeking light
> Against dark ignorances and assaults.
> And yet, this spread of understanding still
> Confronts sly hypocrites and hate-filled groups.
> Too often, words of tolerance and good will
> Slide slinking Gentile prisoners and their dupes.
> Intelligence can never yawn or flinch.
> It must fight hard for progress, inch by inch.
> —"To Israeli Jews and to Gentiles"

In Bodenheim's expression of support for Zionists and mistrust of Gentile efforts on their behalf, he is as one with his friend Ben Hecht, except that Hecht mistrusted not only Gentiles, but many Jews as well.

In 1962 he died with a grin at the fact
That literature and art in America
Were still presenting a mildewed, decorous mien.
—"Simple Account of a Poet's Life"

Max Bodenheim did not live until 1962: he was murdered on February 6 or 7, 1954. By then he had sunk into alcoholism, poverty and misery. His first wife had divorced him and his second wife had died tragically. Like a character in one of his novels, he was living in New York with an attractive younger woman, Ruth Fagan, whom he called his wife. When they became homeless, Ruth befriended a drifter, Harold Weinberg, who offered to let them stay in his room in a seedy hotel. No one knows exactly what happened, but when Weinberg, possibly drunk, attacked Ruth, Bodenheim came to her defense and Weinberg shot him, and then picked up a long hunting knife and stabbed Ruth to death. Weinberg was arrested on February 10 and raved at his trial, "I ought to get a medal. I killed two communists." He was committed to a state hospital for the criminally insane. Bodenheim was buried near Oradell, New Jersey, in the Cedar Park Cemetery. Hecht announced that he was going to pay for the funeral, but some say there is no proof that he ever did.

Bodenheim's place in American literature is uncertain. Like Hecht, he was a first generation American who could not relate to his immigrant parents' Jewish tradition and sought to escape its strictures. It was for this perhaps that he paid a heavy price of suffering and alienation. It is a theme that has appealed to more recent Jewish writers. In Arthur Miller's *Death of a Salesman*, there is a close parallell to Bodenheim's father's relationship with his rich brother-in-law. Budd Schulberg, in *What Makes Sammy Run*, examines Jewish alienation in capitalist society in Hollywood. And Philip Roth, of course, vividly portrays conflicted Jews in a contemporary setting.

MEYER LEVIN: COMPULSION

———

In 1956, WHEN MEYER LEVIN, the well-known Chicago novelist, published *Compulsion*, a thinly fictionalized account of the 1924 murder
of Bobby Franks, Nathan Leopold, about to be released from prison
after serving thirty years for the crime, insisted he had a right to his
own story. The two wound up in court and some of the most horrifying moments in Chicago criminal history became fresh news again.

Levin is probably best known for *The Old Bunch,* a realistic saga
of first and second generation Jews on Chicago's West Side in the
1920s and '30s. Although he produced other well-received fiction and
journalism, he had grown bitter and angry by the late 1950s, believing that he had been slighted by the literary establishment, which did
not appreciate his "Jewish viewpoint." He had recently lost a vitu-
perative legal battle over the dramatic rights to *The Diary of Anne
Frank*, and did not look forward to another public trial which might
stigmatize him as combative and distract from a balanced evaluation
of his work. For his part, Leopold had spent more than thirty years as
a model and even admirable prisoner. Once resigned to life in prison,
he could now, in 1958, look forward to a new life, and to writing his
autobiography. He did not want Levin to dredge up his past and hurt
his very real chance of being granted executive clemency. It was a trial
that would bring each man the wrong kind of publicity at just the
wrong time.

Meyer Levin, born in Chicago's Maxwell Street area on October
8, 1905, was a precocious student who was admitted early to the

University of Chicago and in 1924 at the age of eighteen, became a reporter for the *Chicago Daily News*, one of the most prestigious newspapers in the country. Just months after he started, the Leopold-Loeb case broke. In his autobiography, *In Search*, Levin recalls, "From the day of the finding of the mutilated body of the little boy Bobby Franks, this crime fascinated the world, and little else occupied minds in Chicago. It seemed to us that we were in the center of the world through purest crime—a crime, as we thought, for crime's sake."

When the trial began, Levin was sent to write features. Leopold and Richard Loeb, the two accused murderers, were nearly the same age as Levin and all three had been at the University of Chicago at the same time. But Levin did not move in their circle: like the Franks, their families were wealthy South Side assimilated German Jews, while Levin's parents were poor West Side Eastern European immigrants. The two young men pled guilty to the murder. They would certainly have been sentenced to death if Clarence Darrow had not presented a brilliant defense that relied heavily on the testimony of psychiatrists—a first in Chicago courts. Darrow succeeded in winning them a sentence of life plus ninety-nine years.

After the trial, Levin wrote a series of stories about life in Chicago, and, after graduating from the university, left for a year of study in Paris. He took his first trip to Palestine, returned to Chicago and became cultural director of the Jewish Peoples Institute. Unlike Ben Hecht, whom he once greatly admired, Levin was openly involved in and conscious of his Jewish heritage, despite conflicts with leaders of Jewish organizations as well as with Jews from the old Yiddish-speaking neighborhoods. In 1927, he took a second trip to Palestine and lived for six months at Kibbutz Yagur, an experience that provided material for several of his later novels.

In the '30s he wrote two other novels and became committed to writing about social problems, while at the same time receiving recognition as a serious author. With the outbreak of the Spanish Civil War in 1937, Levin embarked on several years as a foreign correspondent sympathetic to the Republican cause. During World War II, he worked as a director-producer of documentary films for the Office of

War Information, and by the end of the war was a correspondent for
the Jewish Telegraphic Agency and the Overseas News Agency.

He made sure to accompany military forces that liberated concentration camps. His reports of Buchenwald, Bergen-Belsen, Dachau,
and many others, often the first direct accounts by a Western reporter,
were devastating and had an explosive effect, not only on the world,
but on Levin himself. He was traumatized by what he saw in the
camps, he said, which evoked all the fears and insecurity that he felt
as a young Jew growing up on the West Side: "In that moment [on
seeing the camp victims], an anguished hatred arose in me, pure bile
and bitterness against the entire world, the whole rotten putrid human race that could drive its own beings into this. What were these
people? They were just any people from anywhere, just a number of
families and splinters of families scooped up from St. Louis Avenue in
Chicago as well as from Jassy and Bucharest and Wrotzlaw . . ."

Soon after that, he threw himself into efforts to bring Jewish survivors to Palestine, where he had decided to settle. In the course of
this work, he came across an early French edition of *The Diary of
Anne Frank,* published by Anne's father Otto shortly after the end of
the war. Levin was among the first to recognize the literary value of
the *Diary*, and this changed his entire life. The story of Levin's in-
volvement with *The Diary of Anne Frank*—the subject of a 1996
book by Lawrence Graver—connects to his Leopold case, because
while the Anne Frank court struggle was going on, Levin decided that
his next book would have to deal with a subject sufficiently arresting
to allow him to pay off his legal expenses. A novel based on the
Leopold-Loeb case—still referred to three decades later as "the crime
of the century"—would, he was sure, have a guaranteed audience.

Richard Loeb had been murdered in prison in 1936, but Nathan
Leopold was alive and hoping to earn parole. Levin remembered covering the case as a young reporter, remembered the psychoanalytical
studies, the Nietzschean "superman" discourses, and the compari-
sons between the murder and Raskolnikov's crime in Dostoyevsky's
Crime and Punishment. He wanted, he wrote in his introduction to
Compulsion, to explore the role of reporter-detective, "as a Jew of

Russian extraction pitted against the pair of thrill killers with their superman philosophy." He flew to Chicago, met with Abraham Lincoln Book Store owner Ralph Newman, Leopold's literary agent, and received permission to interview Leopold in prison.

Compulsion was published in 1957 to considerable critical acclaim in Chicago and most other cities, but in New York reviews were lukewarm. Levin was already openly hostile to the New York literary "cabal," as he called Lillian Hellman and others whom he blamed for stealing the Diary drama from him, and he believed the denigration of Compulsion was further evidence of s conspiracy against him by a "Stalinist" literary establishment that denied that Jews were the principal victims of the Holocaust.

Leopold had proved to be an exemplary prisoner who, having volunteered during the war to be a test subject for a government project on controlling malaria, had been rewarded with a commutation of his sentence. Some time in the early 1950s, he hired Chicago attorney Elmer Gertz to help him arrange publication of his autobiography. Leopold found Gertz so helpful that he asked him to prepare his plea for parole.

About that time, Leopold gave Levin the requested interview. In his autobiography, Life Plus 99 Years, Leopold says that he was horrified that Levin proposed to "dredge up the past again," but then admitted to Levin that he was in fact writing his own book and was also cooperating on a series of articles about his life that would soon appear in the Saturday Evening Post. For a time, Leopold considered co-authoring a book with Levin, an idea that Levin apparently welcomed. But Leopold, concerned about "what effect such publicity would have on my book," decided against working with the writer, who, Leopold complained, continued "to importune" him and members of his family for personal information. Learning that Simon and Schuster had agreed to bring out Levin's book, Leopold notified the publishers through his lawyers that he would hold them responsible for any libelous statements.

Compulsion is narrated by Sid Silver, a reporter who is trying to understand the motivation of Judd Hirsch Steiner, the young murderer. Leopold, (who called Compulsion "at once a horrible, a fascinating, and a beautiful book—beautiful in the case [sense?] that the irides-cent surface of a swamp is beautiful . . .") was upset by Levin's treat-ment of characters based on Leopold's relatives and others close to him. Outraged by the attribution of violent thoughts, attempted rapes, and homosexuality to Steiner, he wrote, "My God, what I did is hor-rible enough and the load of guilt I bear on my conscience is already heavy enough without this additional source of turmoil." He decided to sue Levin for libel.

Elmer Gertz, in his 1965 book *A Handful of Clients,* says that Leopold, who had been granted his parole in 1958 by Governor Wil-liam Stratton on condition that he avoid publicity, had gone to Puerto Rico to work in a medical facility and stay out of the limelight. In Chicago Gertz kept an eye on the early success of *Compulsion,* and was concerned to learn that Twentieth Century Fox was going to make it into a movie. The success of Leopold's appeal to Stratton for execu-tive clemency, his only hope for true freedom, rested on his keeping a low profile, and Gertz feared that continued publicity about Leopold's "perversity" and bad character might kill that hope.

After consulting with another Chicago attorney, Harold R. Gor-don, Gertz began to develop an unusual argument for Leopold's suit. Gordon had won a case for Al Capone's family, and another for the widow of one of Joe Louis's early managers, by maintaining that there was a "quasi-contractual right to recover unjust enrichment against anyone who appropriated the name, likeness, life story, and personal-ity of another in a work of fiction that was distributed through the usual commercial channels." Gertz thought these precedents could apply to Leopold.

Leopold v. Levin, et al was filed in the Chicago courts on October 2, 1959. In addition to Levin, the suit named as defendants Simon and Schuster and Twentieth Century Fox. Since Levin was a resident of Israel at the time, it was difficult for Gertz to serve him with a subpoena, but he tracked the writer down when he returned for a rare Chicago visit to give a lecture at North Shore Congregation Israel. As Levin mounted the steps of the temple, a sheriff handed him the Com-plaint.

Levin was represented by Ephraim London, a New York attorney who was also representing him in the *Diary* case, and, as local counsel, Leon Despres, whom he had known since the Republic Steel strike in 1937 which Levin covered as a reporter and on which he had based his novel *Citizens*. In a recent interview, Despres reminisced about that strike. Levin was an avid labor sympathizer, and Despres himself was a labor lawyer and a liberal political activist who would eventually become alderman for Hyde Park's Fifth Ward in the Chicago City Council where he was a consistent critic of Mayor Richard J. Daley. Despres wholeheartedly agreed with Levin that Leopold's suit was groundless, and that *Compulsion* was protected as free speech by the Constitution.

The Leopold case dragged on interminably before a number of judges, less in the courtroom than in various legal offices. It seemed to be going nowhere, and weighed heavily on the minds of the two litigants. Several people had to give depositions, including Leopold in Puerto Rico. In the four years since the filing of the initial suit, Leopold had been granted executive clemency, and Levin had written *The Fanatic*, an explosive, angry novel attacking anti-Semites, self-hating Jews, and many others whom he felt were conspiring against him, principally as a result of the Anne Frank controversy. Some reviewers described *The Fanatic* as "paranoid." Finally, on April 15, 1964, Judge Thomas E. Kluczynski ruled in favor of Leopold on Gertz's motion for summary judgment, ruling that both the book and movie "constitute a classic case of an invasion of the rights of privacy. . . ." Leopold and Gertz were of course elated, while Levin, London, and Despres, stunned, decided to appeal.

The Illinois Supreme Court sent the case back to be retried by Judge Abraham Brussell, a prominent Chicago attorney and former partner of Arthur Goldberg, soon to be appointed to the U.S. Supreme Court. For more than a year and a half Brussell studied precedent and weighed the philosophical issues raised by fiction based on real-life events. At last he rendered his decision: Levin had every right to write *Compulsion*. "At last [Levin wrote] another judge, after a year and half, together with the whole background of the fictional use of real persons, issues a lengthy analysis of the important trend in modern documentary literature toward merging of invented fiction with factual material. There could be no distinctions, in purpose, between fiction and nonfiction, as was claimed, and there was no ownership of events; all life was open to writers . . . Costly and protracted, the battle provided a precedent for literary freedom."

The story did not end there. Leopold appealed and the case eventually went again before the Illinois Supreme Court, where it languished until May 27, 1970, when Judge Daniel P. Ward issued an opinion upholding Levin's victory. Judge Ian Levin (no relation), who worked on the opinion as Ward's clerk says that an examination of the opinions of many legal authorities and more recent decisions of the United States Supreme Court had made it clear that Leopold had no right of privacy to his story.

Leopold lost the case, but received executive clemency and lived in relative obscurity until he died in 1971, one year after the final decision in the case, which had gone on for twelve years. For Levin, the Supreme Court decision was vindication, but royalties from *Compulsion* had been held back for ten years and the litigation had hurt sales He did make money on the book, but not the financial windfall he needed to pursue his claim to *The Diary of Anne Frank*.

Levin lived his final years in modest circumstances, bitter at the many people he believed had conspired to keep him from accomplishing his dreams. He died from a stroke in Jerusalem in 1981 while working on *The Architect,* a novel based on the life of Frank Lloyd Wright. He is probably best remembered today as the author of *The Old Bunch* and *Compulsion*, two excellent novels that provide powerful insights into the Chicago Jewish community that so deeply influenced him.

VI
CHICAGO JEWS ON BOTH SIDES OF THE LAW: COLORFUL CHARACTERS

DORA FELDMAN MCDONALD:
SEX, POLITICS AND MURDER

—

DURING THE EARLY YEARS of the twentieth century, a number of arrests and trials involving Jews caught the attention of the Chicago press. In 1901, Emma Goldman and a number of Jewish anarchists were arrested for supposed complicity in the assassination of President McKinley. In 1907, Ben Reitman, known as "King of the Hobos," was arrested and tried for defying police orders by leading a march of indigents. Then, in 1908, was held one of the strangest trials in the annals of Chicago history; this, like the Goldman trial, involved a Jewish woman.

Dora Feldman McDonald, the wife of Michael Cassius McDonald, a notorious Chicago politician and gambler, was charged with the murder of her lover, Webster S. Guerin. The sensational trial began on January 20, 1908, nearly a year after the crime. Col. J. Hamilton Lewis, recently elected to the U.S. Senate from Illinois and one of the most flamboyant criminal lawyers in Chicago at the time, was senior defense counsel. The presiding judge was Theodore Brentano. For three weeks, thousands of Chicagoans crowded into Judge Brentano's courtroom to hear the lurid details of Dora's love affair with Webster. Newspapers supplied their eager readers with banner headlines and front-page stories. Dora was nearly forty years old at the time, fifteen years older than Webster. Dora was Jewish, Webster Roman Catholic. The third figure in the affair, Dora's husband Mike McDonald, had died at the age of sixty-six after her arrest, but before the trial.

Dora Feldman, born in Chicago, had come back from Kansas City, and found work as a chorus girl. She was married to Sam Barclay, a baseball player for the St. Louis Browns. The couple had one child, a boy named Harold. Dora was described at the time as the "prettiest girl in town," with auburn hair, a beautiful face and a shapely figure. Sam, whose baseball career was over, opened a barbershop. In 1898 Dora met Mike McDonald, a wealthy and powerful gambler, politician and businessman. Some historians trace the beginnings of the Chicago Democratic political machine to the reign of "King" Mike McDonald. For a long time, Mike had owned the Store at 176 South Clark Street, a flourishing four-story gambling emporium that also offered lodging. Mike had lived with his wife and two sons on the third floor. Despite his money and influence, he was not a happy man. His wife, Mary Noonan McDonald, known as "Tootsie," and a colorful character in her own right, had caused him great distress by running away to San Francisco with "Billy" Arlington, a minstrel. Mike had followed her there, brought her back to Chicago, and in 1882 moved the family from the Store to a spacious new brownstone on the corner of Ashland Avenue and Harrison Street.

The mansion had its own chapel for Mary's personal use. Claiming she had repented her recent sins, she arranged for her own priest, Father Joseph Moisant of Notre Dame, to join her in her daily prayers in the chapel. It was not long before she ran away again—this time to Europe with Father Moisant. Mike traced Mary to Paris, but did not bring her back. Instead, he divorced her and reportedly smashed her altar to pieces, saying that he had been betrayed by the Catholic religion. Father Moisant left Mary six years later to enter a monastery in Belgium, and she returned to Chicago to run a boarding house.

Mike proposed to Dora soon after they met in 1898, even though she was married and twenty-five years younger than he. He reportedly offered her husband Sam a $35,000 divorce settlement, which was apparently quickly accepted, and began to build a mansion for Dora at 4601 South Drexel Boulevard, then an upper-class Jewish neighborhood. To complete his transformation, Mike renounced Catholicism and seems to have accepted Judaism, although the details of his conversion are unknown. It was reported that the couple chose to be married in a Jewish ceremony in Milwaukee.

Dora and Mike settled into their new Drexel Boulevard home. He was almost sixty years old and easing out of gambling and politics. Dora, now in her mid-thirties, embarked on a secret affair with young Webster Guerin, a friend of one of Mike's sons. In mid-February, 1907, Dora began asking Mike for large sums of money. Then, on the morning of February 21, she told Mike, "I will settle in full today," and left the house. What Mike did not know, among other things, was that Dora had just learned that her young lover was about to marry Avis Dargon, whom he had been seeing for some time "behind Dora's back." At 10:30 a.m. Dora Feldman McDonald entered Webster Guerin's office in the Omaha Building at 132 West Van Buren Street and shot him twice, killing him.

Dora collapsed after the shooting and was taken to the Harrison Street police station, calling for "Papa," her pet name for Mike. He came and retained J. Hamilton Lewis as her lawyer and took "other steps" in her defense—at Dora's trial, the state questioned many of those steps as illegal attempts to subvert the judicial process. In any event, a coroner's jury did not accuse Dora of any crime, and she was released to a sanitorium at 5642 West Washington Boulevard. But some months later, a grand jury indicted her for murder. Mike's health suddenly declined. "He became broken in body and mind from distress over the murder charge against his wife," according to the *Chicago Tribune*. He was taken to Saint Anthony de Padua Hospital at the end of May, and died there on Friday, August 9, with Mary and their two sons at his bedside. Dora had apparently visited him the day before against doctors' orders. While in the hospital, Mike had drawn up a will in which he left one-third of his $2,500,000 estate to Dora, with the rest left in trust for his sons. He also provided a defense fund of $40,000 to defray Dora's legal expenses. Mary, weeping at his bedside, was left nothing.

Mike Cassius McDonald was given the last rites by a Catholic priest and taken by a special funeral train—a common practice at that

time—to Mount Olivet Cemetery for burial on August 12, 1907. Dora
was not present. As her trial opened with the questioning of prospective jurors, her religion became an issue. The *Tribune* reported that
"both sides have an understanding that no Jews will sit on the jury. It
is repeatedly brought out in the examinations that Mrs. McDonald is
a Jewess. Five Jews were among those excused from the jury box
during the day."

"We don't want a Jew on the jury because it would place him in
an embarrassing position," said her lawyer J. Hamilton Lewis. The
prosecuting attorneys too seem to have agreed with this for their own
reasons. The defense made a great effort to keep any men of religious
persuasion—regular churchgoers—off the jury. Mr. Lewis asked one
venireman, "Do you believe in the old Mosaic law—an eye for an eye,
a life for a life?" Proscutor Day objected, "We are not trying this case
under Mosaic law." Judge Brentano intervened: "I think we had better stop discussing the Mosaic law." Lewis was clearly the star of the
trial, much to the delight of the spectators. While Dora sat morosely,
her face hidden by a veil, Lewis paraded before the jury in a high-
styled blue suit, his famous pink whiskers quivering, as he engaged in
verbal pyrotechnics eagerly seized upon by reporters.

The trial began on January 27. The state presented a picture of
Dora as a selfish, immoral woman who had seduced a young lad and
killed him in a jealous rage. Guerin's brother Archie testified that his
brother had met Dora on his way to school when he was just sixteen
years old, and the relationship had gone on for years; that Dora had
once even followed him to California. Archie's wife Avis denied under
oath that she had ever had an affair with Guerin; it was all, she said,
a figment of Dora's imagination. An aunt of Guerin's testified that his
mother had gone to Dora years ago, had fallen to her knees and begged,
"Please let my boy alone," and Dora's reply was, "Oh, won't you let
me have him? I'll kill you! Look out!"

Other prosecution witnesses swore that Dora, at various times—
in a hotel room, in a restaurant and at home—had threatened to kill
Guerin during fits of jealousy, and once had deliberately broken up
Guerin's engagement to Dora's niece Minni. Witnesses testified that

she had bought the murder weapon and that she had been seen pistol in hand at the time of the shooting. The prosecution accused the defense lawyers of bribing witnesses, and presented evidence that Mike McDonald had worked with the acting police commissioner and his detectives, not only to leak information to the defense, but to suppress incriminating evidence—like Dora's confession and her statements at the scene of the crime. State's Attorney William E. Rittenhouse called defense attorney Lewis a "shyster" in open court. At the close of the state's case, a policeman testified that in the course of Dora's confession at the Harrison Street station one hour after the shooting, she had said that she expected to hang for the crime. Dora collapsed at the end of this testimony and was carried out of the courtroom amid great uproar.

Lewis opened the case for Dora's defense, not pleading insanity as many had expected, but self-defense: the shooting, he argued, was "not by her hand but by the hand of the deceased, while she was struggling to turn from her body the deadly hand which was leveled there." Dora, he said, was a victim of blackmail who had paid thousands of dollars to Guerin because of his extortion threats, and who was, on the day of the shooting, "hounded, broken, driven to desperation."

The defense called Minni Sallinger-Hirsch, a daughter of Dora's brother, Harry Feldman. Minni, recently married, testified that she had been Webster Guerin's fiancee but that "religious differences" and not her Aunt Dora, had ended the relationship, and that Guerin had written blackmail letters to Dora. Minni's mother testified that Dora had bought the murder weapon as a present for Harry Feldman. While Rittenhouse fumed and threatened perjury prosecutions, three tailors with shops near Guerin's office swore that when they heard the shots and dashed to the scene, they saw Dora standing amidst broken glass from a smashed door, crying, "He shot himself. Please save him."

When the day arrived for Lewis's closing argument, 2000 people fought and screamed to get into the courtroom. Women fainted and men lost their tempers and slugged policemen. Two wagonloads of police responded to a riot call. The *Chicago Tribune* reported, "James Hamilton Lewis in that human drama, 'The Defense of Mrs. McDonald,' was the attraction that drew one of the biggest crowds in the history of the Criminal Court Building to Judge Brentano's courtroom yesterday. With the art and grace of a consummate actor, Col. Lewis presented his part. Few left the courtroom unmoved at the vivid pictures he drew: one, of the woman of sorrow—his client, and the other, of the man without a heart—Webster Guerin. Though self-defense was given as the basis of the argument upon which the jury will be asked to acquit Mrs. Dora McDonald of the charge of murdering Guerin, nothing was omitted in the sketch of these two soiled and wandering human souls that did not leave insanity still open as a plea."

There never was a woman in all the literature of her sex who forgave as much and as often as did Dora McDonald, Mr. Lewis contended, and he admitted he could not explain it. The complex heart of woman was beyond his feeble comprehension. But there it was—the black story of the years that Guerin spent hounding and threatening the woman who had given him her affections—pure though her love was. As to Guerin's mother's plea to Dora, Lewis maintained that Mrs Guerin had come to Dora to stop the marriage of her son to Dora's niece because "she did not want the marriage of her son, a Catholic, with a Jew. She did not get down on her knees and plead for her boy's soul to Mrs. McDonald." Dora's second lawyer, Patrick O'Donnell, added a religious tint to the portrait of Dora. Speaking on a Saturday, he said, "Her ancestral people lit the candles at sundown last night. Somewhere in this city a light is burning where a Jewish mother is praying and hoping for her errant daughter. You are approaching the moment when you must do your great duty. You are here only to say whether she killed Guerin with a criminal intent in her heart. A daughter of Israel coming to judgment. She may have been wayward, but we are not to judge her past life . . ."

The defense rested its case without calling Dora to the stand. On Tuesday night, February 11, the *Tribune* reported: "Mrs. Dora McDonald, widow of Michael McDonald, the gambler, was acquit-

ted last night of the murder of Webster S. Guerin. The jury returned a
verdict in Judge Brentano's courtroom at 6:20 o'clock after five hours
of balloting and arguing." Dora, holding a bouquet of red roses,
thanked the jurors and left the courtroom. A reporter asked her what
she planned to do. "I want to go away where it is bright and sunny,"
she said. "Why not Florida?" he suggested. "I never thought of that,"
she answered. "I'll do that."

Years later, the *Chicago Daily News* reported that Dora had gone
to California and married a man named Newcomb. On one of her
trips back to Chicago, she remarked, "If anybody wants to know
how I'm getting along, just tell them Dora is getting along fine." She
died in 1931, having apparently spent most of the money that Mike
had left her.

DAVEY MILLER: THE REFEREE'S SCRAPBOOK

———

OVER TEN YEARS AGO, Sylvia Friedman, the daughter of Davey Miller, a famous Chicago prizefight referee, permitted us to make a copy of her father's scrapbook, made up of newspaper clippings, personal letters and photographs covering his public life over the approximately thirty years he was Chicago's best-known boxing referee and restaurateur. The book, which he put together himself in the early 1950s some time after suffering a stroke, is in virtually random order, but, almost like a time capsule, affords us a look back at a tough and generous man who contributed to Chicago and its Jewish community in an inimitable rough-and-tumble way. He first developed a reputation as the "protector" of Jews against anti-Semitic toughs on the old West Side, but the scrapbook picks up his story later, after he had become a respectable licensed referee and well-known man-about-town.

An invitation card to a testimonial dinner given in his honor by the Illinois Boxing Commission on his retirement as a referee in 1950, is the first item in the scrapbook. Arch Ward, longtime sports editor of the *Chicago Tribune,* was the principal speaker, and over five hundred guests attended. Ward pointed out that Miller was a referee in 1923 at the first boxing tournament sponsored by the *Tribune,* and was in the ring at the newspaper's first Golden Gloves meet in 1928. Miller told the audience that his proudest moment came when he refereed the heavyweight fight between Jersey Joe Wolcott and Ezzard

Charles in Comiskey Park in June, 1949. He also revealed, apparently for the first time, that he had turned down a bribe in connection with the Jack Dempsey-Gene Tunney heavyweight fight in 1927.

He was slated to referee that fight, but a few minutes before the bout began, Dave "Long Count" Barry was assigned to it instead by the Illinois Boxing Commission, for reasons never disclosed. On the night before the fight, Miller had been called from dinner and driven to a hotel near 22nd Street and Michigan Avenue, where Al Capone entered the car, put his arm around Davey's shoulders, told him he was betting "50 Gs" on Dempsey, and that "all I want you to do tomorrow night is give Dempsey an even break." Davey said that "there were no actual threats, but . . ." Asked why he never disclosed this incident to the Illinois Boxing Commission, he replied, "I didn't want to get anyone into trouble. After all, nothing came of it." After Miller was abruptly replaced as referee by Dave Barry, Dempsey knocked Tunney down, but did not go to a neutral corner as required, and the result was the famous "long count" by Barry, who did not continue the knockdown count until Dempsey was in the right corner. Tunney subsequently got up from the canvas and won the fight.

Numerous articles in Miller's scrapbook deal with the legendary fighters that he either discovered, managed or refereed. The most famous was Chicago-born Bernard Rosofsky, better known as Barney Ross. A Jewish boy from Maxwell Street, Ross had been running with a bad crowd when Miller discovered him in the 1920s and brought him into the Golden Gloves Tournament. Ross's father had been killed in a hold-up in his Maxwell Street store and Ross, always a provider for his mother and brothers and loyal to his friends, often thanked Miller for his early sponsorship of his career. For a while Miller managed Ross, but turned him over to Gig Rooney, a well-known Chicago manager who was managing Jackie Fields, another successful Jewish fighter.

Ross became welterweight champion and a World War II Marine hero. He captured America's heart because of his courage when, after becoming addicted to drugs during treatment for his wounds, he fought to recover his dignity and good name. In the scrapbook is a clipping of an article by Damon Runyon about the friendship between Davey Miller and Barney Ross, written in Runyon's unique style.

A touching letter from Benny Leonard, another Jewish fighter and lightweight champion, reflects the great affection these young fighters had for Davey. The letter, written in 1930, complains that Miller had not informed Leonard of the sudden death of one of Miller's brothers: "Why didn't you let me know? Dave, I like you. You are a real and sincere pal. You have been in there shooting for me many times and don't think that I didn't appreciate it. . . . Please remember me to your dear ones and tell your daughter that she has my every good wish for happiness, health and prosperity." There are other friendly letters: one from Jack Dempsey in July, 1935, addressing "Dear Friend Davey," and one from Illinois Governor Henry Horner dated November 17, 1932, thanking "Dear Davey" for "his great help," no doubt during the recent successful election campaign.

Miller and members of his family owned various eating and drinking establishments, starting with the E&M restaurant and club at 3216 West Roosevelt Road and including the 2530 Club at Milwaukee and Kedzie. Later, for a number of years the Millers owned a popular tavern at Clark and Randolph Streets, across from the Sherman Hotel. The scrapbook has pages of autographs from famous boxers—Joe Louis and Jack Dempsey—and entertainers like Bob Hope. Davey Miller knew them all.

Miller had several brothers: one of them, Harry, was a Chicago police officer who won lasting fame, or infamy, during the term of Mayor Anton Cermak, when he was involved in an attempt on the life of Frank Nitti, the Capone mobster. Some people believe that Nitti retaliated by assassinating Cermak in Miami while the mayor was with President-elect Franklin D. Roosevelt. Harry Miller was at Cermak's side when he was shot.

Another Miller brother, Hershie, was often a source of pain to the family. In January, 1924, Davey was shot and critically wounded at the LaSalle Theater, apparently by mobster Dion O'Banion. A newspaper reported that this shooting was related to gang warfare involving Hershie Miller, who was a pal of Samuel "Nails" Morton, a Jewish World War I hero alleged to be an accomplice of O'Banion. Nails, like Davey, was a hero to West Side Jews because he protected them from marauding gangs. Hershie and Nails were often in trouble with the law and were charged with murder, but neither was ever convicted.

In 1929 Edward Dean Sullivan published a book called *Rattling the Cup on Chicago Crime,* dealing with more than two hundred underworld characters. Sullivan, in connection with the attack on Davey Miller, asserts that the Miller brothers had been "pushing'" Dion O'Banion around, and generally "pushing into rackets." Davey Miller sued Sullivan for libel in the Federal District Court in New York. During the jury trial, Benny Leonard and Abraham L. Marovitz, then a Cook County assistant state's attorney testified as character witnesses for Davey Miller, calling him "the man who had come from Chicago not to collect damages of $250,000, which he had originally demanded . . . but to clear his name."

Davey Miller testified that O'Banion had shot him "not because he had belonged to the 'mob' of Hershie Miller, his brother and family black sheep, but just out of plain meanness." He sought vindication rather than money, he said, and the smallest sum permitted by law would be adequate. He drew a picture of himself as a hard-working respectable citizen, a member of the Elks, an Odd Fellow, a Zionist, a Mason and a licensed referee who ran a restaurant at 3216 Roosevelt Road, "open for twenty-four hours a day for the last nineteen years." Emil K. Ellis, Miller's attorney, told the jury that both Miller and his daughter, a student at Northwestern University, had suffered because of Sullivan's statements. The judge agreed that Miller had been libelled and directed a judgment in his favor of six cents, a vindication of sorts.

By the end of his career in 1950, Davey Miller had been a fight referee for twenty-seven years, and had refereed five thousand fights in Chicago. Famous boxers were his friends and confidants, among them Jewish fighters Barney Ross, "Kingfish" Levinsky, Davey Day and Jackie Fields. After he retired, he continued to donate his services for intramural fights at Navy Pier and Army and Navy bases. He died in 1956.

One day perhaps we will have a full history of Miller's protection of vulnerable immigrants against attacks by thugs, but the scrapbook gives us a valuable glimpse into an important aspect of the Jewish experience in Chicago. Basketball, football and baseball are today's avenues for minority youth to obtain fame and fortune on the American scene; but in the years in which Davey Miller was a referee, Chicago Jewish youths often used their fists to pound their way out of the West Side. The scrapbook tells us that Davey Miller was often there to lend a helping hand.

BEN REITMAN: HIS UNORTHODOX LIFE

DR. BEN REITMAN WAS born to poor Russian immigrant Jews on New Year's Eve, 1879, in St. Paul, Minnesota. He died more or less a Baptist on November 17, 1942, in Chicago. His last will begins: "I wish to testify that life has been good . . ." and concludes, "$250 shall be spent for food and drink for hobos and unemployed who will be invited by my son to a funeral dinner. I should like the service to be in a big hall, with drink, fun and a happy good time for all." Besides his son, Brutus, who died in a plane crash shortly thereafter, he left four daughters—Mecca, Medina, Victoria and Olive—and several wives, to one of whom he was married legally. There is uncertainty over whether the funeral dinner was actually ever held.

Hundreds of hobos did attend his funeral services and accompany his body to Waldheim—not Jewish Waldheim—Cemetery. He was buried near the monument under which lay the remains of the Haymarket anarchists August Spiess, Albert Parsons, Adolph Fisher and George Engel. A few feet away was the grave of Emma Goldman, another anarchist equally famous or infamous, depending upon one's point of view.

The *Chicago Daily News* editorialized at the time of his death: "It was not that Ben Reitman was a great man or that he was a national figure; but he was a Chicago figure . . . He was a publicity hound and an opportunist. But beneath the phony properties . . . was a man who had a real understanding of his fellow men and a genuine sympathy for those who dwelt outside the pale of social sanctions and in the drab penumbra of the half world . . . With his passing, Chicago loses another of the rugged individuals whose personalities contributed to the vitality that made the Chicago of a quarter century ago one of the most colorful and dynamic cities of the world . . ."

Who was this unique man? A partial answer is provided in *Damndest Radical. The Life and World of Ben Reitman, Chicago's Celebrated Social Reformer, Hobo King and Whorehouse Physician* by Roger A. Bruns, director of publications for the National Archives in Washington. Bruns's story begins after Ben and his mother, abandoned by her itinerant-peddler husband, had moved to a predominantly Irish slum in Chicago's Near South Side vice district. Here the young boy ran errands for the prostitutes he learned to love, and used boxcars in the nearby rail yards as his playrooms. His neighborhood friends called him "Sheeny Ben," and the hobos who frequented the rail yards regaled him with tales of the virtues of tramping.

From the age of ten, Ben was often riding the rails, seeing America. Once he was a fireman on a steamship which sailed to Europe and the Middle East. When he came back to his mother's home in Chicago, he went to work as a laboratory boy for Dr. Maximilian Herzog, a pathologist and bacteriologist. Doctors in the facility were so impressed with the young man that they arranged his admission into the College of Physicians and Surgeons in Chicago, later to become the University of Illinois College of Medicine. Reitman received his M.D. degree from the college in 1904.

While he was still a student he embarked on his first marriage, to May Schwartz, on July 4, 1901. The couple sailed for Europe, where Ben promptly deserted his wife who was pregnant. After graduation Ben taught medicine and opened a private office in Chicago. But he often closed his practice and took to the rails. On one of these trips he learned about the Brotherhood Welfare Association in St. Louis, better known as the Hobo College. This group provided food and housing for the unemployed and disabled, and these men became his pals as the prostitutes had done earlier. He organized a Chicago branch of the Hobo College through which he became involved with unemployed workers in Chicago.

In, January, 1908, Reitman led a protest march of thousands of unemployed on Chicago's City Hall, only to be confronted and dispersed by club-wielding police squads. Reitman was arrested, but the march brought him to the attention of the police, the media and radicals. Two months later, in March 1908, began the great passion of Reitman's life—his affair with Emma Goldman. They first met following a notorious event in Chicago history: on March 2, Chicago's intemperate police chief, George Shippy, shot and killed an apparently innocent young Russian Jewish immigrant, Lazarus "Jeremiah" Averbuch, who had come to the chief's door. Shippy explained the killing by saying that he suspected that Averbuch was an anarchist assassin. The Chicago newspapers immediately launched an anti-anarchist campaign, seeing in this incident a repetition of the Haymarket "conspiracy." Even though no evidence connected Averbuch to any anarchist activity, the police went on a rampage through the South Halsted Street area, arresting any Jews thought to have anarchist connections. Reitman was immediately brought into custody to view Averbuch's body, since the police were convinced they had seen Averbuch in the protest march. Reitman could not identify the body and was released.

The next day Emma Goldman came to Chicago. Her outspoken anarchist views and her earlier arrest in Chicago in connection with the 1901 shooting of President William McKinley by Leon Czolgosz, had made her *persona non grata* to the Chicago police. When no one would rent her a hall in which to speak, Reitman contacted her and offered her the use of his Hobo Hall. The police refused to allow her to use the hall, but Ben and Emma met and the spark was lighted. While the newspapers reported that she was ill and out of circulation, Emma, at the age of 39, was finding ecstasy in the arms of her "beautiful tramp," ten years younger than she. Lazarus Averbuch's name was never cleared, but Emma and Ben began a romance that lasted for over ten years. Their correspondence has been largely preserved, and their astounding letters throb with an explicit passion that might at times shock even today's readers.

Reitman now began a connection with the anarchists in general and Goldman in particular. He became Goldman's manager, wrote articles and gave speeches on birth control, free love and free speech and, for a time, edited *Mother Earth*, the anarchist magazine. In 1911, during bitter labor strife involving the I.W.W. (initials often derided as "I Won't Work" but actually standing for the International Workers of the World, the "Wobblies"), he and Emma went to San Diego, where a mob attacked Ben, dragged him from his hotel and into the desert, where they stripped him and burned the letters I.W.W. onto his buttocks with cigar butts. He was then covered with tar and released, barely alive. He would later often drop his pants at the end of a speech to display his wounds, much to Emma's chagrin

When America entered the war in 1917, Emma Goldman was arrested because of her extreme anti-war and anti-conscription agitation. She broke with Reitman because he disagreed with her. The affair was over. She was deported to Russia in 1919, and except for one brief visit, was never allowed to live in this country again. Reitman, no longer an anarchist, returned to Chicago. In the 1920s he practiced medicine among prostitutes and hobos, and added a new group of friends: notorious underworld characters, Al Capone and his ilk. He took a job with the city as a doctor specializing in the treatment of venereal diseases, earning the nickname "The Clap Doctor." He helped to establish the first venereal disease clinic at Cook County jail, and also treated prostitutes owned by the vice lords.

He was active as dean of the Hobo College, and later in the famous Dill Pickle Club, a saloon on Chicago's Near North Side, where the famous and the infamous sounded off. When the speakers went outside to vent their spleen in Bughouse Square, the crowds would see "Ben and his flowing cape, the walking stick, the fedora and the Windsor tie." He published two books: *The Second Oldest Profession* (1931), a study of pimps; and *Sister of the Road: The Autobiography of Box-Car Bertha* (1937).

Throughout his life he had numerous affairs; his ability to seduce women was said to be legendary. His later political views were strange and often perverse: he thought Franklin Roosevelt to be as much to blame for World War II as Hitler and Mussolini, and he was said to have no sympathy for the Jews being persecuted in Germany, maintaining they could take care of themselves. He died in November 1942, a year after Pearl Harbor, so he did not experience much of the war, and undoubtedly knew nothing of the Holocaust. He remained preoccupied with VD and its prevention until his death at the age of sixty-three.

The Damndest Radical treats Ben and his escapades with warmth and affection. Nostalgia for the "rugged individualists" of the past permeates the book. This is not a book that seeks to explore the psychological trauma experienced by a poor Jewish boy raised among Irish ruffians, or what the impact of living next to whorehouses had on his adult relationship with women. These are left for the reader to explore.

SAMUEL "NAILS" MORTON: 20TH CENTURY GOLEM

———

THE MEDIEVAL TALE OF the "Golem," a clay creature brought to life by the famous Rabbi Low to protect the Jews of Prague against their enemies, has long been part of Jewish folklore. Understandably, Jews have often romanticized those who have acted as protectors, many of whom were eminent leaders—philanthropists or scholars. But in Chicago there have been a number of these champions whom the Jewish establishment and the secular authorities considered disreputable, and who have been forgotten for the most part, but whose lives contain fascinating bits of history, worth retelling.

One of these who lived and died in Chicago in the early part of the 20th century was Samuel J. Morton, nicknamed "Nails." He was born on July 3, 1893, in New York City to Sarah Goodman and Frank Marcovitz, Russian immigrants, and came to Chicago at an early age with his father and stepmother, Sarah Goodman having died in New York.

The eldest of seven children, Samuel was raised in the Maxwell Street ghetto where thousands of poor Eastern European immigrants struggled to make a living in rickety frame houses, one built virtually on top of another, without adequate sanitation, an area filled with sweatshops, pushcarts and rag and junk dealers, and also with vice and crime, and surrounded by other immigrants groups—Italians, Irish, Germans, Poles and Greeks—who were as poor as the Jews and who often engaged in gang warfare with them.

The 20th Ward, which included the Jewish area and its thorough-
fare, Maxwell Street, was often referred to as the "Bloody 20th." One
writer described it in 1906: "Murderers, robbers and thieves of the
worst kind were born, reared and grew to maturity in numbers that
far exceed the record of any similar district anywhere in the world . . .
From Maxwell came some of the worst murderers, if not actually the
worst, that Chicago has ever seen."

Frank Marcovitz was a tailor. The family, apparently Yiddish-
speaking Orthodox Jews like most of their neighbors, first lived on
Johnson Street, a few blocks from Maxwell Street. Samuel and his
brother Paul worked at a young age for Hannah & Hogg, a local
whiskey distributor. One of their bosses was a man named Morton,
and for some reason at around that time Frank Marcovitz changed
the family name to Morton. Young Samuel earned his nickname of
"Nails" in gang fights. It is not clear how he ran afoul of the law early
in life, but according to police reports he was in frequent trouble. Bill
Reilly, a Chicago writer interested in Morton, thinks that he became a
local Jewish gang leader and joined the West Side gambling and sports
crowd who greatly admired prize fighters.

These Jewish gangs protected their neighborhoods against violent
incursions by non-Jewish bands. Nails was arrested once when he
and some friends took on several Poles after a Jewish boy was attacked in Humboldt Park. When he was brought up for sentencing,
legend has it that Morton was offered the option by a local judge of
going to jail or joining the army, a fairly common offer at that time.
Morton enlisted in the 132nd Infantry, the "Dandy First" Illinois regiment, which became part of the famous Rainbow Division after
America entered World War I in 1917.

In France he was awarded a *Croix de Guerre*. He had gone out at
the head of a small raiding squad, and he was the only one to return,
with a bullet in his arm and shrapnel in his leg. He was rushed to a
field hospital where his wounds were dressed. As the surgeons completed their work, he begged to be allowed to return at once to his
regiment. This was refused, but the incident brought him official recognition by the French government. On his discharge from a base

hospital, Sergeant Morton was sent to an officers training school in France, where he was commissioned a second lieutenant. Later he was promoted to first lieutenant and returned to Chicago to be welcomed by the Jewish community as a war hero. Meites' 1924 history of Chicago Jews includes a paragraph about Morton, listing him on an Honor Page of heroes of World War I.

After the war, Morton returned to his old haunts as a gambler and the operator of a "hot car" garage. One reporter wrote: "His willingness to accept almost any kind of odds offered quickly won for him a start of his fortune. He became proprietor of several well-known gambling houses, and his fortune mounted rapidly." By 1920, with the onset of Prohibition, Nails was involved in the bootleg whiskey trade "which honeycombed the city and state." He was a familiar ringside figure at principal boxing matches in Chicago and elsewhere where his "bet five grand on the man in my corner" made him a celebrity. Bets of $5,000 to $10,000 each were "matters of common occurrence with him." He owned a stable of prizefighters. A fancy dresser and nightclub habitue, he was said to be a "cultured gentleman" who fronted for the mob. Women fought for his attention. He often spent time in South Haven, Michigan, where his family owned a cottage, and where many of his Chicago buddies went to relax and watch their boxers train for Chicago matches. In his family life, Nails seems to have been a paragon of virtue. He bought a two-flat building at 3105 Augusta Boulevard for his parents and his siblings, and was generally known for his generosity to family and friends.

Nails was involved with some legendary Jewish underworld characters of the 20th Ward, including Benjamin "Buddy" and Samuel "the Greenie" Jacobson; Hershie and Max Miller, brothers of Morton's friend Davey Miller, the referee; Maxie Eisen; Isadore "Nigger" Goldberg and David Elman. But Nails and his friends could not compete with the other gangs surrounding the 20th Ward. On the one side were the forces of Dion O'Banion, Bugs Moran and Hymie Weiss (who was Polish, not Jewish); on the other were the gangs of Johnny Torrio and a newcomer, Al Capone. Caught between them, the Jews

chose sides. Nails picked an old friend, Dion O'Banion, who in addi-
tion to bootlegging, labor racketeering and bank robbing, ran
Schofield's florist shop opposite Holy Name Cathedral at 738 North
State Street. It was said that Morton had an interest in the shop.

Nails hit the headlines in August, 1920, when he was arrested
with Hershie Miller, accused of having shot and killed two detectives
in a gun battle in the notorious Pekin Beaux Arts Cafe at 2700 South
State Street. Bill Reilly's research indicates that the two detectives had
tried to "shake Nails and Hershie down," and when they refused, the
detectives made anti-Semitic remarks, leading Nails and Hershie to
reach for their guns. Nails claimed he was innocent, and in two trials
both he and Hershie were acquitted by juries, amidst allegations of
bribery and threats to witnesses. A Chicago historian put it this way:
"By spreading a little money around, and by virtue of the fact that his
gang regularly delivered the vote for the Jewish politicians of the West
Side, [Nails] got off on a plea of self-defense."

The Chicago newspapers wrote a great deal about Morton as
powerful and popular, with many friends, leading an elegant, glamor-
ous life high in the razzle-dazzle of the early Prohibition years, while
his people protected Jewish neighborhoods whenever they were threatened by other ethnic gangs. But they reported also that he had been
arrested many times and questioned about liquor hijackings and kill-
ings.

In his classic work, *The Gang—A Study of 1313 Gangs in Chicago,* Dr. Frederic M. Thatcher of the University of Chicago writes
that in the winter of 1920–21 great tension arose in Chicago over
Jewish pogroms in Eastern Europe. When Chicago Poles proposed a
parade down Division Street through Jewish neighborhoods, a gang
of young Jews, age 17 to 23, armed themselves with guns and barred
the path of the marchers, who then chose a Milwaukee Avenue route
instead. A few months later, it was rumored that Jewish boys had
been assaulted passing through a Polish community: "Thereupon a
gang of young Jews (considered sluggers in the neighborhood) as-
sembled and, led by "Nails," made for the Polish district to seek apolo-
gies. They went to the street corners indicated by the boys who had

been attacked and started a free-for-all fight. After a sufficient amount of physical punishment had been administered, they withdrew." But the clashes continued. One Saturday a gang of Jewish boys playing baseball in Douglas Park were attacked by about thirty Polish youths. When news of the attack reached the Jewish poolrooms, Thatcher writes, "A man like 'Nails' went into the fight for revenge. A good many others, including high-school boys, amateur prize fighters and hangers-on of the poolrooms were eager for the fun of 'helping the Hebes hide the Pollocks.' Their slogan was 'Wallop the Pollocks,' and they rushed fifty-strong to the scene of the battle. Finally, policemen dispersed what was left of the Polish gang."

It was along the frontiers of Humboldt and Douglas Parks that Nails Morton's reputation as protector grew. Thatcher found that there were about twenty Jewish gangs in Chicago in the early 1920s, about two percent of all the gangs that he counted in the city. Another gang to which Morton was said to belong, the WWWs, had Jewish and non-Jewish members who were excellent boxers. Thatcher writes that the WWWs "successfully stemmed an invasion of Lawndale from the southwest by Polish gangs intent on following the example of their countrymen across the seas and holding a pogrom in the Jewish residential area."

On the morning of May 13, 1923, Morton, by now an experienced horseman, went riding in Lincoln Park with his friend Dion O'Banion and O'Banion's wife. Morton wore an "immaculate green sports coat, cream colored riding trousers and riding boots." The horse, which Morton had recently purchased, bolted when a stirrup strap broke, throwing Morton to the ground. The horse became frightened and kicked Morton, cracking his skull and killing him. Nails was not yet thirty years old. His body was taken to Piser's chapel at 4936 Broadway, and the funeral was held the next day at the Roosevelt Road chapel, with interment at Waldheim cemetery. His death certificate lists his occupation as "florist."

The *Chicago Herald-Examiner* described the funeral: "Funeral services this afternoon brought dramatically to light a phase of the gang chieftan's character that few outsiders knew while he was alive.

Five thousand Jews paid tribute to Morton as the man who made the
west side safe for his race. As a young man he had organized a defense
society to drive 'Jew baiters' from the west side. Speakers at the brief
services extolled Morton for his work for his race and for his gal-
lantry in the World War. The other side of the career that ended was
not mentioned. There were religious, fraternal, and military services,
with Rabbi Julius Levi, the Elks, and Morton's former 'buddies' of
the One Hundred Twenty-third [sic] Infantry officiating. Officials of
the city, state and federal government attended. Hundreds of dollars
worth of flowers were sent to the chapel by friends." Records show,
incidentally, that Rabbi Felix Levy of Temple Emanuel officiated at
the service, not Julius Levi.

In his will, Nails left bequests of $2,500 to $3,000 to his brothers
and sisters and $5,000 to charities to be chosen by his brother Paul
who was executor; a trust fund of $20,000 for his father and any
residue outright to his father. His stepmother, Bessie, was not mentioned in the will. The inventory of his estate listed only two accounts
receivable, valued at approximately $15,000. The estate was closed
in 1927, an unusually long time for the probate of a small estate, by
which time Nails's father was dead.

If Nails died a rich man, no part of his fortune ever came to the
attention of the probate court. A total of $12,000 in assets was lo-
cated, meaning that only prorated sums could be distributed to the
legatees. No record has yet been found of the money that Nails had
supposedly amassed. In fact, according to court records, his brother
Paul had to donate $2,500 of his own money to Congregation Anshe
Knesses Israel, then located at 3411-19 Douglas Boulevard, to discharge the charitable bequest in the will.

Some Jewish community leaders were very unhappy with the emotional response of the Jewish population to Nails's death. A one-year
anniversary memorial service was cancelled, apparently at the request
of General Abel Davis, a Lithuanian-born Jewish lawyer who had
been Morton's commanding officer in France.

The *Chicago Daily News* quoted him: "Davis said that he thought
'they are making a mistake in flaunting a man's record in the faces of

decent citizens.'" Morton was one of six Jewish soldiers from Chicago who had received awards for valor while serving under Davis, who had himself received the Distinguished Service Cross.

Few people remember Samuel "Nails" Morton today, but oral histories imply that he and his followers were often on hand to protect West Side Jews when outside gangs threatened to invade their "turf." On a few additional points: it was said that Dion O'Banion and his fellow gangsters, "at a loss to express their feelings except through revenge, kidnapped the horse and solemnly 'bumped him off.' The actual assassin of the horse was said to be Nails's friend "Two Gun" Alterie, who owned a ranch in Colorado where Nails had learned to ride. The horse story became one of Chicago's great "Roaring Twenties" legends, turning up in the movie *Public Enemy* with James Cagney. And finally, Morton's friend Dion O'Banion was gunned down in his florist shop in 1924, some say by Al Capone, and his funeral was even more splendid in its floral abundance than Morton's.

AL "WALLPAPER" WOLFF: G-MAN AND UNTOUCHABLE

"How DID A NICE Jewish boy like you become part of the Untouchables?" The question was often posed to Al "Wallpaper" Wolff, the last member of a team of fifteen Federal agents known as the Untouchables, who, led by Elliot Ness, operated in Chicago from 1929 to 1933 against bootleggers who flourished during the Prohibition years, 1920 to 1936.

Al was born in 1903 on Chicago's West Side near Maxwell Street. His father, Harris Wolff, born in Hamburg, Germany, came to this country in the late nineteenth century. He met and married Rosa, a Lithuanian immigrant, earned a medical degree and opened an office at 12th and Canal Streets near the couple's upstairs apartment, where Al was born. Rosa was Orthodox, wore a wig and strictly observed the Sabbath. Harris Wolff was less observant, and his children followed in his footsteps, rejecting their mother's pious traditions.

Al attended the Jewish Manual Training School between Clinton and Jefferson Streets, a school founded by wealthy German Jews to educate children of recent immigrants, that produced many community leaders and successful businessmen during its thirty years of existence. Al grew to six feet, two inches tall with a large frame that stood him in good stead in his rough neighborhood, where he took up boxing and met Jewish Barney Ross, "Zibby" Goldberg, Charlie White and Davey Day, all of whom later became famous prizefighters. In 1918, though he was only fifteen years old, he enlisted in the army and was in Hawaii on his way to the Far East when World War I ended.

In 1921, through his father's political connections, Al got a job in the office of Denny Egan, bailiff of the Chicago municipal court, where he was tagged with the nickname, "Wallpaper" because it was said that when he evicted someone (pursuant to court order, of course), he moved out everything but the wallpaper.

After four years in the bailiff's office, Wolff applied for a job with the FBI under the young J. Edgar Hoover, against the advice of Julius "Putty" Annixter, a distant relative of his mother and the owner of a well-known West Side Jewish restaurant and gambling establishment. Annixter told him that he could make more money elsewhere—FBI agents earned about $2,500 a year at that time—and that there were no Jewish FBI agents anyway. But, Annixter added, if Al was going to be a G-man, he should be an honest one and never be "on the take." Al followed this advice throughout his government career, even though he said there were many times when he was offered bribes.

Assigned to the Alcoholic Enforcement Division, Al was sent to Kentucky to raid illegal distilleries. In 1926 he married Hanna Rubens at Temple Beth Israel in Chicago; the couple were to have two sons and a daughter. In 1929, he requested a transfer back to Chicago, and was assigned to the Elliot Ness team as an undercover agent. The Ness team's scrupulous honesty earned them the soubriquet "the Untouchables." Since he was an undercover agent, he said, no one knew his true role, not even his wife and children. He looked, he said, like a "Kraut," and, when he didn't shave, like an Italian.

In a recent interview, he told many stories about his raids on speakeasies and arrests of bootleggers. He had no particular animus against these people: as he put it, "They were doing their job and I was doing mine." He refused to name people whom he knew were engaged in criminal activities, because he didn't want their children or grandchildren to be brought back into the public spotlight. He said that many of the so-called gangsters really were good guys to their people, that even Al Capone set up soup kitchens for poor Italians at Christmas time. He never gave any special treatment to bootleggers who were

Jewish. He remembered going undercover to bathhouses on 14th Street and overhearing the bootleggers discussing their breaches of the law. On their way out, he would have them arrested.

By the late 1920s, Prohibition was so unpopular, and public patronage of bootleggers so widespread, that they were often thought of as ordinary businessmen. Repeal was inevitable: when it came, the Untouchables were disbanded and Al was assigned to different areas of government service. At various times he was in the Narcotics Division, the Internal Revenue Service and, during World War II, in the Office of Price Administration. After the war, he left the government and returned to Chicago where he owned and operated a number of restaurants ("Wolff's Inn") in the Loop and then a private club at 201 East Superior Street.

Since Wolff had been an undercover agent, no one knew about him until Paramount Studios contacted him as a consultant on the film *The Untouchables*. He was finally able to talk about his undercover days, and about his feelings as an American. "I think my destiny was [to be] a nice Jewish guy overcoming all these obstacles to working in all those departments as the only Jew," he said. "There is no country in the world like America because we still have freedom, we still can pray and do anything we want. We can get married and have children. I am proud to be a Jew, but I'm an American first. I was born and went to schools here. I served in the American Army. I was born an American citizen; I don't know of any other country like America. I was blessed being born here. I am glad my father didn't miss the boat coming here. I would have swum across the ocean to get to America."

Al "Wallpaper" Wolff passed away on March 21, 1998. He was the last survivor and the only Jewish member of Elliot Ness's "Untouchables."

KINGFISH LEVINSKY: FIGHTER COULD TAKE A PUNCH

IN HIS 1988 *The Jewish Boxers Hall of Fame,* Ken Blady says that Chicago heavyweight prizefighter Kingfish Levinsky never bothered to learn the basic art of boxing, but would block punches with his face and attack fists with a blunt instrument—his head! Once in 1930 when he was asked how he had outpointed the great boxer Jimmy Slattery, he is supposed to have replied, "I hitted him where it hoit da most. Da King ain't no sucker you know." Whether he ever really uttered these words is a matter of conjecture, but it is undoubtedly true that the Kingfish was a familiar figure on the Chicago scene in the late 1920s and throughout the '30s, and, justifiably or not, was considered a "klutz," the Jewish clown from Maxwell Street.

He was born Harry Krakow on September 10, 1910, in New York City. In an interview with a *Miami News* reporter in 1981, he said that he was one of seventeen children and that his family moved to Chicago's Maxwell Street area in the early 1920s. "My family sold fish and so did I," he said. "I only went up to the third grade. I fought in the street and finally started boxing out of the Kid Howard Gym." When he turned pro he decided to change his name to something more memorable. He considered calling himself K.O. Hogan, Slugger Reilly or One-Round Hannigan. But his manager convinced him to keep his Jewish identity. So Harry Krakow took the name "Levinsky" because the manager thought he looked a little like "Battling Levinsky," the lightweight champion from New York City. He told the *Miami*

News that he called himself "Kingfish" because it reminded him of his Maxwell Street occupation, though other sources quote Levinsky as saying the name came from one of the characters in the popular "Amos 'n' Andy" radio show.

The new name helped him attract public attention. But it was his brutal overhand right that won him his early fights. One of his managers was Al Miller, a brother of Davey Miller, the Chicago fight referee. Kingfish, tall, husky and not bad looking, had no defense, never raising his left hand to blunt an opponent's jabs. The resulting pounding that he took, coupled with his unique Maxwell Street vernacular, made the Kingfish a favorite butt of the media. Despite his inept fighting style, by the end of 1931 when Max Schmelling of Germany was the world's heavyweight champion, the Kingfish was somehow the fourth-ranked heavyweight in the world. And then came the fight that brought him wide national attention.

Jack Dempsey, America's greatest heavyweight, had been in retirement for over five years after his famous "long count" loss to Gene Tunney in Chicago in 1926. Now he was scheduling a number of exhibition fights with an eye toward making a comeback. The Kingfish, then twenty-two years old, was signed to a four-round exhibition to test Dempsey's stamina. The fight was held at the Chicago Stadium on Thursday, February 18, 1932. Over 23,000 fans saw the Kingfish batter Dempsey, who dropped his plans for a comeback as a result.

The Kingfish now met boxers with national reputations. On July 4, 1932, he lost a 20-round decision to Max Baer in 110-degree weather in Reno, Nevada. (Contrary to popular belief, Max Baer was not Jewish.) But on September 18, 1933, he beat Art Sharkey in Chicago and ended up that year as the third-ranked heavyweight in the world. By now, the Kingfish had a new manager, his sister Lena Levy. She did not like the way the Kingfish had been treated by his managers: he often received a fraction of what his opponents got from the fight proceeds. Lena quickly became a legend.

The English historian Robert Holdone, in his 1948 *Giants of the Ring,* wrote of Lena: "And while he was committing mayhem and legalized manslaughter in the ring, she would bob up and down like an infuriated Jill-in-a-box urging Levinsky to further deeds of dastardly, with a tongue like a cactus and the vocabulary of a chimney sweep, only pausing in the interwake to give the sweating King a neat and fancy rubdown in the best professional fashion."

Lena was up and down in her brother's corner so often that boxing reporters soon dubbed her "Leaping Lena." Under her management, Kingfish met many well-known fighters and took his beatings, but often won and received a greater percentage of the gate than he had before. In 1934, Lena was successful in arranging a third fight with Max Baer, now heavyweight world champion. On December 28, 1934, the two met for the third time in Chicago. Levinsky had been out-pointed in the first two fights, but they had been close and exciting. Baer had spent his six-month reign as champion carousing in night clubs and was out of condition. The Kingfish surged out and repeatedly smashed his right into Baer's midriff. Gilbert Odd, in his 1978 *The Women in the Corner*, describes what happened next: "There was murder in Baer's eyes as he sat waiting for the second round to start and as soon as he saw the timekeeper move to strike the gong, he started across the ring and caught the unprepared King with a right hander to the chin as he was in the act of rising from his stool. Levinsky was knocked cold; he slid to the canvas and remained motionless while they counted him out."

In 1935, a new boxer was appearing on the American fight scene: Joe Louis, the "Brown Bomber" from Detroit. The year had been a disaster for the Kingfish; he had lost eleven fights by knockouts and won just two. Despite that, Lena managed to land a $30,000 contract for her brother to fight Louis in Chicago. The fact that he might be overmatched did not apparently concern her. The fight was set for Comiskey Park on the evening of August 8, 1935. The Kingfish had not heard much about this black newcomer to the boxing scene and had predicted to the newspapers that Louis would be "a sucker for his right."

However, on the evening of the fight, his brother Fishky and others, one after another, told him about the Bomber's record—that Louis had just knocked out Primo Carnera in six rounds, and thirteen of his twenty-three opponents had been leveled in three rounds or less. Suddenly, the story goes, the Kingfish became petrified. Some say he locked himself in a bathroom stall which had to be forced open; others that Levinsky had to be dragged into the arena. A couple of the preliminary fights were cancelled for fear the Kingfish would not stay for the main event. The bout, witnessed by 40,000 fans, lasted two minutes and twenty-one seconds. Louis threw some punches; Levinsky, one in return. The Kingfish fell to the floor and was quickly counted out. Some fans never saw any of the fight, it was over so quickly. It was, of course, a disgraceful moment for the Kingfish. His reputation as a "klutz" was now fixed.

Lena gave up her job as the Kingfish's manager after she was suspended for unbecoming conduct in the ring when a ten-round decision went against her brother. The Kingfish's boxing career went into a steep decline. In 1937 he managed to arrange a fight in London with Jack Doyle, an eccentric British singer and boxer. The fight apparently reached a comic level: the Kingfish was reported to have held onto Doyle so often that the two of them were virtually waltzing in the ring. In London the Kingfish visited Buckingham Palace, which he reportedly called "da joint where dat other King hangs out." He boxed professionally until 1939, ending his career with a record of seventy-two victories and six draws in his 110 fights. He had earned over half a million dollars during his boxing career, but when he quit he was penniless, and forced to take up wrestling for a short time. In Tampa, Florida, he entered a novel match with a Chief Chewaki that allowed both boxing and wrestling in the same fight. He was often battered in these matches and his wrestling career ended when he punched a referee.

The Kingfish was married three times. His first wife, a tap dancer, was said to have divorced him on the grounds that he ate herring in bed and the bones tickled her. Nothing is known about his second wife. His third, whom he married in Crown Point, Indiana in 1938, was Roxanne Glickman, a fan dancer. When he retired from boxing and wrestling, he sold ties. Many Chicagoans still remember, with great affection, seeing the Kingfish in local hotels and restaurants, selling, for about $3.50, the colorful ties with his Kingfish label. Later he took himself and his tie business to Miami, where a bellhop commented, "I've watched him for ten years and know his routine . . . He tells them he's punch drunk. Some of the people believe it and buy 'cause they feel sorry for him. But I don't. I think that's just how he sells his ties."

The Kingfish is no longer selling ties. He has vanished from public life, though no obituary has appeared. If alive, he would be in his nineties. While the media may have seen him as a clown, to many Jews he was a hero of sorts from Maxwell Street. One veteran Chicagoan was quoted in the *Miami News*: "Kingfish was the toast of Chicago. He was an idol of the Jewish community . . . He was such a character, and on any given night he could beat anyone. He fought the best heavyweights on earth."

Ben Bentley, a veteran ring announcer, called the Kingfish a "tough, courageous fighter," despite the Louis bout. After all, he pointed out, another world heavyweight champion, Max Schmelling, suffered almost the exact fate at the hands of Louis in June, 1938. Kingfish Levinsky, whether alive or dead, deserves to be remembered as a representative of those uneducated, impoverished Chicago Jews who used their fists, as well as their heads, to punch out their destiny in the arenas of the Golden Land.

MOE BERG: "CATCHER WAS A SPY"

———

IN *THE CATCHER WAS A SPY*, Nicholas Dawidoff traces the enigmatic life of Moe Berg, a baseball player, linguist, amateur physicist, Columbia Law School graduate and World War II spy. These accomplishments should have made Berg a legend, but he is best remembered for the years he spent as a mediocre back-up catcher in the major leagues, "the guy who was fluent in seven languages and couldn't hit in any of them." Dawidoff's book is carefully detailed, but gives short shrift to Berg's years as a Chicagoan, a White Sox player and, in his time, one of the few Jewish players in all of major league baseball.

Moe Berg was raised in a predominantly Gentile neighborhood in Newark, New Jersey. His father, Bernard, a pharmacist who had come in 1894 from Kippinya, a Ukrainian shtetl, was fluent in several languages even before he settled in America and determined to shed the remainder of his old-world "anachronisms." He wanted his family to meld into American culture and would not allow Yiddish to be spoken at home. But Moe may have become more of an American than Bernard expected. He became something of a baseball playground legend, attracting the notice of coaches and scouts. His father resented that, complaining his son should have used his energy to help build the family pharmacy business. Bernard supposedly refused to watch Moe play baseball even after his son became a major leaguer.

His skill at baseball helped earn him a scholarship to Princeton, a considerable feat for a Jewish student at that time. He was a superb

shortstop, and his Princeton team was called the greatest in the
university's history, winning nineteen games in a row, a record that
stood for many years. After he graduated in 1923, Princeton offered
Berg a teaching position, but he turned it down because he planned to
go to Paris to study languages at the Sorbonne. He changed his mind
when he got an offer from the Brooklyn Dodgers; he decided to sign
with them and try to continue his studies in this country. In 1925 he
entered Columbia University Law School even though he was still on
the Dodger's roster. A year later he joined the Chicago White Sox, a
team whose fortunes had sagged after the infamous 1919 "Black Sox"
World Series scandal, and immediately alienated the team's owner
Charles Comiskey and the entire Chicago sports world by announcing that he would skip spring training and the first two months of the
regular season so that he could complete his first year of law school.

The *Tribune* commented, "It was quite a disappointment to Manager Collins, who had counted upon Berg to handle the shortstop
position when the season opened. [Berg is] intent upon being an attorney and wants to finish his law education now so he can practice
to some extent in the winter while he is playing and then have an
established profession when the time comes that he must quit the
game." It is possible that this decision reflected a compromise with
his father: the son would continue to play baseball, but not at the
expense of his education. Nevertheless, as he was often to do, he had
made a curious decision to undermine his position as a major league
shortstop at the very beginning of his baseball career. He went to law
school and joined the White Sox on May 28, 1926, as a utility shortstop. He played infrequently in his first year and when he did play, the
press often made him an object of ridicule.

In a game against St. Louis, the White Sox lost because Berg made
a fielding error. The newspaper commented, "our aspiring barrister
Moe Berg was guilty of one mistake. He could never convince any
jury of laymen that it wasn't his fault." He played in forty-one games
in the 1926 season, batting an unimpressive .221. His one moment of
fame came in the City Series, the best of seven post-season series of
exhibition games that the White Sox played with the Cubs. In the

seventh game, Berg's double off the left field wall in Wrigley Field drove in the series-winning run for the White Sox. Tribune sports columnist Irving Vaughn reacted sarcastically: "Moe Berg isn't much of a hitter, but this was a game where decorum meant over $300 per individual, so Moe hit one."

Berg reported late again in 1927, after lengthy arguments with Comiskey. When he did arrive in May, he sat on the bench. In August he switched positions, from shortstop to catcher. When Ray Schalk, the White Sox manager and catcher, broke a finger, and a few days later the back-up catcher was injured too, the team was out of catchers and Schalk, in despair, looked for help. Dawidoff says that in the White Sox dugout, "Schalk heard a low, measured voice say, 'You've got a big league catcher sitting right here!'" The voice was Berg's. "All right, Berg," Schalk said, "go in there."

Berg later claimed he had been referring to Earl Sheely, a utility first baseman and that Schalk misunderstood and thought Berg was volunteering to catch. Berg had never caught in the big leagues. As he donned his gear, he is supposed to have said, "If the worst happens, kindly deliver the body to Newark." But Berg proved an immediate success. He became a favorite of the White Sox pitchers, particularly Ted Lyons, a future Hall of Famer with an array of pitches. In one game against the New York Yankees—then led by Babe Ruth, and possibly the best team in baseball history—the Sox won six to three with Lyons pitching and Berg catching. Berg made the defensive play of the game when he scooped up a throw from the outfield and tagged out the New York player sliding into home plate.

Led by Lyons, the White Sox converged on their new catcher. "He went forward like a shortstop and picked up the half hop," Lyons said. "He caught a wonderful game and handled himself like an old timer." Columnist Westbrook Pegler commented on Berg in the *Tribune*, "The distinguished Korean philologist confessed he was secretly a catcher at the time instead of a shortstop, as everyone thought him. He has been catching very nicely, and Mr. Schalk feels faint stirrings of hope that some of his other players will confess to a secret accomplishment, preferably hitting."

Berg decided that catching was his calling, and in early 1928 took a leave of absence from law school for the rest of the year. He joined the White Sox for spring training in Shreveport. Starting on the bench, by mid-season Berg had become the regular White Sox catcher. A *Tribune* columnist compared Berg to Gabby Hartnett, the celebrated Cubs catcher. Hartnett, he said, was the harder hitter, but both "are nifty dressers and single . . . the single big difference between [them] is that Hartnett drives one of the most costly of domestic cars, while Berg still clings to his boyish love for the bicycle. He can be seen every morning, rain or shine, in the vicinity of 53rd Street and Hyde Park Boulevard. Berg speaks from seven to twenty-one languages, while Gabby speaks but one—rock-ribbed English." Berg lived at the South Side Del Prado Hotel, a favorite of many out-of-town ballplayers.

He was obviously becoming popular with the press and the fans. A member of a poor team mired in the second division, he was a "character," a scholar who read literature, in foreign languages no less, between innings. He was also a handsome man, and very witty. In the City Series of 1928, the Cubs won four to three, but Berg, who caught every game for the White Sox, batted .3333. Chicago Jews were certainly proud of him. He is remembered by some of them today, but he was apparently never part of that community and received no special treatment in the city's Jewish press.

Dawidoff says that Chicago fans raised over $25,000 for a "Berg Day" at Comiskey Park, only to have it turned down by Berg. It was rumored in the fall of 1928 that the New York Yankees, eager to have a Jewish player in their line-up, had proposed a trade for Berg. But there was no trade to the Yankees. Berg had trouble during his last year at Columbia. He failed Evidence and did not graduate with the class of 1929, although he did manage to pass the New York State bar exam later that spring.

The 1929 season was a difficult one for Berg, whose mind was often elsewhere. On September 7, he caught a foul pop-up with a runner on third, the score tied at one, and one out. After catching the ball, he threw it toward the pitcher's mound and began heading for his dugout. He had lost track of the number of outs and the runner at third raced home with the winning run. The White Sox pitcher of that day, Tommy Thomas, never tired of telling Berg, "You can speak a dozen languages, but you can't count to three." Of errors such as this one, legends are made. Berg's reputation for "weirdness" was reinforced.

Nevertheless, he batted a respectable .288 for the season and was considered a fine defensive catcher.

Moe repeated his Evidence course in New York, passed it this time, and received his LLB on February 26, 1930. He was now a veteran White Sox player and the team's starting catcher. Despite being considered aloof and preoccupied because of his intellectual pursuits, he seems to have enjoyed good relationships with a number of teammates, particularly Ted Lyons.

On April 6, 1930, as the White Sox were travelling north from spring training, Berg suffered a serious injury in an exhibition game in Little Rock, Arkansas. While rounding first base, he caught his spikes in the turf and felt a sharp pain in his knee. He had torn a ligament and left the team abruptly without telling officials where he was going. On May 2, 1930, a notice appeared in the *Tribune*: "If anybody in Chicago knows how Moe Berg, the first string catcher now laid up in Chicago, is getting along will they please communicate with the ball club."

Berg was apparently not laid up in Chicago, but had gone east to be treated by his brother, a doctor. He soon returned to Chicago, but his career with the White Sox was just about over. Although his torn ligament was healing, it would never be strong enough for the rigors of squatting as a catcher every day behind home plate. He played in a few games for the White Sox in 1930 and was put on waivers in April, 1931, at the start of the season. The Cleveland Indians promptly claimed him. That began the final phase of his big-league career. He lasted several years longer in the major leagues as a journeyman backup catcher before retiring from baseball. Even after Berg left Chicago, he continued to be remembered with fondness. Jerome Holtzman of the *Tribune* and Ira Berkow of the *New York Times* (a Chicago native himself) were two of Berg's admirers. Both wrote regularly about him after his career was over; his unusual intelligence and education made him good copy even when he wasn't playing.

Dawidoff tells a fascinating story of a man too gifted to be successful, unable to settle on any single profession despite having so many from which to select. One vocation did stand out for him, however, the stuff of which legends are made: Berg had toured Japan with Babe Ruth and other American ballplayers in the 1930s and had taken secret films of Tokyo said to have been useful to U.S. Intelligence during World War II. Because of this, he came to know Nelson Rockefeller and William "Wild Bill" Donovan, who asked him to undertake other espionage missions for the government. Berg agreed and became a capable secret agent.

His most unusual mission came late in the war when the government, aware that German scientists were working on atomic weapons, became concerned that they might get ahead of the Americans working on the Manhattan Project. Berg had studied modern physics as an avocation, and spoke fluent German. As a reasonably well-known American athlete, he enjoyed a kind of international carte blanche that few espionage agents could match. He seemed the perfect choice to discover the status of the German atomic project, so in 1944 he was sent to Switzerland to attend a lecture by Werner Heisenberg, the German counterpart to the Manhattan Project's Robert Oppenheimer. Berg was given a gun and simple instructions: if Heisenberg appeared to be making real headway in his work on the basis of the most up-to-date American research and development, Berg was to assassinate him on the spot. But Heisenberg's lecture convinced Berg that his approach was off-base, so the gun remained in his pocket. History proved Berg correct: the Germans never came close to being able to produce an atomic bomb.

Oddly, though Berg was in Europe at the end of the war, he seems never to have commented on the horrors he must have witnessed. There is no mention of the Holocaust in his voluminous correspondence with people at home in the States. But he could be disturbingly erratic in his interests and his behavior. Since espionage requires stability as well as intelligence, Berg didn't last with the C.I.A. Toward the end of his life, he became a drifter who lived off his friends. His final days were unhappy ones. He died of heart disease in 1972, his contributions to the government and to baseball largely forgotten.

His body was cremated and the ashes buried in Newark. A few years later, his sister Ethel dug up the urn, flew to Israel and, with the assistance of an anonymous rabbi, reinterred his ashes somewhere on a mountain in Jerusalem. The actual site is unknown.

There is something appropriate about Berg's ashes being in the Holy Land but lost at the same time. Always a mystery, usually estranged from the Jewish people, he was a remarkable man who led a remarkable life.

INDEX